Deep Focus

Devotions for Living the Word

Stephen R. Graves

Thomas G. Addington

JOSSEY-BASS
A Wiley Imprint
www.josseybass.com

989 Market Street, San Francisco, CA 94103-1741   www.josseybass.com

Jossey-Bass books and products are available through most bookstores. To contact
Jossey-Bass directly call our Customer Care Department within the U.S. at 800-956-7739,
outside the U.S. at 317-572-3986, or fax 317-572-4002.

Jossey-Bass also publishes its books in a variety of electronic formats. Some content that
appears in print may not be available in electronic books.

Library of Congress Cataloging-in-Publication Data

Graves, Stephen R., date.
    Deep focus: devotions for living the Word / Stephen R. Graves,
Thomas G. Addington.
      p. cm.
    Includes bibliographical references.
    ISBN 0–7879–6477–8 (alk. paper)
      1. Bible. N.T. Epistles—Meditations. 2. Christian life—Biblical teaching.
I. Addington, Thomas G., date. II. Title.
BS2635.4.G73 2003
242'.5—dc22   2003015405

Printed in the United States of America
FIRST EDITION
HB Printing   10 9 8 7 6 5 4 3 2 1

Contents

Part Four: Galatians: Living Free   141

On a Mission for God • On Stage Before God • A Changed
Man • Spiritual Pillars • Private Power Supply • The
Law • Losing the Joy of Giving • Stand Firm,
Stand Free • Fruit of the Flesh • Fruit of the Spirit • Keep
in Step • The Original Do-Gooders • Boomerang Living

Part Five: Ephesians: Higher Ground   163

Other Person Prayers • Good Works • We All Need
Peace • How Wide? How Long? How High? How Deep? • The
Value of Unity • Change Your Stinky Clothes • Settle It
Before the Sun Goes Down • Quit Stealing • Not Even
a Hint • Carpe Diem • Dressing for Battle

Part Six: Philippians: Perpetual Rejoicing and Thankfulness   181

God Doesn't Quit • Diagnosing Our Lives • Hardship Has
Its Rewards • Monitoring Your Conduct • Spiritual Cruise
Control • The Final P&L • Working Toward
Perfection • The Winner's Circle • Disagreeing,
But Getting Along • Anxiety-Free Living • Think
on These Things • The Secret Silver Bullet

Part Seven: Colossians: Christ Is Supreme   201

A Hidden Power Source • A Firm Foundation • Follow
the Head • Heavenly Minded and Earthly Good • Spring
Clean Your Life • A Heavenly Wardrobe • Giving Work
Your All • Do Right—Be Fair • Five-Star Dialogue

Introduction

The word *devotional* is the adjectival form of the noun *devotion*. Those words, along with their brother verb, *to devote,* are all hallmarks of a follower of Christ. We are devoted to Him, and to encourage that devotion there have always been—down through the ages—devotionals that help us focus on Jesus.

Devotionals are meant to bring a break, a period of solitude, an interlude to what would otherwise be a day uninterrupted by a busy pace. They are not designed to supply information in the "to know" part of life; nor are they intended to be checked off on the "to do" task lists of daily existence.

Devotionals—and the quiet times they help engineer—are meant to be thought-provoking, bite-sized morsels of truth that give us pause.

A professor at a religious college told me many years ago that he liked to speed-read the Psalms. In his opinion, there was not much substance in those 150 chapters, and themes just kept repeating themselves. I remember thinking at the time that of any book in the Scripture where the need-for-speed-impulse ought to be avoided, Psalms was it. Why? Because essentially each is a prayer between a needy individual and his or her great God. David, and other authors in that collection of poetic intercession and praise, used them as time stoppers and speed bumps. They are supposed to slow us down. They act as brakes on our daily rhythm, not as accelerators.

Any devotional, these included, needs to be read after taking a deep breath. If your days are like ours, time for devotions often looks more like a comma than a period. The venue varies greatly: from quiet corner in the house, to office, to airplane, to hotel room, to restaurant, to Starbucks, to automobile. But whatever block of time we have to give devotions in our schedule and wherever they take place, they ought to redirect our focus for some span of time.

Devotionals sometimes state the obvious, because we need to be reminded of things we already know. In other instances, they bring new meaning to old knowledge, because Scripture is a prism of truth that can be enjoyed from diverse angles. Sprinkled among that old knowledge and the fresh angles on truth ought to be unexplored biblical territories that open our eyes to new spiritual geographies. We hope this volume accomplishes all three of these things for you, the reader.

This is our second volume of devotional material. The first, simply titled *Daily Focus,* used the Old Testament wisdom literature and the New Testament book of James as its home base. This second volume moves to the New Testament letters, most of which were written by Paul, Peter, and John—(along with the possible exception of Hebrews, where the author is not identified by name). In both devotionals, we have worked to use the Scripture as a lens through which to view daily life and issues in a worker's world.

The letters written to churches and individuals in the New Testament are perfect material for men and women whose lives are defined by cell phones, Palm Pilots, laptop computers, and BlackBerrys. Why? Because Paul, who was himself defined professionally as a maker of tents, addresses people in everyday, real life, not those individuals who moved outside mainstream society to dedicate themselves to full-time prayer and study of Scripture. Paul's challenge to each of the audiences he addressed was not to leave current life to follow Christ, but rather to intentionally inject Jesus into current life. He invites us to make our own existence a Jesus existence.

What characterizes our current existence? Distractions, good people and bad people, strengths, weaknesses, opportunities, and threats. Stocks, bonds, wars, terrorism, family, church, friends, and travel. Into that mixed bag of ups and downs, of blessings and challenges, Paul parachutes into our lives with his letters. The devotionals that follow simply isolate snapshots from those letters for us to ponder.

The goal of any time focused on God and His word is a changed life. We are given the opportunity to become different people as we interact with Jesus. Along that line, let us encourage you to inject prayer into your time of devotion. The Holy Spirit mysteriously transforms us from the inside out through the process of prayer, and the combination of meditation on biblical truth and conversation with God through prayer is always life changing—even if it's not what we intended!

We hope this little volume enhances your life of devotion to Jesus.

Acknowledgments

Thank you, Sarah Moser. Your writing and editing assistance helped this project make it to the finish line. You have a great fourth-quarter game. Toward the end of the project you wanted the ball, which is what really capable people do. Thanks.

Thank you to all the Bible writers and translators since the original authoring of the Scripture. This entire project has involved tumbling over the pages of the Scripture, finding selected verses or phrases to do an application drill-down. Having a copy of the Bible, in our common language, thousands of years after it was first written, is an unbelievable privilege. We are grateful to you.

Thank you to our parents, who instilled in us a love for the Scripture. Having something of priceless value gathering dust on the shelf is one thing. Having an intrinsic appetite and love for the truth that is found in the pages of the Scripture is a whole different ball game. Our daily interaction with the Book is in large part because of you. Thanks.

Thank you, Sheryl Fullerton and the team at Jossey-Bass. This is the fourth project we have done with you in a very short time. You are clearly the best team we have ever had the privilege to work with. Your commitment to the category, content excellence, good sell-through, and catalyzing of life change is at times a warm hug and at times a kick in the pants. Thanks for doing both.

Thank you, Chip MacGregor, our agent. It's way past professional. We have simply become good friends.

There is an old proverb that goes: A person with one friend is a fortunate man; a person with a few friends is beyond blessed. We are beyond blessed with friends.

This book is dedicated to two partners who met us on the Life@Work journey and have rooted into our pursuit for commercial and kingdom enterprise. Greg Spencer and Bill Townsend, you and your families have been the best medicine that two road-worn soldiers could have ever had. Thanks for the last few years.

PART ONE

Romans

THE HEART OF THE GOSPEL

Key Elements

Purpose: to introduce Paul to the Romans and to give them a sample of his gospel-centered message before he arrives in Rome

Author: Paul

To whom written: the Christians and Roman believers everywhere

Date written: about 57 A.D.

Key Themes

- The righteousness of God. Straight out of the world of the courtroom drama, Paul delivers the ironclad argument that we are all in desperate need of righteousness that is personally activated by the faith life.
- The human condition. We are lost, helpless, and hopeless left to ourselves. We must have God.
- The sovereignty of God. God and humans are not peers or equals. Humans are creation and God is creator. Romans displays God as being in charge of His world.
- Service to others. To be most useful, we must strive to translate our Christian knowledge into personal service.

The Good Rumor Mill

I thank my God for all of you, because your faith is being reported all over the world.
—ROMANS 1:8

A good story carries itself. When someone does a good deed, going to extreme measures of sacrifice and commitment, others pick up the story and pass it along. Paul certainly heard lots of stories, both good and bad, in his travels around the first-century world. And it seems that whenever he landed in a port or harbor, someone gave him another good report on the church at Rome. So in his letter to the Romans he presents them a verbal trophy—an accolade for the "good rumors" he had heard about them.

Are people passing good rumors about you? Like the men and women of Rome, all of us are building reputations by our lives and our words. Unfortunately, many times our lives do not offer enough substance for people to carry on a good rumor mill about us. If we did live such a life, the stories others passed along would create the ripple effect through the good rumor mill.

It's not our job to make people talk about us in good manner. Our job to live a life that gives people the substance, the fodder, with which to start this good rumor mill.

At the same time, we should ask ourselves whether we are known as carriers of good news or bad. Are you someone who retells a good story when you hear it? Do you generate good stories about others? One of the best ways to start the good rumor mill at the office is to praise an employee or coworker in the presence of other people. Those who hear the praise are likely to pass the good word along to others.

Men and women of faith should be the tracks on which the good rumor mill runs. Every job has great stories about great people. We should be the carriers of those stories.

Ask yourself today, am I living a life that generates traffic on the good rumor mill? Am I building smooth tracks for good news to run on? Or have I developed a negative way of looking at my boss and coworkers—a point of view that creates or adds to a bad rumor mill?

Set a goal for yourself to become a person about whom others will say, "That's somebody I continually hear good things about."

Proud of It

I am not ashamed of the gospel.
—ROMANS 1:16

The gospel will never embarrass God. Neither should it embarrass us. In fact, we should be proud of the gospel—ready to tell the good news to anyone in any situation. Paul certainly was. The word *gospel* appears in the New Testament seventy-two times. Sixty times, it appears in Paul's letters.

Because of bad representations of the gospel through the years, however, many people have never gotten to the point where they can see its incredible power. The gospel gave Paul his identity.

He was an opponent, but then he became its servant—he became a product of the gospel. The gospel also gave Paul his credentials—the highest business card he could float to another.

Are you a product of the gospel? Or do other credentials give you a higher sense of self-image? Have you been changed, as Paul was changed by the good news? If so, then you, like Paul, are not ashamed to share the good news: the story of God as expressed through the life, death, resurrection, and expected return of Jesus.

When you are unashamed of the gospel, you experience its power. Paul used the Greek word *dunamis* (from which comes our word dynamite) to describe this power. This gospel power can blow someone off the seat of traditional religious ritualism. It certainly worked that way in Paul's life, and it will in yours as well when you accept it completely—when you stop hand-picking the parts you like and begin to understand and believe in the complete message of the gospel.

When the gospel for you is Jesus and Jesus alone—not Jesus plus something on top of the gospel—then you will have experienced the life-changing power of the good news, and you will never be ashamed of the gospel.

Lying on the Trampoline

For since the creation of the world, God's invisible qualities—His eternal power and divine nature—have been clearly seen, being understood from what has been made, so that men are without excuse.

—ROMANS 1:20

On many winter nights, my family grabs our sleeping bags—or sheets in summer—and then we run out to the backyard and lie on the trampoline and play games. Soon we find ourselves lying on our backs in the quiet, listening to night sounds and staring up at the stars. We have a contest where we try to be first to identify airplanes and satellites among the stars; I am always quick to misidentify a star as a satellite.

Staring out at the universe, I am reminded of Psalm 19, which begins "The heavens declare the glory of God; the skies proclaim the work of His hands." To the Romans Paul said, in effect, that if you lie on the trampoline long enough, you'll realize that the space you occupy is part of a much bigger universe that has nothing to do with you. It has to do with God.

"Where were you when I laid earth's foundations?" God asked Job. "Have you ever given orders to the morning, or shown the dawn its place?"

Looking at creation around us and above us, we know that only a great God could have created all that exists. Nature reveals to us who God is, and it reminds us who man is—that we are not God.

Give someone who is starving a meal and then ask if the person believes there is a cook; he or she will say, "Of course I do." That's the crux of Paul's argument to the Romans. But just believing in the existence of the cook is not enough. We must take the next step and get to know Him personally.

Nature was never intended to show "the way to God," but rather to settle "the fact of God." Only Jesus can show us the way to God. But every night, the heavens declare court on God's existence. The stars, the moon, the wind, and even the quiet are called to testify that a creator lives. Have you been summoned to court lately?

A Moral Alarm Clock

The requirements of the law are written on their hearts. . . .
—ROMANS 2:15

God puts inside each of us a moral alarm clock, a sense of conscience and awareness that helps us in the initial stages of life to navigate and signal right and wrong. We all know that when the alarm goes off, something's wrong.

We also have within us the ability to hit the snooze button and ignore the alarm. In the artificial silence, we do wrong things so many times that they become habits. We become comfortable with them, and before long we don't have to think about the snooze button, for we no longer hear the alarm at all.

When people fall into this downward spiral of sin, the conscience grows quieter day by day. The sense of right and wrong that they were born with virtually disappears.

In the workplace, you are surrounded with opportunities to ignore your moral alarm clock—to allow lapses that seem insignificant. But each time you hit the snooze button, even on the smallest issues, you create the opportunity for a bigger lapse.

In today's convoluted ethical landscape, the workplace is slippery. If you haven't planted your feet firmly on the side of morality, you may not recognize whether the opportunities that present themselves are right or wrong. There is an avalanche of men and women in today's business landscape who fell from the top of organizations because they lost their intrinsic sense of right and wrong.

Can you still hear your moral alarm clock, even on the little things? As you develop your own sense of hearing, keep in mind that you are not to be the moral superman in your office. Your alarm clock has to do with you personally: how you act minute by minute in ethical situations, whether you veer to the right or lean into the wrong. It's more about your own choices than policing others.

God gave you your moral alarm clock. Don't hit the snooze button.

One Bad Apple

There is no one righteous, not even one.
—ROMANS 3:10

In some way or another, all people are tainted and fall short of the divine goodness or righteousness of God. Theologically speaking, the term described by this verse is *total depravity*. We all find ourselves lacking an excuse that can make a difference in our eternity.

This doesn't mean that we could not be any worse than we are today. We could be. Nor does it mean that there is no moral goodness within us. There is. Rather, total depravity means that each person is as bad as he or she can be, left to his or her own inadequate ability to relate to God.

People offer varying responses to the knowledge that they fall short of God's righteousness. Some build a wall of denial around themselves. Others admit the fact and give up, believing there is no hope whatsoever. Still others offer excuses that they believe will somehow change how they are viewed in the eyes of God.

I am reminded of the time when I was in college and got a speeding ticket for driving forty-five in a thirty-five-mile-per-hour zone. I knew I was guilty, but I decided to go to court and explain my situation to the judge and ask for mercy.

"I'm guilty," I explained to the judge, "but with circumstances."

Over proverbial reading glasses perched on the end of his nose, he raised one eyebrow and asked, "What exactly does that mean?"

"Well, I'd like to explain my story."

He allowed me to present my "circumstances"; then he declared me guilty, and I paid the fine. Nothing I said had made a difference in the way the judge looked at me or the outcome of my case. I could offer no excuse that would change the facts.

So I know that I am not righteous. Now what? Paul's statement was not intended to drive me to self-pity, but rather to highlight God's goodness in contrast to my badness. That knowledge was intended to drive me to the lap of a loving and forgiving God and ask for help.

Crooked Stick Theology

There is no one who does good, not even one.
—ROMANS 3:12

Too often when I find myself guilty, I look around to find someone who is in even worse shape than I am—someone more crooked than me to measure myself against. Why? Because then I look less crooked—sometimes I might even look straight. At least I feel less crooked.

But other people are not measuring sticks in God's eyes. Jesus is the only true measuring stick, and not once in my life have I looked straight when measured by His perfection. There is a world of difference between our goodness and His righteousness; all of our goodness measured against His guidelines of righteousness comes up woefully inadequate. But that does not mean there is no hope.

God also makes it clear that He is not trying to create an unhealthy self-image within people. He does not want to make us feel that we are worthless. However, we know that no amount of self-measuring will make us feel healthy deep inside ourselves.

Nowhere does God say that we as people do not do good things. We do. He acknowledges that if we perform an autopsy on human behavior and motivation, we will find good deeds. Living a life better than the next guy's is good, but not good enough. This is why Paul said in 2 Corinthians 10:12, "We do not dare to compare ourselves with some who commend themselves. When they measure themselves by themselves and compare themselves with themselves, they are not wise."

The Gospel Formula, Part I

> But now righteousness from God, a chapter from law, has been made known, to which the Law and the Prophets testify. This righteousness from God comes through faith in Jesus Christ to all who believe.
> —ROMANS 3:21–22

Sometimes we can go overboard looking for recipes for living—tight little formulas that are easily remembered and guarantee us that if we do these three things or those five things, good results will follow. But most of Scripture breathes and teaches a dynamic relationship between God and His people, not multistep formulas.

Here in the book of Romans, however, we see a recipe that gives us the four critical ingredients of the gospel. The gospel is:

1. From God
2. Through faith
3. In Jesus
4. To all

You can't pick and choose your ingredients; you must combine all four to achieve spiritual success.

My daughters enjoy cooking in part because they like to be in the kitchen, and also because they enjoy entertaining friends. It's quite common for them to try to make up something from scratch. One night my oldest daughter had several friends over and they decided to make cookies without looking at a recipe. They put in what they thought would be the right amounts of sugar and flour and eggs and water. They put the dough in small pieces on the cookie sheet and baked it. After a few minutes, smoke started billowing from the oven. They opened the door; their "cookies" had become a single sheet of smoking mess. They all laughed at their mistake, pulled out a recipe book, and started over.

God never intended for us to figure out the gospel formula on our own. He spelled it out for us clearly in the Bible, and when we tinker with it we always create a mess. Some may say that the gospel is from someone other than God, or that we can achieve salvation through our good works or through someone other than Jesus. Some religions even believe the gospel is exclusive for their label of faith.

But the recipe could not be clearer. It is from God . . . through faith . . . in Jesus . . . to all. The gospel is not a human plan for people who are reaching to God, but a divine plan for God reaching down to mankind.

The Gospel Formula, Part II

> But now righteousness from God, apart from law, has been
> made known, to which the Law and the Prophets testify.
> This righteousness from God comes through faith in Jesus
> Christ to all who believe.
> —ROMANS 3:21–22

A person never realizes the power and strength of the gospel until he or she is lost or at the point of being utterly stranded and needing a massive, miraculous rescue. Then the power of the gospel comes to play as never before. Have you ever been hopeless and helpless, running out of air speed, altitude, runway, and fuel, as a pilot might say? In that kind of bankrupt state, the gospel can come in and make all the difference.

But God's rescue of us is not a single transaction. We don't buy our ticket to heaven and then go about our business. Rather, through the gospel God wants to revolutionize not just the way I spend eternity, but the way I live every day individually.

The heart of the gospel, which is from God . . . through faith . . . in Jesus . . . to all, can be found in 1 Corinthians 15:3–8. Jesus lived, He died, He rose, and He appeared.

One of the biggest misconceptions of men and women of faith in the work world is that the gospel is something with only spiritual dimensions and related only to the hereafter. When we first read through the Bible, we can see where somebody would say that. But when you begin to unpack the gospel in all of its deep and intricate meanings, you find that what God offered to us as people in the gospel was something He intended to have grafted into the persons we are, twenty-four/seven. The gospel was intended to revolutionize our motivation for life and work, transform the way we approach ethical decisions, and alter every aspect of our lives.

Contemplating the gospel formula, I am reminded that I'm not alone. God has committed Himself to me. Through Christ, He has built a giant highway between Himself and me, and I can interact with Him minute by minute, nonstop, wherever I am, whatever I'm doing.

Works, Wages, and Credits

> Now when a man works, his wages are not credited to him
> as a gift, but as an obligation.
> —ROMANS 4:4

Most people who work for a living receive a paycheck every week or every couple of weeks. They do their jobs, and when payday comes around they receive what is rightfully theirs: the money they earned for the work they have accomplished.

For many people, this concept is the heart of their gospel: through their good works they earn their way into heaven, and when the time comes God will pay them what they have earned.

But the one true gospel is based on the concept of giving, not earning.

Imagine you are out looking for a birthday present. But before you decide how much to spend on someone else, you pull out your electronic organizer and you look up your friend on file. You add up all the good or pleasing things she has done, subtract all the bad or irritating things she has done, and you come up with a score that indicates you can spend $39.13 for a gift.

That's not the right model of giving a gift. Giving is based on love and appreciation—on heartfelt enthusiasm on the giver's part to reach out to someone else. In this chapter of Romans, Paul makes a methodical case, almost like a lawyer before a jury pounding the argument over and over in case one of the twelve jurors doesn't understand, or in case someone went to sleep earlier in the testimony.

This gospel he has referred to earlier, this righteousness he has been writing about, this salvation he refers to, is not something we work for and receive as a wage. It has nothing to do with that. It has everything to do with our believing and receiving a gift.

In our capitalist, free-enterprise system, where we earn almost everything we get, this concept of receiving something we have not—and cannot—earn is difficult to internalize. But we must wrench ourselves away from the mind-set that we can earn our way into the presence of God.

We need to pause at our desk, or chair, or in bed at night, and thank God for this incredible gift. We don't deserve it, but we do receive it from Him. That's all God expects from us, as paltry as it sounds. He just wants us to receive His Good Gift.

A Different Kind
of Credit Report

"It was credited to him as righteousness." The words "it was
credited to him" were written not for him alone, but also for us,
of whom God will credit righteousness—for us who believe in
Him who raised Jesus our Lord from the dead.
—ROMANS 4:22–24

I t was credited to him as righteousness." The *him* is the great
Old Testament hero Abraham, a man who found himself having a late-life conversion. Abraham had everything going for him.
He was financially successful. He enjoyed a wonderful family situation. He was an important man in the town where he lived. He
had all the elements that would have allowed him to honestly say,
"I've got life wired!"

Then one day he had this experience between himself and
God, and he learned that God had something else in mind for his
life. From that point forward throughout history, Abraham has
represented a mountain of faith. If we wanted to emulate someone who relates to God, it would be Abraham.

But even Abraham, in all his good doing, was not able to
contrive his own righteousness. Rather, it was something done on
his behalf by a compassionate and loving God.

Abraham was credited with righteousness. The word *credited,* of course, is an accounting term. When you balance your

checkbook, you double-check to be sure that the bank has credited your deposits to the right account. Now, suppose you found an extra deposit, as if someone had direct-deposited money into your account. That's the picture of what happens here. God credited righteousness to Abraham.

This is the most important message in the Scripture—the message that begins in Genesis and flows all the way through Revelation: what God did for Abraham He does for us—through Jesus Christ. God has made a deposit on our behalf—a deposit of righteousness through our Savior. It becomes ours when we choose to accept it. That deposit is the bank account that we can draw upon for a peaceful, fulfilling life of happiness.

Peace

Therefore, since we have been justified through faith, we have peace with God through our Lord Jesus Christ.
—ROMANS 5:1

The gospels record in several places Jesus' warnings that we will face troubles in our world: "In this world you will have trouble. But take heart! I have overcome the world" (John 16:33). He also assures us: "Peace I leave with you; my peace I give you. . . . Do not let your hearts be troubled and do not be afraid" (John 14:27).

Do you know the peace of God? Do you dwell in that peace? Do you keep that peace in your heart?

The early years of the twenty-first century will be remembered as a time of trouble—a time when Americans sought peace in the world and peace in their hearts and had a difficult time finding either. Christ made it clear: in our lifetimes, we may never experience peace in our world. Although a country may not be at war, it will experience economic troubles, physical afflictions, and difficult relationships.

In the New Testament the word *peace* entails the quality of being of a person. Rest, contentment, and self-control all begin with this peace. When Jesus and His disciples are sailing across the lake (Mark 4:35–41), the raging storm around them hurls the disciples into a panic. They allow the external trouble to become internal turmoil. Jesus is in the same storm in the same boat, but instead of standing on the deck and hanging onto the side of the boat in fear, he is relaxing—snug under a cover taking a nap. When the disciples, in their panic, wake Him and express their fears, Jesus says to the storm, "Peace! Be still."

His message to us today is this: whenever you leave shore, God Himself is in the midst of your boat, in the person of the Holy Spirit. You are not now alone and never were. So why are you worried about storms around you? Regardless of the storms you find yourself in, He's in the middle with you, and you have nothing to worry about. You can experience His peace in your soul. There will be trouble around you. You can count on it. However, peace is not the absence of trouble and problems; it is the presence of God.

Three-Legged Stability

> We rejoice in the hope of the glory of God. Not only so, but
> we also rejoice in our sufferings, because we know that suffering
> produces perseverance; perseverance, character; and character,
> hope.
> —ROMANS 5:2–4

Certain things come with suffering that you cannot find anywhere else. Even when you are weighed down heavily with
suffering—especially then—you have the ability to construct one
of the stablest, strongest foundations for life. Through suffering
you can build perseverance, character, and hope.

Suffering is one of the "big ideas" in Scripture, ranging from
why bad things happen to good people to "Why me?" The entire
book of Job is about suffering. Suffering is a big word; it's an idea
the size of an aircraft carrier, and it can mean all kinds of things
to different people. The core concept of suffering is that something
has arrived on the doorstep of my life that initially brings a tear to
my eye and a frown to my face. Suffering is difficult. It is challenging. It can't be eliminated quickly.

But through this life of suffering, I am able to create, discover, and engage in three concepts that at first don't seem to go
together: perseverance, character, and hope.

There always will be elements of difficulty and a certain
amount of suffering in our work. For some folks, the suffering fre-
quency is turned up high. The book of Genesis makes it clear that
we are to provide for ourselves and our families "by the sweat of

your brow" (3:19). Our sweat may create physical, mental, or emotional stress because of our jobs.

But Paul reminds us that we have an opportunity to go to school on the topic of suffering and graduate with a degree in perseverance, character, and hope. You've seen people who have earned these degrees. They stand out from the crowd at work, among your friends, and at church. Are you one of them?

Perseverance

We know that suffering produces . . . perseverance.
—ROMANS 5:4

Someone said that perseverance is not a long race, but rather many short races, one after another. It is certainly true, in theory and in life. In life we all are on a mountain-climbing adventure of one sort or another. The road is rugged. The weather is challenging. There are and there will be knockdowns as we walk along the path. We are reminded of what the apostle Paul, told the church in Corinth: "We are hard-pressed on every side, but not crushed; perplexed, but not in despair; persecuted, but not abandoned; struck down, but not destroyed" (2 Corinthians 4:8–9).

The biblical concept of perseverance is patiently and faithfully enduring under the load. As mountain-climbing adventurers, we all strap on a fifty-pound backpack even before we begin the journey. Sometimes life has that sense of heaviness. Things don't always turn out as we would like as we trudge through the valleys and shadows, through the "downers" and the deep end of the pool. We find ourselves treading water, no longer standing on bottom, and we wonder how much more we can endure.

We must be careful when we attempt to sort out people by one characteristic or another, but this is clear: humanity can be categorized by those who give up and those who do not.

We all get knocked down physically. We all face spiritual challenges and become emotionally bruised. Only some of us, however, hop up and get back into the game. Some of us persevere through suffering with an iron will in our psyche and personality. Although many do not persevere, all of us can, with God's help through prayer, endure any amount of suffering.

God does not ask us to joyfully whistle a tune while storms batter us against the rocks. He's not looking for stilted optimism. Nor does he care for our complaints in our suffering.

How strong is your perseverance muscle?

Character

We know that suffering produces . . . character.
—ROMANS 5:4

Our society is enamored with leadership. It ought to be enamored with character instead. Character is the internal quality that combines morality, attitudes, and behavior. It has been said, rightly, that our reputation is what others think of us, but our character is what we really are. The estimation of character is determined by what we would do if no one ever saw or knew what we were doing.

Paul uses the Greek word *dokime,* the same word for metal that passes through the fire so that everything base has been purged out of it. He gives us a clear picture of what happens when affliction is forged with internal purity, and something good is produced: character.

Some of the deepest work of God in any of our lives is the sifting and testing of our motives. He uses a Job model of suffering and pressure and trials to unbutton the depths of who we are and to bare our souls.

When people talk about the experiences that shaped them into who they are, how often do they point to a season of suffering? Many older Americans, for example, are thankful for having lived through the Great Depression, not because they enjoyed enduring the pain but because on the backside of hardship and suffering a model of character was created in them.

We spend untold millions of dollars and working hours growing the leadership component in corporate America. If we would instead embrace the graduate school of suffering and allow it to grow the right kind of character in us, we might wonder if good leadership is but a by-product of good character.

Hope

Suffering produces . . . hope.
—ROMANS 5:4

Hope is more than human-contrived optimism. The shallow optimism we too often display rarely stands up against real difficulties. Real hope is not my deciding to smile and be happy this morning. Hope is more than a personality type or a temperament. Certainly some people are more naturally hopeful than others. They are jolly and optimistic, and they look at the bright side of life. They have a real sense of optimism, seeing the highest, happiest, biggest, and best potential.

The biblical concept of hope is much more than optimism, even genuine optimism. Biblical hope is a cardinal virtue of the Scripture, a core idea that is central to the Bible from Genesis to Revelation.

Real hope is constructed on reality, not just dreams and illusions. Biblical hope is built on the indestructible God and His truth. In other words, because God is who He is, and because He is indestructible and trustworthy, I can have hope. I can believe what He says.

Henry Wadsworth Longfellow said, "'Tis always morning somewhere." We can take hope that at every moment, the sun is rising somewhere. But here's the real hope of the Bible: when sunrise stops, life doesn't end. Rather, we are deposited into what God calls eternity. There again, God is the stability and the security of eternity, and still we have hope.

It's easy in a workplace setting to distinguish people with hope, those with a sort of internal foundation where they have driven pillars deep down below the surface of life. They rely on these pillars of solid rock. That's where they get their hope.

Even though the last chapter has not been written, they understand and believe that God is in control, even if in a dark moment they consider the possibility that the sun might not rise tomorrow. When a company is experiencing market gyrations, someone with the ability to discern genuine hope is extremely valuable. This man or woman of faith can impart the concept of hope into any job, and import that hope into the entire company.

Reconciliation

For if, when we were God's enemies, we were reconciled to Him through the death of His Son, how much more, having been reconciled, shall we be saved through His life! Not only is this so, but we also rejoice in God through our Lord Jesus Christ, through whom we now have received reconciliation.

—ROMANS 5:10–11

What drama there is in these two verses, as they picture the ultimate "before and after"! We were enemies, but now we have become something different—what is called "reconciled." Through reconciliation we can rejoice. We can celebrate. Before, we learned to take on the posture of an enemy, a prisoner of war, despondent, with no true hope. Now we are reconciled.

Reconciliation has its root in the concept of alteration. Think about a tear in a garment—a gaping hole in your shorts or britches. A seamstress, with needle and thread, puts it back together, altering the garment and making it whole again. At its core, that's what reconciliation is about. It requires someone from the outside to mend the tear in our garment, which is our very soul.

When we apply this concept to the whole of humanity, we see clearly that we as humanity are torn in our relationship with God. But God is the divine tailor, and with his loving, skillful, tender hands He patches up our relationship.

Reconciliation is a beautiful picture in the Scripture. Remember the parable of the prodigal son, who ripped himself away from his father? To be mended, he had to come back and ask to be sewn back into the family. The loving tailor, his loving father, reconciled the son back to himself and the rest of the family. That's the picture of reconciliation.

Any reflection on the topic of reconciliation should create a range of emotions within the reconciled son or daughter of faith, from tremendous gladness to be home and sewn up, to a tremendous sense of guilt and shame for what we did to create the tear. The apostle Paul here does not ask us to wallow in guilt and blame; rather, he asks us to get up and live as a privileged member of the family enjoying the possibilities that come with reconciliation with God.

Have you experienced this kind of reconciliation? Are you enjoying the benefits?

Grace, Part I

But the gift is not like the trespass. For if the many died by the trespass of the one man, how much more did God's grace and the gift that came by the grace of the one man, Jesus Christ, overflow to the many!
—ROMANS 5:15

Not too long ago, my kids watched the old-time movie *Flubber* (which Disney has recently remade). The premise of the movie is simple: an inventor creates this blob of substance he calls flubber, which alters everything it touches. When flubber touches an ordinary basketball, the ball bounces higher. When flubber touches tennis shoes, they run faster. When it touches an automobile, the car begins to fly. Flubber alters the constitution of everything.

In the New Testament, there is a concept called grace. It acts like flubber when people effectively rub against its true biblical understanding. It alters their lives. How they approach God, how they handle life, and how they see other people is dramatically changed. The very constitution of their life is altered.

What is grace? We use the word to describe a dancer's movement, the elegance of a queen, the smooth beauty of a deer running through the woods, and even the perfunctory pause before a meal. But what is grace, as the Bible uses the term?

One Bible teacher has defined grace as "a demonstration of deep love toward me that I do not deserve and that I could never repay." Anything less is really not grace at all. Are you trying to establish a relationship with God based on anything but His grace?

All of history will record that there has been every color and flavor of religious formula on this earth, but every single one can be put in one of two groups: those religions that base salvation on our ability to do something to get ourselves to God or to get ourselves in good standing with God, and those that say our salvation is something God has done on our behalf. That's the dividing line of grace—something God has done for us that we don't deserve and we can't repay.

Grace, Part II

> But the gift is not like the trespass. For if the many died by the trespass of the one man, how much more did God's grace and the gift that came by the grace of the one man, Jesus Christ, overflow to the many!
>
> —ROMANS 5:15

Grace is (again, as the Bible teacher wrote) "a demonstration of deep love toward me that I do not deserve and that I could never repay." Are you living out your faith experience under daily grace? Some people initially accept the gift of grace from God to them as the way to relate to God. But we as Americans are so independent, so utilitarian, so work-oriented, that many of us men and women of faith have migrated away from a grace-based relationship with God to an amalgamated concoction of a little bit of grace and a little bit of works—in other words, my salvation is a little bit of God and a little bit of me. Actually, I must live out my faith in the understanding of what God has done for me and that I don't deserve it.

Daily we must ask ourselves, "Am I treating other people with grace? How do I balance the concept of grace in a workplace setting, between letting anybody do anything they want and becoming so legalistic that I overpower the abilities of others?" If I have experienced grace, I must extend grace. I must give others a chance to mess up so that we all learn the art of forgiveness. I must allow people to forgive me so that we can all move on.

In a classic short story, Ernest Hemingway wrote of a distraught father in Spain who wants nothing but to be reunited with his estranged son. He places an ad in the newspaper that reads, "Paco, meet me at Hotel Montana noon Tuesday—all is forgiven." Paco is a very common name in Spain, and when the father goes to the square he finds eight hundred young men named Paco waiting for their fathers.

Our society is filled with "Pacos" who are in desperate need of tasting grace, of sensing forgiveness. None of us deserves it; none of us can repay it. But we all need it more than life itself.

As men and women of faith, we are bound and obligated to figure out how to extend grace into the workplace setting—in small companies and large, public and private, and government offices as well. When we do, people around us will be transformed.

Open Under New Management

For we know that our old self was crucified with Him so that the
body of sin might be done away with, that we should no longer
be slaves to sin—because anyone who has died has been freed
from sin. Now if we died with Christ, we believe that we will
also be alive with Him.
—ROMANS 6:6–8

It was one of my favorite restaurants. It was quaint. It had good
food, and great atmosphere—one of those fun restaurants that
became a landmark in our area and was a must for people who
drove up for ballgames. But over the years, the food quality steadily
declined. The quaint turned into dirty, and the great atmosphere
turned into too much clutter.

One day while eating lunch there with a friend, I overheard
a conversation at the next table. "Someone needs to take this joint
over and give it a remake," the man said. Well, that is exactly what
happened. Within two weeks it was closed. The doors were
boarded, the windows were locked and dark, the parking lot was
empty. After the long, downward slide, I wondered whether anybody would be able to bring the old restaurant back to glory.

Then one day I noticed a sign: "Open under new management." Sure enough, someone had bought it out, taken it over,
cleaned it up, and brought it back—better than ever.

In Romans 6, a similar story unfolds of God the Father accomplishing the same thing with a man or woman who is in need

of major renovation. Man's original blueprint had God in the center; our lives were originally intended to be constructed around God. But selfish sin took over and moved God out. Mankind needs a serious makeover.

There is hope for the most rundown and dirty individuals to be restored to full use and glory, but to enjoy that renovation, we must be willing to come under New Management.

Breaking Free from Bad Habits

> Don't you know that when you offer yourselves to someone to obey him as slaves, you are slaves to the one whom you obey— whether you are slaves to sin, which leads to death, or to obedience, which leads to righteousness? But thanks be to God that, though you used to be slaves to sin, you wholeheartedly obeyed the form of teaching to which you were entrusted. You have been set free from sin and have become slaves to righteousness.
> —ROMANS 6:16–18

What's so bad about a habit? It depends on whether it's a good habit or a bad one. As good as good habits are, bad habits are just as bad. They have a destructive element that can be devastating. One might ask, "Can one pet sin or bad habit really be that destructive?" It certainly can be.

Many times, one bad habit is the weakest link in our character. That weak link can be transferred to our family and our friends. This is called a cycle of bad behavior. Bad habits can build deception and dishonesty—a cover-up style of life that is anything but authentic and transparent.

A bad habit can be a blind spot. More often it's something we know is wrong but we keep on doing it. Is it really possible to break the ball and chain of a bad habit?

Joyfully, Paul argues in Romans 6 that it is possible for any man or woman of faith to break this cycle of bad behavior. Paul gives us a tip that I believe worked for him daily. The tip is to realize that we are slaves to whatever or whomever we obey.

That is the key to a spiritual jailbreak. When I repeatedly follow the impulse of a bad habit, I dig a rut that my life enters by default. I must wrench myself out of the rut and take at least a baby step in a different direction. A decision to not do the same bad habit over and over again is the beginning step of establishing a good habit. By becoming a slave of righteousness, I am set free from the bondage of a bad habit.

Total Wipeout

For the wages of sin is death, but the gift of God is eternal life in Christ Jesus our Lord.
—ROMANS 6:23

Surfers started it, balancing on the blade of their board, relaxing and riding a wave until it played out. Often, however, surfers find themselves at the crest of a wave and they can't hold on. They tumble beneath the salty foam while their board goes flying high into the air in what they call a total wipeout. The result may or may not be physical harm, but one thing is for certain: a wipeout in the midst of competition means disqualification.

Racecar drivers experience it as well. They're flying around the track inches from each other, engines screaming, fans screaming. Then someone blows a tire, and it's a total wipeout. Disqualification, at best. Fatal, at worst.

Our daughter came home from summer camp the other day, and she told her mother that the clothes in her bag were extremely dirty. As a matter of fact, one bag had some clothes that probably needed to be thrown away. I entered the conversation and said, "No way, let's wash them." But our daughter insisted, "Dad you don't understand. We had a mud war in the rain. They're filthy—totally ruined. We might as well throw them away because we'll never get them clean."

Our souls are the same way. No amount of self-directed laundering can clean our stained selves enough to rightly relate to God. In reality, we have all experienced a total wipeout. We've all been engaged in a mud war in the rain. Although it seems illogical, the very best plan is to toss our dirty, stinky self-righteousness out the window, register it as a total wipeout, and appeal to God for new spiritual clothes.

A Spiritual Jailbreak, Part I

I do not understand what I do. For the things I want to do,
I don't do and the things I don't want to do, I do.
—ROMANS 7:15

I've always enjoyed reading letters, diaries, and memoirs. When someone takes the time to write a letter, you get a little peek into his or her soul. I recently was cleaning out a bookshelf where I discovered a book titled *I Love You, Ronnie,* more than two hundred pages of handwritten letters from President Ronald Reagan to his wife, Nancy. I began to thumb through and read some of the things he had written, realizing that it was impossible to read those letters without looking deep inside the man and acknowledging his intimate, unending love for his wife. They were written from the White House, from Air Force One, from hotels around the world, on all kinds of stationery with all kinds of closing signatures. He used many nicknames for himself, including "The Ranch Hand" or simply "Ronnie." This was President Reagan's love language for the woman he loved. When you read that, you see the man, the president, his heart, and his passions. You look into his soul and get a glimpse of what was going on in his world.

Paul, in Romans 7, gives us the closest thing to a personal diary of his own spiritual pilgrimage to be found anywhere in the New Testament. It is emotional, and it is personal. He has recorded for us a little bit of insight of what he was going through.

Every Christmas our family receives holiday letters from friends, and the news almost invariably is good ("Billy's made the honor role at Harvard; Patty is the piano solo champion; the dog and cat are best friends; all our stocks are up; Jim's job couldn't be better"). I'm still waiting for the Christmas letter that resembles our life: a typical family struggling with day-to-day issues.

Romans 7 is the apostle Paul's Christmas letter. Written in mid-winter in A.D. 57 or 58, it is a diary of what was going on with Paul—how his year unfolded and what his spiritual condition was, including several confessions—in this emotional, transparent letter.

If someone discovered the intimate letters that chronicled your relationship with God from the last few years, what would they find? Paul gives us his. As we read them we see him pulling back the curtain and exposing his struggles. What are the issues deep inside you that are keeping you from living like a child of the King?

A Spiritual Jailbreak, Part II

For I have the desire to do good but I cannot carry it out.
—ROMANS 7:18

Romans 8 exclaims the victory speech of a man who has just been set free. The question is, "Free from what?" The apostle Paul's own spiritual condition is outlined in the form of a confessional in "A Spiritual Jailbreak, Part I." It would surprise, if not stun, many of us to know how confused and desperate Paul was. Through his Christmas letter diary, he gives us five insights into his soul. Here we'll examine Paul's self-revelation and seek similarities in our own lives. Then we will see how Paul dealt with these issues, and find guidance for dealing with them ourselves. When Paul looked into the mirror, what did he say?

"I am confused."

On my drive home, I pray that I will walk in the door cheerfully from work. I plan to smile, but ten minutes later I turn off the car and Darth Vader steps through our front door. What happened? Like Paul, I set out to do one thing and end up doing another. I get up in the morning and am determined to bring optimism to my job, but between my house and the parking lot I become someone different. Why can't I follow through with my good intention?

I resolve not to cast my eyes on filthy things. I even pray that God will strengthen me in looking only to the good. But when temptation arises before me, I do not turn away from it. I find myself in Paul's confused state of grace and corruption.

Even the most disciplined person among us finds it difficult to always do the right thing. We struggle. We shake our heads in discouragement, desperately wishing our lives were not so confusing.

Do you identify with the confusion that plagued Paul? I sure do. Where do we go for help, and what can we do? Don't give up yet. There is hope around the corner.

A Spiritual Jailbreak, Part III

But I see another law at work in me waging war against my mind and making me a prisoner of the law of sin.
—ROMANS 7:23

"I am in a battle."

When Paul looked into the mirror and then picked up a stylus to chronicle how he was feeling about his spiritual state, not only did he describe an internal sense of confusion but he also chronicled a nonstop battle between doing good and bad within himself: "I see another law at work in the members of my body, waging war against the law of my mind and making me a prisoner of the law of sin at work within my members."

Even when I am in a spiritual state, I find myself standing at the front lines battling my temper, impatience, self-control, sexual desires, dishonesty, laziness, and all kinds of secret skeletons that would breach my defenses or outflank me and come in from behind. Sometimes I can almost swear that I have a split personality, or that I am a walking civil war. I long for perfect holiness, but when the opportunity arises to step closer to that goal I choose to reject it and I fall away, wounded on the battlefield.

The good news is that there *is* a battle going on. I haven't completely surrendered to the dark side. However, at the same time, the bad news is that there is still a daily struggle going on.

Inside my chest are two competing voices battling for control. I am in a battle.

"I am a prisoner."

Paul clearly had the sense of being trapped. The description of his spiritual state is like a descending stairway that leads from confusion to battle to prison. When he reached the bottom, we find that Paul felt he was behind bars regarding being able to do the right thing.

Like a man who is sentenced to solitary confinement or ten years behind bars, Paul said, "I am a prisoner."

When we attempt to live by the law—when we rely only on the law for our salvation and righteousness—the law becomes our prison. "Who will rescue me from this body of death? Thanks be to God—through Jesus Christ our Lord!" (Romans 7:24–25).

Fortunate for us the diary doesn't end here. This is depressing news, but there is a jailbreak in the making. Stay tuned.

A Spiritual Jailbreak, Part IV

What a wretched man I am! Who will rescue me from this body of death?
—ROMANS 7:24

"I am exhausted."

Paul exclaims to the Romans, "What a wretched man I am!" The Greek word for *wretched* also translates to *callused*. In other words, Paul had tried everything he knew, the deeper life, the shallow life, this theology and that theology, praying hard, and fasting long. He talked it out, held it in; he tried every trick he knew. After all that, he opened himself up surgically—spiritually speaking— looked at his inner man, and saw that he had become blistered and then callused. He had done everything he knew to make the Christian life work for him, and then he found himself exhausted.

Paul often used athletic analogies. He writes of running a race. Every runner who has run any distance knows that there comes a point when you hit the wall. You are absolutely exhausted, and you would just as soon drop out of the race and watch the rest of the runners pass by. You also know through experience, however, that if you press on you can break through the wall and reach a state where you are running almost effortlessly.

Paul is at the wall spiritually—that place where he believes he cannot take another step. The great coach of the Green Bay Packers, Vince Lombardi, said, "Fatigue makes cowards of us all."

"I am hopeless."

Exhaustion leads to hopelessness. Paul asks, "Who will rescue me?" One word is the key to the rescue: *who*. Paul does not ask *what* will rescue him. He's not looking for a magic formula to follow. He's not going to any seminars or to the doctor for a pill.

It is a historic lament. Even Job cried, "Since I am already found guilty, why should I struggle in vain? If only there were someone to arbitrate between us . . . someone to remove God's rod from me" (Job 9:29, 33).

You and I are fighting the same battle that Paul and Job and all the spiritual giants and midgets have fought throughout the ages. Even in the Hall of Fame of Faith, we find hopelessness. What can we do?

Finally Free

> Therefore, there is now no condemnation for those who are in Christ Jesus, because through Christ Jesus the law of the Spirit of life set me free from the law of sin and death.
> —ROMANS 8:1–2

Finally, Paul adjusts his thinking. He breaks free, beginning with the answer to his question: "Who will rescue me from this body of death? Thanks be to God—through Jesus Christ our Lord!" He no longer sees himself a prisoner, and neither should we.

Two things are true about Paul and about us as men and women in Christ: we are forgiven, and we are freed. This new state overcomes our previous state of confusion, exhaustion, and hopelessness after being taken prisoner in our battle with the enemy. Forgiveness and freedom have no rivals. They bring with them a real and lasting peace as our bonds are broken—a deep sense of acceptance from God toward our person.

Notice, though, that Paul never says he does not deserve condemnation. He does, and we do as well. There may even be consequences of sin in this world. But there is no *condemnation*.

With the freedom of that knowledge, we no longer need to live a performance-oriented Christianity. We need not burden ourselves with a sackload of guilt slung over our shoulder.

Many times on the news these days we see images of men or women standing before a judge in a prison jumpsuit and shackles. That is the image Paul has painted for us in Romans 7 and 8. But in our case, the Judge has already served the time for us, so he tells the Marshall to remove the shackles and give us new clothes. The indictment has been quelled before the trial begins.

Not only that, but the Judge assigns a Helper to go with us as we walk out of the courthouse, One who will guide us in our new spiritual walk. So we step out into the sunshine feeling lighter, free and forgiven, praising the Judge for the new nature He has given us.

Mind Games

Those who live according to the sinful nature have their minds set on what that nature desires; but those who live in accordance with the Spirit have their minds set on what the Spirit desires. The mind of sinful man is death, but the mind controlled by the Spirit is life and peace; the sinful mind is hostile to God.
—ROMANS 8:5–8

If you're watching your weight, you're probably mindful that people like to admonish, "You are what you eat." If you're watching your spiritual diet, the phrase "You are what you think" fits the bill. In this verse from Romans 8, Paul makes it clear that the mind, as it relates to living and walking in the Spirit, plays the role of influencer. I know that when I desire to walk in the Spirit, I must absorb my mind in spiritual things. If I saturate my mind in things of the Spirit, I increase the likelihood that I will behave in a spiritual manner. This is about spiritual soaking.

For example, picture what happens when you marinate a steak in teriyaki sauce. The meat absorbs, or takes in through the pores, the flavors and juices of the marinade it's soaking in so that when I take a bite the flavor of the marinade has penetrated the flavor of the meat. When you and your children color Easter eggs, the same process happens. The eggshell absorbs the dye you've left it to sit in.

Paul is telling us that our mind acts as an impressionable sponge. It sits and it soaks. If I subject it to continuous office gossip, negative complaining, immoral television, and unhealthy music, those flavors will take hold. If you allow yourself to be influenced by such negative things, you hamper your ability to please God and walk in His spirit.

To further illustrate the point, take the world of commerce. Import and export gates allow or restrict product flow in and out of any country. Your mind, likewise, employs import gates that you as a follower of Jesus must monitor: the eye gate, ear gate, and imagination gate. I, too, must monitor what I read, what I see, and what I watch. What comes through my eyes affects my mind. What I listen to, including music, sounds, and words, affects my mind. My imagination gate monitors what I think and fantasize about. If I don't monitor those gates, I subject myself to the sinful nature of man, not the peaceful nature of the Holy Spirit.

I must allow only good and healthy things into my mind. In Philippians 4:8, Paul reminds us of this point again, saying, "Finally, brothers, whatever is true, whatever is noble, whatever is right, whatever is pure, whatever is lovely, whatever is admirable— if anything is excellent or praiseworthy—think about such things."

Are your thoughts noble, pure, and lovely? Are they absorbing the nature of the Holy Spirit? Or are they soaking up dirt like a sponge, getting your mind black and dirty?

Abba, Father

> For you did not receive a spirit that makes you a slave again to fear, but you received the Spirit of sonship. And by Him we cry, "Abba, Father." The Spirit himself testifies with our spirit that we are God's children. You receive the Spirit of sonship.
> —ROMANS 8:15–16

The term *daddy* is full of relationship, energy, and spiritual meaning. When you hurt yourself as a child, you likely cried out, "Daddy!" Or when you were excited, you called out for daddy in the same way. At other, more reserved times, you likely said "Dad" or "Father." That's because *daddy* carries some huge relational power. A child releases a real family force field in calling out "Daddy."

This is evident in Romans. Paul goes to great lengths to construct the family force that comes to play when a follower of Jesus cries out to the Lord. He uses the Aramaic word *Abba* in conjunction with "Father" in a very familiar, relational way to illustrate the fact that we are God's children, and we can cry out to Him just as we would to our earthly father.

Do you think of God as your father? We all have concocted understandings and images of God through life experiences, songs, movies, and past relationships. Some of these images are incomplete at best and heresy at worst, picturing Him as everything from the cosmic killjoy to the heavenly policeman. He wants us, though, to think of Him as our Father, someone we can cry out to in times of pain, sickness, disappointment, loneliness, or even excitement and joy.

The word *father* is used in the New Testament in relation to God 189 times. Selectively attached to *father* through the New Testament is the term *Abba,* giving those verses a more personal, relational feel. God has given us a picture of Himself as our father in Romans, showing us that you can't use the word *Abba,* Father, without uncovering a depth of personhood. That's what He wants: for us to draw closer to Him, to curl up in His lap and spill out our troubles to Him.

God Works It for Good

And we know that in all things God works for the good of those who love Him, who have been called according to His purpose.
—ROMANS 8:28

When your coworker finds himself a victim of the company's recent layoffs, his colleagues comfort him with "It'll work out for the best." When you flub up a presentation and lose an account, people quickly assure you that "It wasn't meant to be." Even at church you might hear, "It just wasn't God's plan," when something fails to happen that a person hoped for.

People use this verse in Romans 8 to lend credence to their comforting thoughts. Although famous, it is quite misunderstood. The verse does not say that all the things that happen every day are good things. Bad, disappointing, even evil things happen every day around the world. We all know that to be painfully true.

Nor does the verse say that good comes from all things for all people. Rather, it's a promise that God works all things for good for those who love Him, who have been called according to His purpose. God promises only that He will work things for good for those of us who love Him and work toward His purpose. That's why those pat responses people give others in times of pain, about all things working out in the end, don't hold water. God never promises that all things will turn out rosy, especially for those who don't live for Him. Even the most righteous among us experience pain and suffering. Just ask Job from the Old Testament and Paul from the New Testament for a testimony.

Nor does it say that God's goodness is the same as personal happiness. The key difference here is that God works all things to benefit His plan—not just to make us happy. Some things happen in our lives that don't seem right at the time. We may pray and pray for a new job or a promotion, and when it doesn't happen we assume that God ignored our requests, or that it wasn't His plan. But we must remember that His plan happens on His time, not ours.

Many times people can't fathom that our current circumstances could ever work out for good. The Scripture says that God does promise it will happen. But we must define good as God defines good. He defines good as that which serves His purpose—not just what puts smiles on our faces and makes our lives easier.

Five Staggering Questions

If God is for us, who can be against us?
—ROMANS 8:31

Boxing matches don't just take place in the boxing ring. Many offices host boxing matches, without the boss ever knowing. Just ask anyone who's ever had a fellow worker out to get him. Let's face it, not every office is full of nice people who want the best for everyone. From time to time a person finds himself or herself in the way of another's career, and that means being undermined at meetings, lied about, accused of untrue things, and separated from success.

At a time like this, it's likely that the person being beaten up by a coworker feels alone and discouraged because bullies have a way of turning everyone against the victim, no matter the circumstances. What the victim—you and I, in some situations—must understand is that we greatly underestimate God's willingness and ability to stand in our corner as we engage in these boxing matches of life.

In Romans 8:31–39, Paul asks five staggering questions that put our lives and faith into perspective. They help prove that God is on our side; He's in the boxing ring with us, standing on our side and lifting us out of reach of the bully situation intimidating us. In essence, these are the questions:

1. Who shall oppose us?
2. Who can accuse us?
3. Who can condemn us?

4. Who or what shall separate us?
5. Who or what shall defeat us?

The simple answer is that no one, or no thing, can ever oppose us, accuse us, condemn us, separate us, or defeat us so long as we have Christ on our side. God gave us His son to save us from sin. Don't you think that if God goes so far as to give us His son, He will protect us in the boxing match, that He will accept us, love us, forgive us, give us confidence, and free us from the trials that bullies bring?

When feeling cornered and down for the count, remember that God is on your side. He's in the ring with you at all times, and He won't let you down. Life was never meant to be slugged out by oneself. God is willing and able to enter any situation of conflict and pressure with us. He is pulling for us to make it and win in life, not to get beaten up day after day.

God and Mankind in Perspective

For from Him and through Him and to Him are all things. To Him be the glory forever! Amen.
—ROMANS 11:36

Perspective is a funny thing. From a distance, everything looks hundreds or even thousands of times smaller than it really is. Zoomed in tight, things look much larger than they really are. How things appear all depends on your viewpoint.

From a distance, God might not seem large or powerful to you. Because we are so close to our daily lives, the needs, wants, problems, and triumphs of life, it's easy to think of ourselves as larger than life and make God some small aspect. But that's a distorted, one-sided view.

God is greater than humans. He always has been; He always will be. Romans 11:33–36 tries to illustrate the vastness of our Creator. Verse 33 talks about the depth of the riches of the wisdom and knowledge of God. Try picturing how deep the ocean is, or how high the sky travels. It seems infinite from our perspective. Guess what? God is bigger.

Verse 33 continues by saying that His paths are beyond tracing. Picture the most complicated garden maze you've ever seen— and not been able to complete. God is much more complicated to track down than that. His ways are a mystery, and no sleuth, not even Sherlock Holmes, can figure out His path.

In verse 35, the writer asks who has ever given to God, that God should repay him. When a friend helps you out of a bind— such as finishing a project for you while you're out sick, and thus saving you from being in the next round of layoffs—you feel you owe this friend more than you could ever possibly repay. There is nothing, however, that you could do to make God feel He must repay you. In fact, you'll live in eternal debt of love to Him for all He has done in your life.

Clearly God and humans are two different beings. Our perspective on Him is limited, but these verses help us understand that He is much bigger than us, and much bigger than we can even comprehend.

I remember sitting at the top of a football stadium at an NFL game. The players looked like ants from where I sat. From my perspective, I was much larger, and much tougher, than any of the guys on the field. But after the game I had the occasion to go down to the sidelines and meet a bunch of the players. I was absolutely staggered at the size of these guys. Up close—and in proper perspective—I looked like the ant I thought they were from afar.

As long as I sit up in the stands, perched in the upper decks looking out at God, I'll have a big view of myself and a small view of Him. To put things into perspective, I must come out of the upper deck and walk close to Him on the field. Then I'll find myself measured correctly.

A Living Sacrifice

Therefore, I urge you, brothers, in view of God's mercy, to offer your bodies as living sacrifices, holy and pleasing to God—this is your spiritual act of worship. Do not conform any longer to the pattern of this world, but be transformed by the renewing of your mind. Then you will be able to test and approve what God's will is—His good, pleasing and perfect will.

—ROMANS 12:1–2

Nothing is as good as the original. Case in point: my wife usually does the grocery shopping. She knows exactly what we need and which brands work best for her recipes. I recently offered to do a quick shopping run one busy afternoon, on condition that she make a (very) detailed list, which she did. Only problem was, I lost the list on the way to the store. Instead of admitting defeat and calling for help, I tried to complete the shopping from memory. Needless to say, I brought home the wrong brands, sizes, and quantities of most things. My substitute list just didn't cut it.

Likewise, substitutes don't work in our spiritual life. As a follower of Jesus, nothing substitutes for unceasingly placing our lives on God's altar. Nothing. You can't read *Cliff's Notes* of the Bible, send God an e-mail, and call it good. You can't count the religious or goodwill deeds done and think that God is impressed. This is why God says over and over in the Bible that he would rather have personal obedience than sacrifice. God doesn't want a substitute for you; He wants you. You must regularly put yourself on His altar, sacrificing your own life to Him.

In these verses, the writer grabs the thread of so much of the Old Testament, bringing in the idea of sacrifice and altars, of worship, and of God's mercy. He calls our bodies "living sacrifices." But this isn't meant, obviously, in the same way sacrifices were meant in the Old Testament. When God gave us Jesus to die on the cross for our sins, Jesus fulfilled the ultimate sacrifice. The sacrifice He wants from us is the daily pledging of our lives back to Him and His purposes. He wants us to do it in our first awakened breath of every morning to announce to Him, "Lord, here I am. Forgive me. Fill me. Take me. Use me. I am available for you."

It's our job to establish a relationship with God, pray daily, read His word, and give of ourselves regularly as thanksgiving to Him for His ultimate sacrifice. He didn't cut corners in creating us, in comforting and loving us, or in giving His son to us. He deserves so much more than we can give, so why would we ever try substituting what we give Him for something less? It just doesn't cut it.

Watch Out for the Squeeze Play

Do not conform any longer to the pattern of this world, but be transformed by the renewing of your mind. Then you will be able to test and approve what God's will is—His good, pleasing and perfect will.

—ROMANS 12:2

Poured concrete sets in the shape of its frame. Lay out a six-foot-by-eight-foot square of wood frames, pour in the concrete, and you'll get a concrete slab the size of the frames. You can't expect anything different of the concrete in those circumstances.

My life is the concrete: moldable, easily influenced, and susceptible to my surroundings. The wooden frames represent the place I put myself in life. Whatever I frame around my world is what I will become. If I constantly frame myself in the world—meaning, surrounding myself with music, movies, activities, and people who believe what the world believes and live by the world's standards—then I will become like the world. But if I set my frames around God, surrounding myself with things that are holy and good, I will become more like God. Isn't that the goal?

Twenty-five years ago, I first heard Howard Hendrix say, "Don't let the world squeeze you into its mold." I was reminded of this admonition the other day when I was driving through Los Angeles on a six-lane highway, squeezed between two semis. It was late in the evening, so the traffic was moving at a fast pace. Driving a small sedan between two huge semis is always a little scary, but when those semis start crowding your lane, you start to panic. When that squeeze play happens you must either speed up or slow down, but one thing is clear. You must get out of the squeeze zone.

The picture that Paul is trying to relate in this verse from Romans 12 is that I need to be very careful not to let unhealthy things squeeze me out of the lane I'm driving in, or become shaped into something other than God's design. Allowing this to happen means I'll start thinking things I don't want to think, acting in ways I don't want to act in, and surrounding myself with people who won't influence me for good.

Unlike the frame set for concrete—a quick, deliberate process—setting the frames of your life is a slow and sometimes unnoticed process. Evaluate your life now, while you're soft and malleable. Make sure you're not setting yourself into a mold that will set you into a hard person of the world. If you're getting squeezed into the wrong lane, get out. It could end up ugly.

A True Estimate of Yourself

> For by the grace given me I say to every one of you: do not think of yourself more highly than you ought, but rather think of yourself with sober judgment, in accordance with the measure of faith God has given you.
>
> —ROMANS 12:3

Some people think too much of themselves. They see themselves as more important, more skilled, more intelligent, more talented, and more charming than they really are. Clearly their self-image is not suffering a bit.

On the other hand, some people think too little of themselves. They see themselves as unimportant, irrelevant, having nothing to offer, and not worth anyone else's time.

Just because these people have inflated or deflated images of themselves doesn't mean that's reality. The problem is, these people—possibly including you and me—aren't seeing themselves through the eyes of God. Instead, they're using a warped worldview to value their skills, intelligence, or beauty. Good news: the Scripture calls for us to have a true estimate of ourselves. This means we are to measure ourselves on the basis of our identity in Christ.

The author of Romans makes it clear that God calls for us to have a true estimate of ourselves. He says if we are to think clearly of ourselves, we must have sober judgment when we look in the mirror, and we must see ourselves according to God's design.

What does he mean by telling us to have "sober judgment"? He means to not be intoxicated through self-deception. Don't look into the mirror and think that your high title, big toys, quick wit, or huge bank account gives you self-worth. Put aside the meager comparisons between you and others that leave you thinking, *Well, I'm really not that bad. Just look at so-and-so.* Instead, begin to see yourself for what you're worth in God's eyes.

Figure out exactly who God created *you* to be—not who He created your boss or coworker to be. When I tap into God's reality and discover that I have God's creative fingerprints on me personally, I gain a tremendous sense of confidence, and a healthy self-image starts to take shape. The image is grounded in the security of having God's prints on me. Now, that is a sobering thought. God created me, and He created me with a purpose in mind.

Although all believers are created equal, all of us have our own sense of unique contributions. God made us different from each other for a reason: to serve Him in the best way we can as individuals. Look inside and figure out who He wants you to be—and judge yourself only against that expectation.

Unique Spice
in a Bitter Society

Love must be sincere. Hate what is evil; cling to what is good.
Be devoted to one another in brotherly love. Honor one another
above yourselves. Never be lacking in zeal, but keep your
spiritual fervor, serving the Lord. Be joyful in hope, patient
in affliction, faithful in prayer. Share with God's people who
are in need. Practice hospitality.
—ROMANS 12:9–13

I remember the first time I bit into authentic Indian food. It was seasoned heavily with cumin. I'm not an adventurous eater, and this was stepping out on a limb for me. The pungent spice assaulted my senses; my eyes watered, I felt a catch in my throat, and I'm sure my face contorted into something very unattractive as I tried getting past that first taste. The bitter spice left an unpleasant aftertaste, one I was determined to never experience again.

In life, just as in eating new things, we sometimes bite into something bitter that leaves us feeling less-than-pleased. Our society is full of attitudes, words, and actions that leave us looking for something sweet to erase the memory of the bitter.

In Romans 12:9–13, as in 1 Corinthians 13, God gives us an answer to the bitterness that surrounds us: agape love. Agape love is a faith-based kind of love that's different from any other kind of qualitative love. It softens the bite of any mean taste this world throws into the soup.

The verses in Romans 12 list seven qualities of agape love. First, it is sincere. There's nothing self-serving or fake about this kind of love. It's true and pure, something that surely leaves a pleasant taste in your mouth. Second, it develops loyalty and devotion. Third, agape love builds others' self-esteem. Remember, it's not self-serving; instead, it's about building up others and encouraging them. Fourth, this pure love is fueled from serving the Lord. A spiritually lazy person may struggle with knowing true agape love, but one who fervently seeks the Lord will know its true nature. Fifth, the love Paul talks about in these verses grows from the correct response to adversity when you find yourself in tough times. Sixth, agape love is faithful at all times. Last, it's what makes you reach out to those in need.

We live in a world in which, every day, we're likely to find something that turns our stomach, makes our eyes water, or elicits a groan of disgust. This is why finding something so pure and true, this agape love, makes us rejoice. Who wouldn't prefer a taste that makes us smile rather than a bitter one that leaves us regretting eating our food?

Operation Sandpaper

> Bless those who persecute you; bless and do not curse. Rejoice
> with those who rejoice; mourn with those who mourn. Live in
> harmony with one another. Do not be proud, but be willing
> to associate with people of low position. Do not be conceited.
> Do not repay anyone evil for evil. Be careful to do what is right
> in the eyes of everybody. If it is possible, as far as it depends
> on you, live at peace with everyone. Do not take revenge, my
> friends, but leave room for God's wrath. . . . Do not be
> overcome by evil, but overcome evil with good.
> —ROMANS 12:14–21

OK, admit it. There's someone in your office who just drives you crazy. Perhaps it's the coworker who noses into every conversation you have, offering her opinion on subjects that don't involve her. Or maybe it's your boss, the man who gives you an assignment—and then takes it back three days later to rethink the direction of the project.

Have you ever thought that God uses those people to knock the rough edges off you, like sandpaper? I know that in every irritating relationship I've had, God has used those people to soften my character and bring some shine and luster to my life.

God has wired us for good, healthy, relational dynamics. So when we find ourselves in a healthy environment but getting rubbed raw, we must see this as sandpaper in the hands of God. Here's how He wants us to respond to conflict:

1. *Go against our first impressions and reactions.* Verse 14 says "Bless those who persecute you; bless and do not curse." This

definitely goes against my natural inclinations. I'd be more inclined to give back more fully what my persecutor gives me: he curses me, I curse him louder. He hurts me, I hurt him more. But God directly instructs us to do otherwise.

2. *Develop empathy for other people.* A person who can't empathize with others constantly struggles with relationships. But being able to rejoice or mourn with others makes us better people and leads us into the agape love God calls for (verse 15).

3. *Strive for harmony within a sense of personal humility.* Some people don't strive for harmony, but God calls them to seek harmony *and* humility. Don't break your arm trying to pat yourself on the back for your harmonious efforts (verse 16).

4. *Leave the avenging to God.* It's God's job to right the wrongs, repay bad actions. Get that? It's God's job, not ours. End of story (verse 19).

5. *Meet your enemy's needs.* You've heard the phrase "kill 'em with kindness." I've found this to be of particular help when facing a driver afflicted with road rage. Smile, wave, and allow the person into your lane. The aggressive driver certainly doesn't expect you to react that way, and your kindness will baffle the driver for days—or at least until the next angry driver gets in that person's way.

At the end of the day, God is the only one who has the ultimate perspective on rights and wrongs. There are so many times in life when we don't know the whole story of why a coworker is acting the way she is; why your boss is so uptight this week; or why you are surrounded by people who rub you raw. But God is really committed to balancing right and wrong, whether we recognize it or not. In the meantime, He's rubbing off our rough edges with His own special brand of sandpaper.

Government Has a Role

> Everyone must submit himself to the governing authorities,
> for there is no authority except that which God has established.
> The authorities that exist have been established by God.
> Consequently, he who rebels against the authority is rebelling
> against what God has instituted, and those who do so will
> bring judgment on themselves.
> —ROMANS 13:1–2

There's no disputing the fact that we must obey God's rules, since He is the ultimate authority on our lives. But a harder concept to grasp is that we must obey government authorities, too, because God established all authorities. God says in Romans 13 that rebelling against government is the same as rebelling against God. Four principles emerge from Romans 13:1–7 to help us frame our thinking and behavior regarding our role with government.

First, God has established all authority (verse 1). It is interesting that God does not distinguish between conservative and liberal, modern or traditional, Christian or otherwise. He says that He established governments. It is one of His four divine institutions to help mankind live peacefully and successfully. Of course, the immediate question comes to mind, "What if the government is not God-honoring?" To that question we call upon the Old Testament leader Daniel for testimony. He had a career tie-in with the government officials of at least four pagan leaders. But he demonstrated both the need as well as the model for following Godless rulers and holding one's faith intact (Daniel 2:20–21; 4:17, 25, 32).

Second, rebellion against authority brings consequence

(verse 2). One of the side lessons from understanding and embracing authority is the portrait of seeing human governments as a snapshot of the concept of divine judgment. In other words, breaking the law has consequences.

Third, the government's job is to police injustice (verses 3–5). People in government are God's servants. They are to protect order and good. They are to punish wrong and evil. This is why God ordained them.

Fourth, the believer is to submit to and support the government (verses 6–7). Although we may not always agree with what those in power say, unless it clearly goes against God's word it's our moral obligation to obey. This idea is sometimes a hard pill to swallow, but knowing that our Lord instructs us to obey makes all the difference. Daniel spent a tremendous amount of time praying for those over him. We should pray for those in every government service. It keeps us in the correct frame of thinking and holds them up before the Lord for His help.

Resumes and Game Plans

I myself am convinced, my brothers, that you yourselves are full of goodness, complete in knowledge and competent to instruct one another.

—ROMANS 15:14

I've heard that a good way to build your resume is to write out what you want your resume to look like eventually. Fill in the types of skills you hope to learn, the accomplishments you want to achieve, the places you might like to work. Note when you expect to hit each of these goals. Then post this future-looking resume somewhere you're be able to see it regularly. Putting your plan on paper and reading it regularly helps you work toward your goals.

In our walk with Christ, we too must set goals. Staying stagnant won't do us any good. So where do you hope to be in your walk by this time next year? In five or ten years? Do you want to read the Bible in a year, or become more involved in certain aspects of your church? Perhaps you'd like to concentrate on spending more quiet time with God, aligning your will with His. All great goals.

Paul encourages the Romans in their walk with Christ (in Romans 15:14). Paul saw in them a sense of goodness and moral excellence, that they were striving to do the right thing. This is a quality that ought to receive a trophy in today's world. He said they were complete in knowledge—meaning, they were practicing what they had learned in the area of spiritual matters. Telling them they were competent in ability to instruct one another encourages them to push on. He's inspiring them to become someone different, holding their hand if necessary, taking them to a new horizon.

Paul ends the book of Romans with this vigorous affirmation of what he saw in the Roman believers. The application of his statements to our lives is clear: all of us have a chance to write out our own spiritual resume and draft our game plan for spiritual life. What does your game plan look like, and are you playing to win?

PART TWO

1 Corinthians
ORDER IN THE CHURCH

Key Elements

Purpose: to identify problems in the Corinthian church, to offer solutions, and to teach the believers how to live for Christ in a corrupt society

Author: Paul

To whom written: the church in Corinth and Christians everywhere

Date written: about 55 A.D.

Key Themes

- Human leadership and wisdom are shown to be inferior to divine leadership and wisdom.
- Freedom of choice in religious practice is explored and encouraged in all areas except where expressly forbidden in Scripture.
- Orderly worship; divisions of all sorts had crept into the Corinthian church and Paul was pleading for the high role of a Godly love.
- Spiritual diversity and giftedness are the backbone of authentic personal and corporate worship.

Enriched by God

For in Him you have been enriched in every way—in all your
speaking and in all your knowledge. . . .
—I CORINTHIANS I:5

A sure way to soften a person up before dealing a blow is to
offer a compliment. Chances are you've been on the receiving end of this action during an annual performance review at your
job. In many organizations, employees know they'll hear several
compliments before the dreaded word "however" strikes ("Jimmy,
you're doing a great job drumming up business for the company.
And clients rave about the way you handle their accounts. However, you still have areas of improvement we need to discuss . . .").

In case you thought all of those business gurus and consultants thought up the "three positives for every negative rule,"
think again. Paul used the rule when speaking to the Corinthians,
as evidenced in the verse here. The Corinthians were struggling
with their place in the world as new believers and often found
themselves grappling with idolatry, immorality, and spiritual im-
maturity. In his letter to the Corinthian church, Paul sought to address these issues in rather straightforward language. But before
diving in, he praised their strong points. Paul points out that the
people of Corinth spoke out about Christ, and that they were wise
enough to understand His truth.

Many times people employ this buttering-up tactic to deliver harsh news. It smoothes things over and paves the way for an
audience to hear what you have to say. But when done lovingly
and for the right reasons, this communication method serves an-

other more meaningful purpose. When your boss lists three positive things about you before offering constructive criticism, he is reminding you of the good in you—showing you that he has noticed your strong points and values you as a worker.

Paul reminds the Corinthians of the good in them—of their faith in God and ability to spread His word and perform good works in His name. It never hurts to remind others of their positive qualities, and it always helps to be reminded of all God has given you and your devotion to Him. Such simple reminders not only soften the blow of what you're about to hear next but also make the directions or criticisms that follow more meaningful. If you understand that someone cares for you and your well-being and reminds you of the context in which he or she is speaking, you more fully understand the situation.

Paul did not speak harsh words because he meant to offend or hurt his beloved churchgoers. He spoke because he wanted to draw them back to Christ and remind them for whom they live.

Power of Unity

Is Christ divided? Was Paul crucified for you? Were you baptized into the name of Paul?
—I CORINTHIANS 1:13

Is Christ divided? What a powerful question. Writers use what they call word pictures to make their points vividly; Paul employed the tactic when speaking to the church of Corinth, whose members were quarreling among themselves about pride in their leaders, misunderstandings about God's teachings, and many other questions of morality and worship. To make his point, Paul painted the word picture of Christ divided.

It is hard to allow yourself to think about the graphic picture of Christ (the human form) divided. But Paul is talking about Christ as the church—not just the building we worship in, but also the church as a whole body of believers following God.

Paul's words were written hundreds of years ago, but they're relevant today. It's not hard to find examples of squabbling and division in just about any local church over rules, doctrines, and disciplines. God gave us freedom in many areas of our life, and this freedom often leads to differences of opinion. But what we must understand is that we're not just hurting our pastor, our congregation, or ourselves when we disrupt the church; we're dividing Christ, and the spirit of our fellowship in the process.

Jesus desires His followers to live in harmony and love. During His final evening on this earth prior to His crucifixion, He labored through a prayer with His Father. It is recorded in John 17. What did He have on His heart that last night? The unity of those who would be His followers, those who claim His name as theirs.

Once we realize that our actions, words, and thoughts are splitting Christ, it's hard to keep the fight going. Take action to put Christ back together in your church and relationships, if necessary. Take a big-body-of-Christ approach to life. Make it a point to live with a wide road of acceptance of others, not a skinny, rigid, everyone-must-do-as-I-do religion. Pray for another church in your community today. Call upon the Lord to bless them.

Hidden Wisdom

". . . we speak of God's secret wisdom, a wisdom that has been hidden and that God destined for our glory before time began."
—I CORINTHIANS 2:7

The office gossip mill works faster than Jeff Gordon rounds a NASCAR lap. Tell someone any piece of information and ask that person to keep it a secret, and the juicy news will be around the building in ten seconds flat. It doesn't matter whether the story's about Suzy's new boyfriend, Fred's health problems, or Tom's run-in with the boss. Everyone wants in on the story.

In most cases, keeping a secret is considered a virtue. But not in the case of the "secret wisdom" Paul talks about sharing with the Corinthians in this verse. The secret wisdom is that of God's plan for our salvation, a plan God revealed within the resurrection of His Son.

God didn't intend for this information to be kept secret. From when time began, God knew He would send His Son to save us. He knew Jesus would be crucified on the cross for our sins, and that His resurrection would make God's plan known.

Still, God's plan remains secret for those who don't believe in Him. It's only upon learning about God as our savior, and upon accepting Him into our hearts, that we truly get in on the secret He keeps.

So here's one time when exercising our information-passing skills comes in handy. It's our job to spread the news about Jesus and what He does for our lives, to give as many people as possible a chance to be in on the best news ever. God wants us to shout it from the rooftops, broadcast it loud and clear. He wants everyone to find out His secret, even if it means spreading the word by whispering it to a coworker by the water cooler. Sometimes people listen closer when we speak more softly.

Do you remember the song we sang as children, "This Little Light of Mine"? It illustrates the point that we aren't to hide it under a bushel; no! We're to let our knowledge of Christ and His salvation for our lives be known to everyone. Hopefully your actions and demeanor in life show it, but as St. Francis of Assisi says, use words if necessary.

Freely Given

We have not received the spirit of the world but the spirit who is from God, that we may understand what God has freely given us.
—I CORINTHIANS 2:12

How often can you say that you freely give something to another person? It seems that so often we must give more of ourselves at work, home, and church than we really want to give. We might give to the office collection for a colleague's birthday out of a sense of obligation, or to keep tricky office politics at bay. Or we may give extra money to a visiting missionary at church, because guilt prompts us to do so. But when we freely give something, most often we do so because of love and because we genuinely care for the person we're giving to.

Understanding that concept makes this verse so powerful. Before we knew about God, He gave us the most precious gift He could give. The Bible doesn't say that we asked, begged, or cajoled Him into giving us His gift of salvation. Nor does it say He grudgingly offers salvation, or that He asks for payment in return. It says He has "freely given" us His gift.

The only condition placed on salvation is that we must accept it in order to understand it. A gift isn't a true gift if you say, "Great, thanks, now how much do I owe you?" It's a gift when you accept it—untie the bow, tear off the wrappings, and claim it as yours. This is what God wants us to do with His gift. He wants us to accept Him graciously, and return His gift with our love for Him. That's all.

Out of love, we'll find ourselves *wanting* to live for Him, doing things in return. Not out of a sense of obligation, but out of love and devotion. With God's gift, so freely given, we must do the same as we would with a birthday present from our parents: untie the bow, tear off the wrappings, and claim God as our own.

God's Field

For we are God's fellow workers; you are God's field,
God's building.
—I CORINTHIANS 3:9

A field is obviously an integral part of achieving a farmer's plan. Without a field to plant corn, wheat, and other crops in, or to keep cows and pigs for food production, a farmer wouldn't be able to earn a livelihood. Without a field, the plan would crumble.

I am the soil that God grows his crop in. My soil can be rich and full of nutrients, allowing the roots of truth to grow deep. Or my soil can be shallow, full of rocks beneath the surface and thorns above it. Jesus must have had this image in mind when He told the parable of the four kinds of soil in Matthew. I am not responsible for the seed. I am not in charge of the weather. I am not in charge of the organic growth of the seed. What I am in charge of is the soil. It is my job to keep the soil plowed up. Hardened, rigid soil will not let the seeds of life in. It is my job to keep the soil moist and healthy. I am not the farmer. God is the farmer. I am the field.

Paul also says we are God's building. I am the construction project that He wants to inhabit. Not all buildings look alike; that is not the point. The point is that God wants to move in and take up residence in my life. The many rooms of my life are to be taken over by His presence and good pleasure. He wants to own and operate the secret closets of my life. He wants to renovate my entertainment room. The public gatherings in my building are to become gatherings with a divine agenda. It is this kind of thinking that caused Paul to say we are not just the field, we are the building.

Knowing God has called you personally to work for Him, to live every day building up His kingdom, spreading His word, and drawing others to Him, ought to show you how important you are in His eyes. He didn't just say, "Whoever feels like it, come spend some part of your life with Me." No, He asked you personally to be a part of His work. He has planted His seed in you. It's up to you to spread it. He was the architect behind your blueprints and wants to construct His building in you. Remember that you're His field and His building.

Foundation of Christ

By the grace God has given to me, I laid a foundation as an
expert builder, and someone else is building on it. But each
one should be careful how he builds. For no one can lay any
foundation other than the one already laid, which is Jesus Christ.
—I CORINTHIANS 3:10—11

A building is only as strong as its foundation. Without a steady
base, anything will fall. It doesn't matter whether you're
talking about a tree house, a log cabin, or a skyscraper. Or your
life, for that matter.

When calling yourself a follower of Christ—or any varia-
tion of that terminology—you are in effect a leader. People look
to you to know what to believe. What you lay as your foundation
means the difference between success and failure as a leader. At
work, if your coworkers know that you follow Christ—and let's
hope they do know that by the way you live, talk, and think—then
they perceive you as an "expert builder," as Paul calls himself in
this passage. They are looking to you to decide whether they too
want to follow Christ. Like it or not, those of the world will scru-
tinize you, looking for reasons to prove your faith wrong. It's up
to you to live in such a way that you leave them no choice but to
believe in Him.

To build such a steady "empire for Christ," you must put
Him as your foundation in everything you do. Let Christ lead the
way, whether you're deciding what terminology to use in a meeting, handling a difficult client, or working to persuade a business

to sign on with yours. Many times, just stopping to think about what He would want you to do, and putting tough situations in His hands—or even pausing to give thanks for a successful presentation, for meeting a deadline, for blessing you with a kind coworker—helps build that foundation of Christ.

This doesn't mean you'll never experience cracks in the foundation, because at some point you will. But as you well know, the power of prayer can patch those cracks and keep the foundation strong. The major structural faults are what you're trying to avoid by building your life from the ground up in Christ.

An Enduring Work

If what he has built survives, he will receive his reward. If it is burned up, he will suffer loss; he himself will be saved, but only as one escaping through the flames.
—I CORINTHIANS 3:14–15

High-quality work comes highly valued. In a day when we hire so many services on the basis of who has the largest Yellow Pages ad, a listing on a Website, or through a flyer that someone tapes to our front door, we're lucky to ever get anything done well. More often, we find a fly-by-night company that wants to make a quick buck, get the job, and not really care about quality and durability.

A friend recently bought a house. The previous owner had designed and built the home himself and then sold it as soon as he was finished—clearly for more profit than it was worth. For several weeks after moving in, my friend found cracks forming along the ceiling in the bedroom. Shortly thereafter, more foundational errors became evident. After an expert inspected the home, the new owner learned that shoddy workmanship would cost him thousands of dollars to repair—and a soured relationship between him and the former owner and homebuilder.

What about the construction of our spiritual life? What kind of quality and workmanship are we injecting? How is the foundation of our life with God? Are there hairline cracks in the frame? The point here is that we must build our lives on a strong foundation—Jesus Christ—and we must use high-quality materials. Just as my friend's house looked great upon first glance (and even second and third), serious inspection revealed many flaws. A smooth, superficial layer of paint and plaster covered up the weak foundation and cheap materials. In our lives as well, a superficial layer of good deeds, Sunday-only worship, and obligatory prayers won't cover up the flawed foundation when judgment day comes.

God knows our true hearts. He knows what others can't see. He knows what we're made of, inside and out, and no amount of plaster and patchwork can repair or conceal what lies beneath. So have you used a strong foundation in Christ, or are you sitting on poor-quality materials—and a foundation that won't stand the test of time?

Faithful Stewards

Now it is required that those who have been given a trust must
prove faithful.
—I CORINTHIANS 4:2

Airlines no longer call those who assist you on flights "stewards" or "stewardesses," saying those terms are no longer
politically correct. If you travel much, you've probably had to ad-
just to this terminology change, now calling the people who welcome you, instruct you, and sometimes still dole out peanuts and
soda pop to you "flight attendants."

The dictionary defines a steward as "one appointed to su-
pervise the provision and distribution of food and drink in an in-
stitution," or "one who actively directs affairs." Yet we often hear
this word in association with those who follow Christ. We are faithful stewards when we follow His will. We are faithful stewards
when we bring our tithes and offerings to Him, meaning we "super-
vise the provision and distribution" of our hard-earned money to
whom it belongs: our Savior.

But money isn't the only thing we're entrusted with in this
life. We have time and talents over which He has asked us to be
the steward. God also provides for us His words, encouragement,
direction, support, and many blessings, and He calls us to use His
blessings wisely.

Paul was entrusted with the secret things of God, as referred
to in 1 Corinthians 2:7. God expected Him to use the information He gave him wisely. This meant carefully teaching others

about God, showing them what He had done for Paul, and helping bring many others to know God fully.

Are you being a faithful steward to the One who gave you life? Think about everything God has given you: love, knowledge, health, talents, and many other things, including money. Are you using God's resources to the best of your ability, and in a way that's pleasing to Him? He has trusted you with whatever it is He has given you specifically. It's up to you to find out what He wants you to do with those things, and then be a faithful steward.

All from God

For who makes you different from anyone else? What do you have that you did not receive? And if you did receive it, why do you boast as though you did not?
—I CORINTHIANS 4:7

I once heard someone say that whenever he receives a compliment from someone else, such as on a well-prepared and delivered presentation, he says, "Thank you" to the person complimenting him, and then a silent—or sometimes audible—"Thank you, God, for all you've given me." He says it keeps him humble, helping him remember that he didn't prepare that presentation and deliver it flawlessly on his own. He thanks God for his talents and asks God to help him use his skills for good. We must always acknowledge that all we have comes from the hand of God.

When things are going well, we have this air of confidence about our life. It is a wise man or woman of faith who doesn't wait for the days to turn bad before coming to terms with frailty and the role God plays in personal success. I must never forget that I can plant, I can water, I can pray, I can sweat over a seed; but at the end of the day it is God who causes things to grow. All I have and all I can do comes from the good hand of a good God.

Praise and admiration from our fellows feels great, there's no doubt about it. In our society we spend a lot of time, money, and energy striving for praise from our friends, family, coworkers, and superiors. Hearing a "Great job!" or "Attaboy!" from a peer brings a sense of satisfaction. But receiving affirmation from the God of the universe is even better. When He says good job to us, our hearts leap with fulfillment.

All you are, all you'll ever be, you owe to Christ. He is the one who gave you what you have and enabled you to accomplish good things. Check your ego at the door, and give all the praise to Christ.

Imitation

Therefore I urge you to imitate me.
—I CORINTHIANS 4:16

In the corporate setting you often see acts of imitation. A young worker watches a more experienced, knowledgeable colleague carefully to see how the elder worker handles situations. For example, at a dinner meeting, a fresh-from-school employee may not know business dinner etiquette, so he watches his superior and takes her lead. Not sure which fork to use? Look to the superior. Not sure whether to stand when someone joins the meeting, or how high-priced an entrée you can order? Look to the superior. Evidently the superior knows something if she's still with the company and seemingly doing well.

This doesn't mean the young worker will copycat every action his elder colleague makes, and occasionally he'll slip up. But patterning his work actions after another more experienced, mature coworker helps him learn the ropes and be more pleasing to his boss.

In the verse here, Paul instructs the Corinthians to imitate him. He wants his fellow believers to take cues from him on how to act, what to say, and how to believe—not on how to dress, what to eat, or which fork to use. Paul was in a position to instruct this, after having followed Christ for so many years of his life. Paul walked closely with God, praying to Him and seeking His guidance. He knew that God made him in His own image (Genesis 1:26), and he wanted to act in God's image as well.

By telling the Corinthians to imitate him, Paul meant for his believers to imitate him as he imitated Christ. He wanted to draw them closer to God, and for them to follow the Heavenly King.

Who do you imitate? Who have you picked up your positive work habits from? Who have you picked up the negative elements of your work from? What do those imitating you look like in their work? Are your daily actions and interactions inherent in a coworker, boss, or celebrity? Or are you patterning your life more after Christ—the only one whose judgment matters in our lives?

With a Rod
or in Gentleness

What do you prefer? Shall I come to you with a whip,
or in love and with a gentle whisper?
—I CORINTHIANS 4:21

Management styles vary greatly, as you well know if you've
read books by management gurus, attended seminars,
or just paid any attention to the way the leaders in your office work.
You may be a manager yourself, with distinct thoughts about how
to rule the roost. Some believe in ruling with an iron fist; others
opt for a more gentle management style.

Those who use the iron-fist method—or, as Paul puts it in
this verse, "come to you with a whip"—feel they must be in control at all times. They often want their subordinates to obey out
of fear. Fear might keep people in line, but it certainly doesn't in-
spire love, devotion, or respect. It also leaves no room for creativity, innovation, or change. Fear only works for a little while, until
employees get tired of the strain and head for greener pastures.

In contrast, those who manage "in love and with a gentle
whisper" have other motives in mind. They want to draw their employees into the fold, teaching them how to act and showing genuine care for their lives. These managers motivate their subordinates
to try harder, striving for the kind word and affirmation. They in-
spire loyalty and devotion, because they've treated their employees
so well that the employees don't want to leave. The employees in
turn respect their managers and want to please them.

Sure, both methods work for a while. But leadership that is built around fear, intimidation, and coercion is leadership that finds followers leaving quickly when they have an option.

Remember Paul's challenging question next time you're put in a position of leadership. Remember that Paul loved the Corinthians, and it was his job to lead them to Christ. He could easily have used the iron-fist management style to scare them into obedience, but his loving words and gentle spirit did more than fear could ever do.

A Little Leaven

Your boasting is not good. Don't you know that a little yeast works through the whole batch of dough?
—I CORINTHIANS 5:6

Sin is a cancer. You've heard it before. It starts small, often in unnoticeable parts of the body. Left undetected, the sin cancer grows and spreads. Left untreated, it soon affects the entire body and eventually kills it off.

The sin cancer is deadly, not only to the person sinning but to people close to the victim. Unlike the devastating medical condition, sin is contagious. Left undetected and untreated, the sin cancer spreads among the rest of the body. Others find themselves infected and affected by our sin patterns.

Just as a little yeast works through the whole batch of dough, the sin cancer works through the whole body of Christ when believers choose to ignore it. This is Paul's message to the Corinthians, one that we'd do well to heed today, as well.

It's not our place to judge. The Bible says so in James. But we can't let the sin cancer, the small bit of yeast, destroy the church. This means we can't ignore blatant sins among our fellow believers. We must gently point out their sins and make it clear how their sins are affecting their brothers and sisters in Christ.

This message also works the other way. Maybe you're the one whose sin is spreading. Maybe you're the one blatantly ignoring God's rules—and other people are noticing, and it's affecting their walk with Christ as well. You've got to pitch the yeast out and treat the cancer, or you'll destroy everyone.

Sin is serious business, and no one should have to live with its effects. Luckily we have God to heal us, to treat us, and even to point it out when we do not realize how our actions play into the lives of others. Sometimes He uses those who love Him most to point it out to others.

Unbelieving Spouse

For the unbelieving husband has been sanctified through his wife, and the unbelieving wife has been sanctified through her believing husband. Otherwise your children would be unclean, but as it is, they are holy.

—I CORINTHIANS 7:14

Y ou get a flat tire on the way to work and show up forty-five minutes late. You spill coffee on your slacks—narrowly avoiding serious burns—and have to attend a meeting you called dressed like that. As if this is not enough, your computer crashes every time you attempt to open the document you were supposed to have e-mailed your boss an hour ago.

If you're like most people, you can't wait to get home after a day like this, hoping to find sympathy in a spouse who loves you, cares for you, and, yes, prays for you. But for so many followers of Christ, this is not an option. Many who come to know Christ after getting married struggle with a spouse who doesn't believe—and who doesn't understand his or her spouse who desires to follow the Lord.

So what should someone with an unbelieving spouse do or think? We're told in 1 Corinthians 3:13–14 that to stay with our spouse and know that our children are considered holy until they're able to choose the Lord for themselves. As for the believing spouse, he or she must keep praying that God will touch the unbeliever's heart.

God puts us in a situation for a reason. In so many unequally yoked marriages, God's purpose is certainly for the believing spouse to be the bridge to lead the other to Him. What better way to do so than by being a constant source of witness in the home, living as close to God's will as possible and praying continuously for salvation for the one he or she loves so much?

God says to love our spouse as Christ loves the church, and He doesn't stipulate that we can only do so if our husband or wife loves Him, too. So even if you can't find a source of constant love and prayer in your spouse on the toughest of days, you can take comfort in the fact that God is using you to reach out to your spouse. Keep praying, keeping loving, until death do you part.

Remain in Your Calling

Each one should remain in the situation which he was in when
God called him.

—I CORINTHIANS 7:20

Prostitutes who find Christ obviously must leave their profession, or else they'll continue sinning in their faith. Drug dealers and hit men who find Christ also must leave their profession.

But what about truck drivers, waiters, store clerks, receptionists, marketing directors, computer programmers, or company CEOs? Paul says they should remain where they were when God called them.

Why would God care where you work? Because this is exactly where God has called some of us to do ministry. Yes, he calls people to be truck drivers and nail drivers, plumbers and planters, nurses and contractors. Not all ministry takes place within the four walls of the church. I must understand that it is not that I simply go to work every day as a front to talk about Jesus. My work is my calling. This is where I have been assigned and called.

Certainly there are occasions when a person who comes to faith needs to change a career path. However, this is not the norm. The norm is that we all must figure out what it looks like to be "salt and light" in the place we have been planted. By remaining in the same job and living out the transformation of meeting Jesus, I begin to demonstrate the irresistible influence of the good news.

I must make sure that my passion for my job doesn't suddenly get put on the back burner. My commitment to excellence and skill should grow when I meet Jesus. However, for many people the ability to deliver a great day's work for a great day's pay becomes suspect. Bloom wherever you're planted, says the apostle Paul.

Knowledge Puffs; Love Builds

We know that we all possess knowledge. Knowledge puffs up, but love builds up.
—I CORINTHIANS 8:I

The heart is wiser than the intellect," said author J. G. Holland. This is essentially what Paul said in 1 Corinthians 8:1 several hundred years before Holland's quip. What does it mean, though?

Anyone can acquire knowledge who wants to. With the proliferation of the Internet alone, one can read up on just about any subject in a matter of minutes and become a self-professed expert on a given topic. Our culture values and encourages knowledgeable people. God doesn't say He doesn't want intelligent people serving Him. The more knowledge, the better.

So, is Paul down on knowledge? When you read through the book of Romans, you certainly think he's a smart fellow. No, Paul is not down on learning. Rather, he is making the simple case that knowledge can become one of those tools that prop up someone inappropriately. Knowledge can make us think we are more important than we are. Knowledge can keep us from crying to God, "I need some help." Knowledge can be a divider of people. Paul is saying knowledge can be dangerous.

Too much knowledge, something you can acquire without God's assistance, doesn't get you any closer to God. Love, on the other hand, is something you gain directly through God's grace. It is given to those who love Him and seek to serve Him, not just something you pick up in a book along the way.

Knowledge puffs up our ego. It is self-serving to those of us who use our smarts to impress others. Love builds up others—it's about making others feel good, and in return we feel good too. Don't quit learning and gaining knowledge; just put love first on your list every day and you'll build up others more than you could ever build up yourself with knowledge.

One God

... yet for us there is but one God, the Father, from whom all things came and for whom we live; and there is but one Lord, Jesus Christ, through whom all things came and through whom we live.
—I CORINTHIANS 8:6

R on leaves for work at six every morning. He sits through meetings, takes calls, and crams in business over lunch. He doesn't leave work at five, like many of his colleagues; *You can't make it to the top that way,* he thinks. Meanwhile, his wife and son are waiting for him to go to a school play—but they don't really expect him to make it. They're used to his late nights and inattention at home.

What is driving Ron to such devotion to his job? It could be that his company is in the middle of a strategic crunch and all the partners have to burn the candle at both ends. That's OK; even Nehemiah in the Old Testament found himself in this situation. It could be that Ron is deriving all his identity from his work. Or perhaps he does not realize that real success is juggling all the balls, not just one of them.

Or Ron could have an idol. He could worship his work and the tangible and intangible outcomes from that work.

Making an idol out of things seems to be the American way. Anytime we place something or someone on the throne of our lives, we are creating an idol. Everywhere you look people are worshipping pop stars, movie stars, fame, cars, possessions, and fortune. You may have made something an idol in your life without even knowing it.

Paul tells us quite clearly in this verse, however, that there is only one God. There's no mistaking the meaning of the verse. If there's only one God, one person whom we should worship, then there's no room left for any other idols in our lives.

Have you been putting anything or anyone else first in your life, other than God? Has something slipped onto the throne of your life? Have you made an idol out of your career, your car, your home? Yes, those things are important. But they were never intended to do for us what only God can do.

Run to Win

Do you not know that in a race all the runners run, but only one gets the prize? Run in such a way as to get the prize.
—I CORINTHIANS 9:24

Running isn't easy. Even diehard, lifelong runners will tell you that. Every morning, a runner must drag out of bed, long before the rest of the world rises; suit up; stretch; and then start down the same path run the day before, and the 2,067 days before that.

Paul uses a number of images to illustrate the journey of followers of Jesus. But none are more developed than this one. The athlete. The runner. There is something about the daily-ness and the discipline of running that captured Paul's thinking. We don't know whether Paul was a marathoner himself. He probably was not. We know him as a short, bowlegged fireplug. But Paul and every other person of the first century knew firsthand of the athletic games that were the early world's Olympics. There was something about the winner bursting across the finish line and being crowned that captured Paul when he thought of his own marathon run with Jesus.

In a race, a runner is never satisfied with just finishing. He wants to push on, to beat his last time, to beat the time of his neighbor, to beat the time of all others in his age category—and maybe of the next youngest, too—and eventually he's not satisfied until he wins the overall race.

In this race we call life, the prize is spending eternity with our Heavenly Father. Like a runner, to win this race we must train diligently, feverishly, with the utmost dedication and desire. Our training in God's race involves following a diet of His word daily; exercising our brains, hearts, spirits in praying to Him; and stretching our lives to always improve and be more like Him.

Running God's race isn't easy. No one ever said it would be. But the prize, winning a lifetime with Him, is well worth the pain it takes to get there. Don't give up. Train hard, push yourself even harder, and know that He is waiting for you at the finish line.

Take Heed Lest You Fall

So, if you think you are standing firm, be careful that you don't fall!

—I CORINTHIANS 10:12

It's when we're feeling most confident of ourselves that we fall the hardest. In gymnastics, men and women sprint across the balance beam, seemingly mindless of the fact that the beam is mere inches wide. I know I'd have trouble balancing on something a foot wide, especially attempting the feats they perform! Backbends, back handsprings, and split leaps on a board narrower than the length of my shoe. Yet to me, they appear to perform their stunts without effort.

But ask any gymnast, and he or she will tell you that concentration, never losing sight of the beam, and never feeling too secure in his or her position is what makes for the best routine. From time to time, we see a gymnast, even one in the Olympics or other major competition, fall during a routine. *What went wrong?* we may wonder. The gymnasts who fall likely say they lost their concentration, forgot their footing, felt a little too sure of their performance . . . "Be careful that *you* don't fall!"

This is a good reminder for all of us, no matter whether we're balancing on a thin beam doing a gymnastics routine, walking the high wire of corporate life, or swinging from the ropes in some other position. Keeping our eyes always on the prize, our Lord, will help keep our footing. We too could suffer a fall if we feel too sure of our standing in God's eyes. A night off from doing our devotionals? No problem! Too tired to pray? No problem! Not really up for church this morning? No problem! Rather not drive across town and help a friend in need? No problem!

But guess what? Feeling too sure of ourselves and our relationship with Christ is not a good thing. Not paying attention to the little things is a first step in falling. Moving from concern for others to a self-centered me-first mind-set eventually causes even the best runner to stumble and fall. Keep an eye focused on the little things.

Flee Idolatry

Therefore, my dear friends, flee from idolatry.
—I CORINTHIANS 10:14

I dols come in many shapes, sizes, colors, and styles these days. One person's idol might be different from the next. Some people idolize money; others, their looks; still others, fame; and another group worships their showcase homes and priceless possessions. In our culture, the word *idol* doesn't always come with negative connotations. It's not uncommon to hear that someone *idolizes* a friend's new home, meaning she thinks it's smashing. More evidence of the word as something to be admired comes in the form of a popular TV show, "American Idol."

But idols aren't something to toy with, and they're definitely not to be admired. Notice that in 1 Corinthians 10:14, Paul doesn't say, "You ought to consider putting idolatry aside." Nor does he say, "It might be nice for you to cut down on the amount of idols in your life." No, he gently, lovingly says to *flee* idolatry.

We usually think of the word *flee* in terms of something you do when in grave danger, when you're narrowly escaping harm. That's exactly what's going on in this verse. Worshipping idols puts something or someone between you and God. In Exodus 20:4–5, we're told, "You shall not make for yourself an idol in the form of anything in heaven above or on the earth beneath or in the waters below. You shall not bow down to them or worship them. . . ." The name *Exodus* even means a mass departure.

God clearly wants us to get the picture that there is no place for idolatry in our lives. Why? Because worshipping something else—money, position, power—means we're consumed with thoughts of something other than God. It means we want to spend all of our time with something other than God. If we do that, we're unable to fulfill our duty as His children.

What idols do you worship in your life?

Seek Others' Well-Being

Nobody should seek his own good, but the good of others.
—I CORINTHIANS IO:24

Picture the most powerful, influential person in business. Now picture this business icon telling people he won't lay them off, even though it would be good for his bank account, because he knows these people need the work. Picture him singing the praises of a recent hire to the press, giving the new employee credit to boost her career, instead of keeping the glory for himself. It's hard to picture someone being so selfless, isn't it?

Yet that's what we're called to do in 1 Corinthians 10:24. We're told to put the good of others ahead of our own. The concept is contrary to the norm of our world—a world that's all about me, my job, my career, my bank account, my possessions, my power. But as a follower of Jesus, we're to put the good of others first.

How can you do that? Easy. Your company is offering overtime for the next six weeks, until a major project is complete. You provide well for your small family and don't really *need* the money—though it would always be nice. Your coworker, however, could really use the extra pay. Her husband just lost his job and she has another baby on the way. Let her have the overtime.

Seeking the good of others is as simple as thinking, *How can I help her? What could make his life easier?* instead of *How will this benefit me?* It is putting myself in the shoes of those around me. An easy way to remember to do this is to think about Jesus in whatever situation you're facing. Would He offer to share credit—

and the bonus that comes with it—with a coworker, or would He pirate the praise for Himself? Would He stay late on a Friday night to help a coworker finish a pressing assignment, or would He head home to relax on the couch instead?

It's easy to see that putting others first is a concept many of us aren't used to. But it's what God wants us to do, and it's just what Jesus did for us.

Open God's Gift of Faith

. . . to another faith by the same Spirit, to another gifts
of healing by that one Spirit. . . .
—I CORINTHIANS 12:9

On your birthday, you sit down at a table filled with presents from friends and family. You blow out your candles, eat your cake, and then get to the good stuff: the presents. One package catches your eye right off the bat, a big gold box tied with red bow—obviously a lot of love went into this package. You notice the tag; the gift is from God. You tear open the wrappings, eager to learn which spiritual gift you've received from your Creator.

God bestows different spiritual gifts to all of His children, expecting them to use their gifts for good. God gives out such gifts as wisdom, knowledge, faith, healing powers, prophecy, speaking in tongues, and interpretation of tongues. He doesn't give the best gifts to His favorite children. No, each gift is equally important, and all gifts combine to work toward God's glory.

So, what is in your box? What spiritual gifts did God give you? His Word says that every child of His has received at least one. Think about that. Not only was I created with purpose but I was given the tools to make a real contribution. Every one of us adds value to the mix of life. You say, "Well, I really wanted this or that gift." That is not your option. It is not up to you to dictate—or even have input on—how the gifts are dispersed. You must not sit around desiring to be someone else, or great at something else. Learn to develop the gift within you.

It certainly seems that God has given each of us a unique personality. His fingerprints of creation are stamped on our soul. But He has also given us a package of spiritual gifts that are to be used for His kingdom. More often than not, those two things line up in partnership.

It's your birthday every day when you open the gift God has given you. Remember your excitement in opening a special present and how you cherished it, and lavish the same affection on what God has given you, His birthday child.

One Body, Many Features, Part I

The body is a unit, though it is made up of many parts;
and though all its parts are many, they form one body.
So it is with Christ.
—I CORINTHIANS 12:12

It's easy to take your body for granted—that is, until something happens to one part to remind you how each part helps the next part function. I'm not a scientist or a medical doctor, but I do know a little bit about how interrelated all the parts in my body are. I've also experienced firsthand the effects of a noncooperating limb or organ.

Have you ever sat with your legs crossed for too long, only to feel your leg go to sleep? Then all of a sudden you have to move quickly to get up from the table; you swing your legs around, but they don't work correctly. It is a strange feeling to have a limb go to sleep and not participate in the command to walk that is being sent from your brain.

Many times throughout the Bible the church is referred to as the body of Christ. Thinking in terms of different functions of one's body working together for a common purpose—to keep alive and kicking—it makes sense to call us Christ's body. What is our role in the church? Are we members of the choir? Leaders in the children's ministry? Are we exercising gifts of serving, teaching, or giving?

We all have our parts, our roles in the church. No one part is more important than another; we need all organs functioning correctly for this body to survive. Even the pastor, the most visible part in many churches, couldn't do his or her job well without people in the congregation to hear his message, a musician to lift praises to the Lord, or a janitor to help keep the physical church in working condition.

Where do you fit in this body of Christ? Are you performing at peak condition, or leaving the rest of the body struggling to keep up in your absence? Have you gone to sleep on the rest of the body? Do you feel like a nonparticipating member of the body?

One Body, Many Features, Part II

> But in fact God has arranged the parts in the body, every one
> of them, just as He wanted them to be.
> —1 CORINTHIANS 12:18

Many men and women might guffaw when reading this verse: ". . . God has arranged the parts in the body, every one of them, just as He wanted them to be." You may even think, *This body—how He wants it to be? Yeah, right!* Lucky for us, however, that He's talking about the body of Christ, not our own, flawed physical bodies.

Even as a part of the body of believers, you may feel out of sorts with the role you play. Are you in a position in your church or in your walk with God that you don't feel is right for you? Maybe a friend in the church pressured you to join the welcome committee—and you just can't break out of your comfort zone to greet hundreds of faces each Sunday morning. Are you more comfortable with baking cookies for new-member receptions, or working in the parking lot in anonymity?

God has a place for each and every one of us in His body. It's up to us to pray, asking that He guide us to the position He has in store for us. Paul tells us that God has arranged the parts in the body. But that doesn't mean we automatically understand our role. We must first nail down with clarity and enthusiasm what our gifted role is. Have you ever discovered the gift(s) God has given you? Begin by realizing you have gifts and start asking God to show you. Perhaps you should call a friend and talk through the list of spiritual gifts found in Ephesians, Romans, or 1 Corinthians, and begin to get a bearing on exactly what gift God has given you.

The next step? Be content with where He places you. Sure, some roles in the church are more glamorous than others. But not every person is cut out to do a high-profile job. Besides, the true rewards come from God, not our peers. So, happily lead kids through Sunday School lessons, bake the cookies, or copy lesson materials. Repaint the new office, or make calls on behalf of the church on a Saturday morning. Whatever it takes—and whatever He calls you to do—do it joyfully, and know that God put you there on purpose. Serve Him where you're planted.

One Body, Many Features, Part III

But eagerly desire the greater gifts.
—I CORINTHIANS 12:31

In the corporate world, the mantra is to push for more money, more power, more prestige. You hear consultants and corporate coaches tout pushing on for the next big thing; don't be satisfied with what you've got. In a way, it's good to push on to become better, but not just to see what else you can get.

It's our nature to always want more, whatever "more" is in a given situation. God wants us to have more, too. But the more He's talking about is more of His love and more power to use the gifts He has given us to glorify Him—not ourselves.

Many people read 1 Corinthians 12:31 and assume it to mean that you shouldn't be content with the spiritual gifts God has given you. Believers often think one spiritual gift is better than another—not true—and that Paul is saying in this verse to push on till they achieve the next big gift. Again, not true.

God wants us to push on to do more with the gifts He's already given. Are you gifted in outreach? Then don't stop at talking to your coworker about coming to church. Pray for guidance, and reach out to your neighbors, your relatives, and even the strangers who serve you coffee every morning or at dinner out on the weekends. Push yourself. God gave you these gifts for a reason: He wants you to use them.

Afraid to push out of your comfort zone? No one said being a follower of Jesus was easy, or comfortable. Just read any of the passages in your Bible that deal with persecution. Remember that your spiritual gifts are not for you; they're for Christ. When you think of them in perspective, it makes it easier to understand our role in Christ's church. He made us; He gave us our spiritual gifts; He instructs us how to use them; and we use them for His glory.

It's not about getting more for ourselves. It's about giving more to Him.

Clanging Cymbals

If I speak in the tongues of men and of angels, but have not love,
I am only a resounding gong or a clanging cymbal.
—I CORINTHIANS 13:1

Have you ever heard anyone play music solely on the cymbals? No other accompaniment, no singing, no strings or horns, just the cymbals? It doesn't happen very often, and for good reason. The cymbals just don't sound melodic when played alone. However, when played as part of the orchestra as a whole, the cymbals add a lot of emphasis and intrigue.

Paul compares the way we perform actions in life without love to the way the cymbals sound without a full orchestra. Actions without love clang like the cymbals: loud, irritating, and out of place. It's not hard to spot the person who's helping you at work with an ulterior motive (say, to get on the boss's good side). You know she's not putting in extra time on your project out of a heart of love, and it doesn't make you appreciate her help.

You might be able to relate with this concept at home, too. You know your children hate picking up their rooms. It's a constant source of strife. Yet when you get home and find two spotless rooms and then a quick request for a trip to the water park, you might know that the cleaning wasn't done out of love, but as bribery to get what they want. Although the result would thrill most parents, the motivation concerns us.

In fact, it's hard to think of any action that is pleasing without love as a basis. That's the point of Paul's words in this verse. Love is the cornerstone of life.

Are you feeling something other than love in your life right now? Are your actions clanging like a cymbal, or resounding like a gong? Pray to God that He will help put the melody back in your life, so that your actions sound more like an emphasis rather than an empty clang.

Profits Me Nothing

If I give all I possess to the poor and surrender my body to the flames, but have not love, I gain nothing.
—I CORINTHIANS 13:3

This verse may speak to you if you give a hefty amount to the Salvation Army each Christmas or donate clothes to a women's shelter just for the tax write-off. Or you may take note if you spend time at a soup kitchen during the holidays because you "feel it's your duty" to do so.

What have you gained from any of these actions if you don't do them out of love? Nothing, Paul says in this verse. Love is something you can give to anyone, and anyone can give it away. It means more than any other gift you could ever give—even to a person who has nothing. A person in need may need new clothes, a warm supper, and some money for personal items. But that person will benefit much more from a kind, sincere word from you; a gentle prayer whispered together over a bowl of soup; an afternoon of talking through problems; or just a few laughs to lighten the load of stress.

Some of the richest people in the world are also the unhappiest. They have material things, they visit beautiful places, they can buy anything they want—and probably do. But without a true and sincere love for Christ, for other human beings, and for life itself, they'll never gain a thing. Their hefty bank balance can't buy them love. The end of that part of their balance sheet is nothing but a bunch of zeros. It amounts to nothing without love.

Are you doing good things for the right reasons? Don't spend another day just putting in time on good deeds. Make a difference by showing others that you act out of love.

Edify Others

But everyone who prophesies speaks to men for their strengthening, encouragement and comfort.
—I CORINTHIANS 14:3

We carry on myriad conversations in a given day. Some conversations produce results in business, such as hammering out details for a new product, service, or project, or cementing relationships with colleagues. Some conversations are for mere enjoyment, such as talking about weekend plans with your coworkers, sharing stories about your children with a colleague, or telling your friends a joke. Some talks, unfortunately, bring harm to those involved.

But think for a moment about how many conversations you have daily that strengthen, encourage, and comfort the people you're speaking with. Can you come up with a number? Are you pleased with the ratio, compared to all of the other conversations you participate in? How much of an encourager are you in your speech?

Paul says in this verse that everyone who prophesies—meaning everyone who communicates with God and spreads His love to those around them—must strengthen, encourage, and comfort fellow men and women. Words must edify others. Edify, meaning build others up, not tear them down. Sometimes that's a hard pill to swallow.

Let's face it; pride sometimes gets in the way. A coworker—or shall we say *competitor*—louses up a task, gets called on it by the boss, and just feels miserable, torn down at this point. You, however, think of how your boss should have asked you to do the task instead, and feel gratified in knowing your coworker is hurting. You may even say as much to a friend about the situation. But is this what Jesus calls us to do? Are those words building up someone who is hurting? No, of course not.

This verse applies to your home life, as well. Your spouse and kids deserve your kind words just as much as your colleagues do, but sometimes they are the ones who get the short end of the stick. You give your all at work, listening to other people's problems and doling out advice. Do you have any left at the end of the day for your family? The Bible says that you must strengthen, encourage, and comfort those you speak to. I sure hope you're speaking to your family.

Don't let your words tear down others. There's enough hurt in the world for that. We need more people strengthening, encouraging, and comforting others—edifying those around them and building a better world.

Be Mature in Understanding

Brothers, stop thinking like children. In regard to evil be infants, but in your thinking be adults.
—I CORINTHIANS 14:20

Life is such a contradiction. People always talk about how wonderful childlike innocence is, singing the praises of a child's simple observations, candid remarks, and merry laughter. But when an adult talks foolishly, makes silly mistakes, and acts unbecoming, people say, "Grow up—quit acting like a child."

There are times in life when being like a child is best; at other times our lives call for more mature understanding and handling. In your own life, you can probably identify situations in which acting like a child—silly, innocent, fun-loving—is good, as when laughing and carrying on with your family or letting loose your creative side. Likewise, you can probably remember many times when your life calls for a more mature, adult touch—such as the face you put on while at the office.

Paul calls on the Corinthians—and all of us, for that matter—to be like infants in regard to evil, but like adults in our thinking. What does this mean? It means infants don't understand evil; their lives are full of love, laughter, and lightheartedness. They don't understand life's evil ways, and they don't relish taking part in them. Paul talks about this in regard to the Corinthians misusing some of their spiritual gifts. One example was the misuse of the gift of speaking in tongues, a practice that uses the spirit to talk with God but leaves out the mind as well as others who are witnessing the event.

To be adult in thinking means to be rational, calm, logical, and mature. It means that although we may feel things, our logic must take over and do what is right. So even though the Corinthians may feel like speaking in tongues, logic says they must refrain from doing so in the presence of others, especially nonbelievers, who might not understand the practice and surely can't gain anything from a bunch of sounds they do not understand.

We can apply this principle to many areas of our lives. Put on your childish face when confronted with evil thoughts, actions, or desires. When a coworker says something that can be taken two ways, choose to be like an infant and assume the better meaning. When you really want to say something harsh to an uncaring boss, be like an adult—even-tempered, logical, and practical.

Evil Company Corrupts

Do not be misled: Bad company corrupts good character.
—I CORINTHIANS 15:33

*C*orruption is a word we've heard a lot about in recent times, with the Enron scandal and other corporate misdeeds. *Corrupt* means "marked by immorality and perversion; depraved; marked by venality and dishonesty."

In many instances, we don't have much choice in whom we spend time with. At work, you spend time with a lot of people who might not be of your choosing. Your boss might be a perfectly nice person, and the men and women you work most closely with might make your work interesting, but there is a chance you wouldn't choose them as your best friends. But are they people who will corrupt you?

Jesus spent a lot of time with sinners. He instructs us to do the same. How else can we spread the light and love of Jesus if we are not spending time with people who don't know His word? But there's a difference between my influencing others for good and others influencing me for bad. With any and every relationship, those two options are possible. I must be on guard to make sure the influence is tending upward, not downward.

Paul says in this verse that "bad company corrupts good character." In previous verses, we learn that he's telling the Corinthians about not putting themselves in the presence of people who don't believe in the resurrection of Christ; without that belief, there's no point in what they do on earth to please God. So when he talks about corruption, we can believe that he means not regularly, willingly surrounding ourselves with people who are God haters and who vocally defile the story of Jesus.

Corruption is all around us, but we don't have to let it get to us. If your coworkers are corrupting you—from the words they say, or their conversation topics, even debates about Christ that leave you questioning your faith—you do have a choice. Try to talk with them and steer them to the good side of thinking. Ask for a reassignment. But ultimately you just might have to leave your job. Leaving a job you like, or even need, may seem like a huge risk. But an even bigger risk—the biggest one you could ever face—is putting yourself in danger of a corruption that eventually turns your core rotten. Think about it.

The Image We Bear

And just as we have borne the likeness of the earthly man,
so shall we bear the likeness of the man from heaven.
—I CORINTHIANS 15:49

What do you see when you look in the mirror? What characteristics stand out: a new wrinkle? a pleasant smile? vibrant eyes? graying hair? How about the image of God? Do you see Him in you somewhere?

In Genesis 1:26–27, God says, "Let us make man in our image, in our likeness. . . . So God created man in His own image, in the image of God He created him; male and female He created them." Again, in Genesis 9:6, we read, ". . . for in the image of God has God made man."

God clearly set out to make you resemble Him. When you look in the mirror, such traits as being gentle, loving, kind, just, full of grace, and forgiving (to name a few) ought to pop out at you as traits you've inherited from your Heavenly Father.

The other day, a friend walked up to me and quietly whispered, "Your daughter is looking so much like her mother. I have watched her since she was a baby and she has so taken on the physical features of your wife." Another day, some out-of-town clients were in my office. I keep a funny family picture there that we made a few years ago; it is all of us doing something goofy in front of the photographer. This client looked, laughed, and then remarked as he pointed to my middle child, "She sure looks like you. There is no mistaking who she belongs to."

Worried that you look nothing like your Father? Unlike your physical self, you can remedy your spiritual self through nurturing a relationship with Christ. Praying to be more like Him, for strength, discipline, love, and a gentle and quiet spirit transforms your image and helps you see Him too, when you check your face in the mirror each morning.

Another sure way to bear His likeness? As we learn in this verse, after living our lives for Him, in His image, we'll also bear even more of His image in heaven. That's great news! The wrinkles, gray hair, and tired eyes will be gone. In their place, we'll revel in healthy new bodies—that look and feel a whole lot more like the image we were made in.

The Twinkling of an Eye

Listen, I tell you a mystery: We will not all sleep, but we will all be changed—in a flash, in the twinkling of an eye, at the last trumpet. For the trumpet will sound, the dead will be raised imperishable, and we will be changed.
—I CORINTHIANS 15:51–52

Every time I read this verse or hear a pastor speak on it, I think about a few specific things. One is the phrase "in the twinkling of an eye." Have you ever caught a twinkle in a loved one's eye? It's the most wonderful thing to see, especially if you're the one who put the twinkle there. But it's also a short-lived event. A twinkle is just that—a quick flash in the course of a regular event.

My next thought is of how quickly I can lapse into old thoughts, old attitudes, and old actions that don't glorify God. I might be at work as a coworker messes up an assignment for the third time in a week—and just like that, in the twinkle of an eye, I'm saying the wrong thing, harboring resentment and angry thoughts instead of being "always full of grace, seasoned with salt . . ." (as we're instructed in the book of Colossians in the New Testament).

I think about how terrible it will be if God comes back for us just as I'm lapsing into one of these unattractive moments in the life of a sinner. I shouldn't be content with my negative actions, thoughts, attitudes at any point, not just "in the twinkling of an eye" as the trumpet sounds.

So what's my take-home lesson? To live my life—every single second of it, to the best of my ability, and with God's help at all times—as if it is the moment God raises us to the Heavens. To think of Him in everything I do, every word I say, every thought I think, and wonder if He might come calling in that twinkling of an eye. His return will be sudden. His return will be personal. His return will be glorious. His return will be final.

Are you prepared for God's return?

PART THREE

2 Corinthians

SAD HISTORY OF A BRIEF REVOLT

Key Elements

Purpose: to affirm Paul's ministry, defend his authority as an apostle, and refute the false teachers in Corinth

Author: Paul

To whom written: the church in Corinth and Christ's followers everywhere

Date written: about 55 to 57 A.D.

Key Themes

- Paul came under attack as not being an authentic apostle. He took time in this letter to tackle that challenge.
- The mystery and meaning of suffering are diagnosed in chapters six and eleven.
- Paul argues and defends his beliefs about giving out of abundance, with joy, to those who are in need.

God's Comfort

Praise be to the God and father of our Lord Jesus Christ, the
Father of compassion and the God of all comfort, who comforts
us in all our troubles, so that we can comfort those in any trouble with the comfort we ourselves have received from God.

—2 CORINTHIANS 1:3–4

Knowing what to say to a coworker in need isn't easy. At
work, we often become friends with those around us, but
sometimes we wonder whether we're crossing the line. When a
coworker/friend offers up details about personal struggles—an un-
happy marriage, children in trouble, financial struggles—it's hard
to find the right words to say.

However, a hurting friend doesn't always want us to make
the pain go away, though we would if we could. The friend just
wants us to listen and offer comfort the best way we know how.
God calls on us to draw from our own painful experiences, think
about how He loved and comforted us, and then offer that same
comfort to others. In fact, according to this verse, that's one reason God comforts us during our tough times. It's not to make the
pain go away; it's not to remove whatever is causing us pain; it's
simply to show love, offer a shoulder to cry on, and listen; it's to
teach us how to show others the same compassion.

God also comforts us to make us more dependent on Him.
He wants us to learn to seek Him as a first response, no matter how
bad (or even how good) the situation. Turning to Him should be
automatic. The more we learn that He comforts us in tough times,
the quicker we turn to Him the next time.

If you are a parent, surely you understand this concept. Your child scrapes his knee or breaks her arm. You can't turn back time and take away the hurtful action, but you can offer sympathy, love, hugs, and kind words. Your child knows this, because who does he call for, a second after he falls off his bike? Mom and dad, the ones who offer love and comfort. Children imitate what they witness in the home. As we see our earthly parents and Heavenly Father comfort us, we will be like Christ to others and dish up our own serving of comfort to others.

Promises of God Are Yes

For no matter how many promises God has made, they are "Yes" in Christ. And so through Him the "Amen" is spoken by us to the glory of God.
—2 CORINTHIANS 1:20

Upon hiring you, your boss made lots of promises. He might have guaranteed a hefty bonus at the end of your first year. He heavily hinted at a promotion in two years. He told you about all the wonderful business opportunities opening up at this fast-rising company. And he promised that you'd be a part of them all.

Does this sound familiar? Now the economy's not doing so well. Those perks you were promised? Sorry, the boss says no dice. Your company has been forced to restructure. As a result, you've been downsized. Counting on the promises of man is always a gamble. So here's a sure thing: God always keeps His promises. No exceptions. Always.

As we're told in this verse, God's promises are Yes in Christ. We're shown this in the fact that God promises us what the Messiah would be like. He delivered exactly as He promised. Jesus lived a sinless life, died for us, and intercedes for us, just as our faithful God promised.

Paul tried explaining to the Corinthians that because God was so faithful in His promises, he too would strive to keep his promises. But we aren't Christ, and circumstances change that redirect our intended actions. Paul wasn't able to return to Corinth at the time he promised because the Corinthians still had far to go in cleaning up their act. Sometimes circumstances change in our lives too, which keeps us from holding true to our promises.

But God has it all planned. He knows the circumstances and He knows how His promises will fit in. We can always count on Him to say yes to what He has promised.

Forgive Others; Gain Forgiveness

If you forgive anyone, I also forgive him. And what I have forgiven—if there was anything to forgive—I have forgiven in the sight of Christ for your sake. . . .

—2 CORINTHIANS 2:10

Have you ever erred grievously with a friend or family member, and then realized the error of your ways? You probably have. So you repent and ask the person you hurt for forgiveness, truly and sincerely. But that person doesn't accept your plea for forgiveness; instead you are met with a further haranguing of your sins. Hearing a listing of your grievous errors—when you already know them too well—doesn't do much to help you feel better about having taken steps to seek forgiveness. In fact, the other person's actions may drive a wedge further between the two of you and stunt your efforts at repentance.

The Bible tells us that a repentant sinner doesn't need more grief from us. He's already suffering enough and has made right with God. Our job is to welcome him back to the church with comfort, love, forgiveness, and acceptance. Otherwise we may permanently separate him from the church. Seek restoration. Besides, if God can forgive and forgive, there's no reason we shouldn't, too. There are many reasons God tells us we must forgive others.

In Matthew 18:21–22, Peter asks Jesus how many times he should forgive his brother when he sins against him. Jesus replies, "I tell you, not seven times, but seventy-seven times." Jesus also tells us in Matthew 6:14–15, "For if you forgive men when they sin against you, your heavenly Father will also forgive you. But if you do not forgive men their sins, your Father will not forgive your sins."

That's strong motivation to forgive our fellow humans, isn't it? I know I can't live my life without God's forgiveness. So I'd better forgive others when the need arises. Living life as a follower of Jesus means acting in the way we know Jesus acted. Not forgiving truly repentant sinners is definitely not a Christlike action.

Is there anyone in your life who seeks your forgiveness? Have you denied forgiveness out of bitterness and anger? Let these verses spur you on to take the next step. Call up your friend, or visit your coworker or relative, and do what God instructs. Forgive.

Aroma of Life

For we are to God the aroma of Christ among those who are being saved and those who are perishing. To the one we are the smell of death; to the other, the fragrance of life. And who is equal to such a task?
—2 CORINTHIANS 2:15–16

The smell of ginger, curry, vinegar, teriyaki, and soy sauce appeals to some people—and repulses others. Numerous smells strike people as either love 'em or can't stand 'em. Generally speaking, people feel the same way about Christ—they're either for Him or against Him, but generally not in between.

Paul is appealing to our senses when he says followers of Jesus are to leave a sweet smell in the air as they leave a scene. Now just picture walking past the perfume counter in your local department store. A fragrance fills the air and unmistakably alters the smell of the whole area. Some smells make you lean into the counter and the bottle. Others make your eyes water and your nose burn. This is the very argument Paul is making for those who bear the name of Jesus.

I am to leave a lingering, sweet aroma at the workplace. Now, it is not some sweet smell that will make people sick. It is an impressive, deep, rich aroma. It makes them sniff the air, not cover their noses and run. Unfortunately, many times I leave the latter effect on my workplace. My conduct, my speech, my reactions, my integrity cause those in the smell zone to cover their noses and run.

We are to have the same positive impact on any environment we find ourselves in. Whether it be our home or our neighborhood, we are to be sweet-smelling sauces that make those around us want to discover more of the claims of our faith.

How is your perfume working? Dish up the strong smell of Christ in small amounts. Prepare it in ways that might appeal to your friends. You wouldn't serve up a full meal of Chinese food if you knew your guests didn't like Chinese food. But you might introduce a few small hints of flavor with a meal they find more acceptable. Do the same with dishing up the message of Christ. Present it in small bites, fashioned in ways your friends will accept. Then slowly introduce more and more as they acquire a taste for the aroma of God.

God's Light in Our Hearts

For God, who said, "Let light shine out of darkness," made His light shine in our hearts to give us the light of the knowledge of the glory of God in the face of Christ.
—2 CORINTHIANS 4:6

Camping trips reveal a lot about people. You see things about your friends that you don't want to see; you learn things about their personalities that you wish you hadn't learned. Being stranded in the middle of nowhere without the comforts of home has a way of making the most joyful people less than a joy to be around. But you also learn who thinks ahead, who comes prepared. You learn who's done this camping thing before and has thought out the logistics of fixing dinner and setting up tents in the dark. Those friends are the ones who usually bring the flashlights and the lanterns for the dark nights.

Tough times in our lives, like camping, also reveal a lot about people. You see your coworkers, friends, and relatives in moods you wish you didn't see; you hear words from them you could live without hearing; and you sometimes experience tantrums with them you would miss otherwise. But, like camping, you also see who comes to life prepared. You see who is in touch with God, knowing that He's in control. You see which people don't let tough times get to them, because they're grounded in Christ. They, like your prepared camping buddies, are the light in the darkness, reflecting the light of God's glory.

Allowing God's light to shine through you relies on your devotion to Him. You must have firm faith in God, knowing that He is in control and that, whatever curveballs you're thrown, He saw them first and will help you handle them.

Tough times hit anywhere, whether at home with family troubles or at work, with a bad boss, incorrigible coworkers, or even a layoff. But these tough times are also when you're best able to witness your faith in God to others, and show them how He guides you through the light and the dark. Feeling calm, showing joy in all things, and reflecting God's love will make your heart shine in the darkness.

Be the prepared life camper. Stock up on God's light, and be ready to shine the next time the sun goes down in your life.

Earthen Vessels

> But we have this treasure in jars of clay to show that this all-surpassing power is from God and not from us.
> —2 CORINTHIANS 4:7

Some friends recently bought a large-screen television, because their family enjoys watching movies and entertaining friends. After much deliberation, agonizing about the cost of something they didn't really need, they chose a moderately large television and arranged for delivery. Imagine their surprise when the delivery men showed up the next night with their weighty purchase loaded unsecured in the back of a truck—the same truck our friends said they had just observed racing up and down their street, much too fast, trying to find their house.

Once the deliverymen arrived, they took the television out of the flimsy box that was supposed to protect it—*before* they even entered the house. They said it was too awkward to carry while still in the box. My friends held their breath until the deliverymen managed to carry the 170-pound piece of entertainment up two flights of stairs and into their living room. The wife said, "The thought of them handling something we'd just spent a fortune on so carelessly made us cringe with each step they took."

Let's reread Paul's thoughts on valuables: "But we have this treasure in jars of clay to show that this all-surpassing power is from God and not from us." God is infinitely more valuable than a silly television. The TV means nothing, nothing at all, in comparison with God. Yet we have this invaluable resource—God—living inside our flimsy, fallible bodies. He has entrusted us with delivering His message of salvation, and He has chosen to use our earthly bodies as the vessels by which we carry Him and His message.

Our bodies fail us; we're often weak with tiredness, plagued with illness, or demotivated by difficult circumstances. Thankfully, we don't rely on our own power to go about our business. We have Him, our living Savior, housed in our weak vessels. We have His power there to help us do the work He has entrusted to us. Our bodies are just that: physical bodies that house God and allow us to do His work.

Do you treat the contents of your vessel—your God—as you would a fragile package stamped "handle with care"? Do you realize that the power you have for living comes only from the One who lives inside you?

Perplexed, Not to Despair

> We are hard pressed on every side, but not crushed;
> perplexed, but not in despair. . . .
> —2 CORINTHIANS 4:8

Everybody experiences a rock-bottom point in life. Each person's bottom point, though, differs, and coming at its own stage in each life. Have you experienced yours? Some people consider rock-bottom being laid off from work; others think it's going through a divorce; still others, understandably, feel their lowest when they lose a loved one to death.

During these rock-bottom times, it's easy to feel hopeless, struck down, hard pressed. It's even understandable. But there's a difference between how followers of Christ and those who don't believe in Him handle these low points. People who lack faith in God believe there's no hope left. They wonder how life can go on during such a miserable period. Sadly, many contemplate—and some even go through with—a life-ending "solution."

The good news for believers, though, is that no matter how far we fall, God is always, always, always there to catch us. Isn't that great? It's such a simple truth, but one that we so easily forget and sometimes fail to believe. God tells us that when we have Him living inside us with our eyes ever focused on Him, no low is too low for Him.

". . . hard pressed on every side, but not crushed; perplexed, but not in despair. . . ." Why would God allow us to plunge to such depths? Because there's a lesson in everything we experience. Because God never said serving Him would be easy. But every time we suffer, we learn more about how powerful God is. We become more and more dependent on Him. We learn how to let Him use us to teach others the wonderful lessons we've learned. Feeling perplexed about life allows us the chance to seek God for comfort, and in turn it gives us another story to share with nonbelievers about how our God never lets us fail.

Next time you're feeling down and out, take heart in the truth that God will never let you fall. God loves you, God comforts you, and wants you to seek Him in everything. He will never let you despair.

Renewal

Therefore we do not lose heart. Though outwardly we are
wasting away, yet inwardly we are being renewed day by day.
—2 CORINTHIANS 4:16

When you're in a bad situation at work, it can easily sour
your existence. Putting up with a negative boss, poor relationships with coworkers, undue criticism, and harsh behavior
has a way of making you want to quit. Those around you surely
see the way you're suffering and wonder how much longer you'll
be able to keep it up.

You go home from work and spill your troubles to family or
friends, but somehow you feel even worse than when you first
started talking. Instead of feeling comforted, you feel even more
victimized. But then you remember who renews you. You remember where to turn for the best comfort, strength, and love. You
pour your heart out to God, asking Him for strength to face each
day. And you're renewed.

Going to God in prayer, especially during times of hurt and
despair, accomplishes several things. First, it establishes that He is
in control and that we are submissive to His plan. Second, talking
with God about our problems helps put life in perspective, weed-
ing out what is and isn't important. Third, pouring out our hearts
to our Heavenly Father allows Him to comfort us. One of the
greatest things about seeking Him during tough times is renewing
our faith in Him.

Every time we go to God in prayer, we renew and cement
our relationship with Him. Bad situations draw us to our knees

more than anything else in our lives, and that's when God fills us with His spirit and renews our spirit, giving us strength to continue.

So even though we sometimes want to quit work, we're still gaining something: a better relationship with God. Others may see the harsh reality of a miserable job, but we who follow Christ know it's a temporary reality. In the midst of misery, we're one step closer to Heaven.

Our Eternal Home

Now we know that if the earthly tent we live in is destroyed, we have a building from God, an eternal house in heaven, not built by human hands.
—2 CORINTHIANS 5:1

How much time do you spend taking care of your body, thinking about your body, and worrying about what might be wrong with your body in a given day? I know, it sounds like an absurd question, but bear with me. Think about how your back aches when you wake up, your knees pop when you head downstairs for breakfast, and your eyes burn with tiredness. Think about how long it takes you to shower, shave, and prepare your outward appearance for the day. More time than you'd like to admit, right?

Now consider how much time you spend thinking about things eternal—your relationship with God, what it will be like in Heaven, how you can better serve Him. *Less* time than you'd like to admit, right?

To put it all into perspective, read this verse again: "Now we know that if the earthly tent we live in is destroyed, we have a building from God, an eternal house in heaven, not built by human hands." In 2 Corinthians, Paul spells out for us the fact that our earthly tents—the bodies we spend so much time on—are temporary. It doesn't matter in the grand scheme of things what happens to the shell that carries us around and houses our beautiful spirit, because in heaven we'll receive a new and perfect "eternal house" from God that will cause us no stress.

Sounds great. What's the catch? The catch is that we must be right with God in order to receive the eternal home built by God. We must spend more time thinking about, praying for, and devoting time to things eternal and spend much, much less time thinking about the spare tire around our middle and the crows feet we've earned from smiling so much with our families.

God doesn't care what our outsides look like; He just wants a beautiful heart to reside in. In exchange, He'll give us the body of our dreams when we get to His house.

A New Creation

Therefore, if anyone is in Christ, he is a new creation;
the old has gone, the new has come!
—2 CORINTHIANS 5:17

Every other day, it seems, another TV program comes out that helps a singer, actor, politician, or everyday person reinvent himself or herself. Just like that, the person sheds the old persona and trades it in for a sleeker, more glamorous one, or a harder, more grown-up look. Everyone cheers, until the chameleon decides it's time for another new look. The reinvention starts over again.

I know there have been times when I haven't been proud of myself. I've wished I were someone else or that I could start again, doing things better the second time around. Once I found Christ, I realized the dream was possible.

Luckily for me (luckily for all of us), we only have to reinvent ourselves once. Unlike the chameleons who change every few years to gain a new pop following, we get to undergo our new creation without the embarrassment of being on national television. How does this once-in-a-lifetime reinvention take place? This verse says that in Christ we are a new creation; the old has gone, the new has come. Most of us couldn't be happier to get rid of our pre-Christ selves and start again.

Have you been looking for a way to shed the self you once were? Are you ashamed of your past, wishing you could wipe the slate clean and start again? Now's your chance. Without undergoing plastic surgery, buying an expensive new wardrobe, or subjecting yourself to hours of hair and make-up, you can create a new and improved you.

God says the old has gone, and He means it. Once you accept Him into your life and repent of your sins—no matter how huge you think they are—He will give you a new life. Not just an improvement over your old one, not just an altered life, but a new life altogether. Your new life, under a new master, will be better than any makeover you can imagine.

Ambassadors for Christ

We are therefore Christ's ambassadors, as though God were
making His appeal through us. We implore you on Christ's
behalf: Be reconciled to God.
—2 CORINTHIANS 5:20

Most businesses would be in trouble if not for couriers, mes-
sengers, and quick-delivery services. Couriers serve a
great need in today's business world, ferrying packages, files, and
documents from one business to the next, sometimes within the
hour they're called upon. Even the proliferation of the Internet and
e-mail in business can't eradicate the need for couriers.

Whether we like it or not, we're couriers, too. God often uses
us in surprising ways. One of the most surprising things about our
relationship with Him is that He chose us—such sinful, fallible
creatures—to carry the most important message ever: that of His
ability to save us. You'd think He would have created something
more foolproof to deliver His precious word, but instead He has
entrusted us with this privilege. He even goes so far as to call us
His ambassadors in this verse.

An ambassador is a diplomatic official of the highest rank
appointed and accredited as representative in residence by one government to another. Although an ambassador can be any of various diplomatic officials of the highest rank, a diplomat isn't just
any ordinary messenger. A diplomat isn't given a note and asked
to deliver it to someone without knowing and completely understanding and believing in what the note says. An ambassador is of
the highest rank.

God must rank us pretty high to entrust us with His message. We're ambassadors, and we're made in His image (Genesis 1:27). If ever we should doubt our ability to spread the word of His gospel, these verses should prove otherwise. God chose us to do His work. He created us, He is the power within us, and He trusts us to be His ambassadors. He believes in us. What more do we need to do His work?

Godly Sorrow Leaves No Regrets

Godly sorrow brings repentance that leads to salvation and leaves no regret, but worldly sorrow brings death.
—2 CORINTHIANS 7:10

In the last couple of years, several companies that don't need to be named here have come under fire for immoral and illegal financial reporting tactics. These events obviously took place over several years, at least—enough time for anyone involved to have felt remorse and sought forgiveness, and to have changed their ways. But without fail, the head honchos for those companies, and for their accounting companies, have expressed great sorrow for what they've done wrong by way of press statements, press conferences, or newspaper reporters.

I'd venture a guess that some of the people involved in these scandals were truly grieved for having done wrong. Getting caught was the wake-up call they needed to change their ways. However, I'd also venture a guess that some of those involved felt remorse not by what they did wrong but by the fact that they got caught. Paul calls that "worldly sorrow" in this verse.

Worldly sorrow often brings about no change—or, even worse, spurs on more serious events. A person caught red-handed may lie low, wait for the scandal to blow over, and then go right back into the activities he or she has always known. Worse yet, being caught and raked over the coals for wrongdoing may lead to further criminal activity, or in the most extreme case loss of life.

So what's the difference between worldly sorrow and Godly sorrow? "Godly sorrow brings repentance that leads to salvation and leaves no regret, but worldly sorrow brings death." A person who feels true sorrow for having committed a sin repents of that sin and draws closer to God. Because God says He forgives and forgets all of our transgressions, we too are free to forget our sins once we've given them over to God. Godly sorrow means people realize the error of their ways, seek forgiveness, and seek God— not just a chance to save face in front of peers while begging for forgiveness. God changes the hearts of those who truly grieve over their sins.

Worldly sorrow, on the other hand, leaves sinners with grief, heartache, and more troubles—and lots of regret that no back-pedaling, no press conference, no tears shed on camera can get rid of. Those who grieve only in the worldly way just feel more sorrow.

The only way to rid yourself of sorrow, pain, and regret for your sins, no matter how big or small, no matter how recent or ancient, is to give them over to God.

Giving Beyond Ability, Part I

For I testify that they gave as much as they were able,
and even beyond their ability.
—2 CORINTHIANS 8:3

Every year, many churches participate in a giving campaign. The funds support missionaries all over the world, paying for medical supplies, travel expenses, food, shelter, and teaching materials, among other things. A few weeks ahead of time, we learn that the giving campaign is approaching, and we're instructed to pray about how much we will give in the coming year. The way the campaign works is we can give a lump sum at a specified time or, more commonly, indicate how much we'll give each week or month in addition to our tithe.

I remember one such event happening. The first year I participated, I wrote down a number I had carefully calculated after reviewing my budget, figuring how much I could afford—without cutting into my personal expenses (vacation, new toys for the house, fancy dinners out). I easily wrote out that check each month, thinking nothing of what the money was going for. But the next year, our pastor challenged each of us to figure out how much we could sacrificially give—and then stretch the amount, maybe even double it. He said he and his wife had prayed over the campaign, and they were giving twice the amount they'd given the previous year, though he had no idea how they'd do it. But they prayed and believed that God was in control and that He would make a way. And He did.

So I upped the ante and gave more also. Not double, but still a stretch for my meager budget. And an amazing thing happened. Because I had prayed over this giving and stretched myself beyond my means, I was watching my money more carefully all the time. Being creative about how to save money each month made me think more often about what my money would be used for. So I couldn't buy a new pair of shoes this month; that's OK, a missionary somewhere in the world needs that $50 for food. I gave up one meal out at a restaurant each week; that's OK, the amount I would have paid for my spouse and me to eat out once would feed many more starving children in an undeveloped country.

Giving beyond your means, as Paul calls the Corinthians to do, not only serves those in need but also nourishes your relationship with Christ. Put your trust in Him and know that He will provide, as long as you're faithful to His calling. Stretch yourself, and watch your relationship with Him grow.

Giving Beyond Ability, Part II

And here is my advice about what is best for you in this matter: Last year you were the first not only to give but also to have the desire to do so. Now finish the work, so that your eager willingness to do it may be matched by your completion of it, according to your means.

—2 CORINTHIANS 8:10–11

Afriend in our town shared this story with me. "Each year, when our congregation fills out our giving campaign forms, we pledge to give a certain amount over the next year to fund missionaries. Most families choose to give a specified amount each month instead of in a lump sum, thinking they'll be able to come up with the money easier that way. And that's mostly right. But somewhere around October or November, when buying Christmas presents and decorating the house takes over, the giving fund goes out the window."

What my friend needs to remember is that pledging to give to the fund is a promise to God. He even gets that reminder of his promise sometime in late third quarter: a letter from the church's administrative office politely points out how much more he owes on the pledge he made the previous year. Oops.

This verse is Paul's polite reminder in late third quarter to the Corinthians, reminding them they started collecting money for the Jerusalem churches the year before. Obviously they've forgotten about that pledge and need a gentle nudge to get them to pay up. Paul doesn't want them to leave unfinished the enthusiastic willingness they exhibited the year before to fund people in need.

What kind of gentle nudges and polite reminders do you need in your life? Are you giving what God has called you to give? Or are you keeping the windfall for yourself? Complete what you've promised, and be faithful and obedient to God, even in your financial matters.

You Reap What You Sow

> Remember this: Whoever sows sparingly will also reap sparingly, and whoever sows generously will also reap generously.
>
> —2 CORINTHIANS 9:6

Many medical professions pay doctors according to production. A medical doctor or veterinarian often receives a base salary and then a percentage of production—meaning, the amount he or she brings in from services rendered. This increasingly popular payment method encourages doctors to work more efficiently and charge for all of their services, and it rewards them according to their work. If Dr. A works the bare minimum, spends twice as long in the exam room as her colleagues, and gives away lots of services, that's her choice—but she won't make as much on her percentage of production. If Dr. B schedules patients efficiently, leverages his nurses well, and charges fairly for his time, he will earn a larger piece of the pie because he's brought in more revenue for the practice.

Sowing and reaping is a simple mathematical formula that applies to all of life and is never broken. The doctors reap what they sow; they only earn as much as they give. The verse says, "Whoever sows sparingly will also reap sparingly, and whoever sows generously will also reap generously." When it comes to giving money to the church—to the cause of Christ—do you give sparingly or generously?

True, it's hard to feel able to give generously when you're struggling to pay the rent or mortgage bill each month and have money left for groceries. But that's exactly the point Paul is trying to make with this verse: if you worry about meeting your own needs and give very little, you'll earn little back from your relationship with God. But if you give generously—as much as you can with a joyful heart—God will take care of your needs.

Giving generously is a leap of faith. Every time you write that check for a bit more than you're comfortable with, you're putting faith in God to take care of your material needs. When you give sparingly, worrying about making ends meet, you're not trusting God to care for you.

God will provide if you put your trust in Him.

Cheerful Giver

Each man should give what he has decided in his heart
to give, not reluctantly or under compulsion, for God loves
a cheerful giver.
—2 CORINTHIANS 9:7

The office fundraiser and office collection for a coworker gift strike fear in the heart of every man and woman. There's no escaping the flyers, e-mail pleas for help with a child's fundraising campaign, or guilt-ridden requests for money for a coworker's wedding, baby, birthday, or retirement gift, or anything in between. In many offices, not a day goes by that there isn't a flyer, catalogue, or announcement asking for money tacked to the break room bulletin board.

How many people give to these collections out of compulsion? Does anybody give to them with a cheerful heart? God doesn't want giving to His church to be an obligation, like buying a raffle ticket from your secretary's son. He wants you to give with a cheerful heart, because you love Him.

Giving up hard-earned money isn't easy. There's no doubt about that. God's giving up His son for us wasn't easy either, I'm afraid. But He did it, because He loves us. No amount of money we give can ever repay Him for the gift of His son, but it can help our churches affect their communities, spread the word, continue running, and support their role in our lives.

This is not a guilt trip; God doesn't work by guilt trips. But He does make it clear that He wants us to give what we can. He wants us to make this decision not by checking our bank balance but by looking to our own heart and by determining what we feel led to give.

Have you checked your own heart lately and asked it how it feels about giving to God? Find out whether you're giving cheerfully or reluctantly. If it's the latter, talk to God about it. See how He can help you give with a cheerful heart.

God's Mighty Weapons

The weapons we fight with are not the weapons of the world.
On the contrary, they have divine power to demolish strongholds.
—2 CORINTHIANS 10:4

A football player preparing to play a game knows he's up against harmful opponents. He prepares by donning protective gear: mouth guard, shoulder pads, helmet, gloves, all meant to ward off injuries from members of the opposite team. The football player knows ahead of time that he can't prevent harm to himself on his own once he steps onto the field. He realizes that he needs the help of protective gear, and he never steps onto the field without it.

Why is it that so many of us who claim to follow Christ step onto the playing field of life without donning protective gear? Every day we face the devil, our opponent in life. Yet we often approach the arena unmasked, unarmed, and wholly unprepared.

But God tells us to "put on the full armor of God so that you can take your stand against the devil's schemes. For our struggle is not against flesh and blood, but against the rulers, against the authorities, against the powers of this dark world and against the spiritual forces of evil in the heavenly realms. Therefore put on the full armor of God, so that when the day of evil comes, you may be able to stand your ground, and after you have done everything, to stand" (Ephesians 6:10–13).

God not only protects us with His armor, He also equips us with custom-made weapons, prepared for us to fight evil strongholds. The people of the world use manipulation, harsh words, violence, doubt, and immorality to fight; God prepares us to fight with prayer, love, hope, faith, encouragement, and His Holy word. We can pray to Him for strength, knowledge, patience, love, and hope to get through any difficult situation. We can read His word to remind ourselves of our place in life and of His love, warding off the devil's schemes of planting self-doubt in our hearts. We know that in Him we have hope and that we are loved. What better weapons with which to fight back against the devil and his evil ways?

Are you wearing the full armor of God? Do you have His weapons ready for the fight? Good, because you're going to need them in this world.

Self-Commendation

> We do not dare to classify or compare ourselves with some who commend themselves. When they measure themselves by themselves and compare themselves with themselves, they are not wise.
> —2 CORINTHIANS 10:12

It seems natural to compare ourselves with others. Some people call it keeping up with the Joneses. It's the destructive and depressing—or elating—habit of regularly seeing how we fit in with everyone around us. It happens all the time in the workplace. You wonder whether you're closing as many deals as the person in the office next to you. You see how she dresses and compare your shabby suit with her new, expensive one and start feeling inadequate. You check out what kind of car she's driving or the house she just bought, and compare it to yours. You feel depressed or elated, depending on how you rate yourself compared to another person.

But what standards are you basing your comparisons on? Many times standards are inferior and worldly ones. The problem is that God doesn't want us to compare ourselves to anyone at all—except Him. He is perfect; no human is perfect. So if we're going to compare and strive for better and better, we should strive for the best: our Lord Jesus Christ. He knows how we should live; He knows how we should act; He's got everything we'll ever need in this world. It only makes sense that we should set our sights high, and aim for the best.

Comparing ourselves with others leads us to feel pride in ourselves. But the point is that God gave us everything we have, so there's no basis for our pride. He wants us to be like Him, not like the coworker who appears to have it all.

When setting standards for yourself and ranking your standings, don't compare yourself to a flawed human; compare yourself to God. Only then will you put your life into perspective and see just how far you have to go.

The Lord Commends

For it is not the one who commends himself who is approved, but the one whom the Lord commends.
—2 CORINTHIANS 10:18

In our society, people live for commendations from others. An employee strives for recognition from his boss; the boss craves praise from her employees. Companies base their value within their industry on awards, ratings in the market, and other pats on the back. Too often, doing good work isn't enough; people need a pat on the back from someone else to feel good about what they've accomplished.

It feels nice to hear kind words from others, especially your boss or a friend or loved one, but it's not the greatest of all commendations. In this verse, Paul warns against relying on commendations from mankind. He reminds the Corinthians—and all believers—that praise from God should be all that matters in our lives. God sets the standards for living, and He alone is in a position to dole out judgments, which includes words of commendation.

Another reason not to rely on praise from others is that praise can inflate our sense of pride. Pride causes us to think only of ourselves, about what we can do, what we have, and how great or important we are. Pride turns our eyes away from God, focusing our eyes and our heart on ourselves. Proverbs 16:18 says, "Pride goes before destruction, a haughty spirit before a fall." Obviously, the process of seeking, accepting, and relying on the praise of people, not God, intervenes in and impedes our relationship with Christ.

Imagine what would happen if every believer in Christ put all the effort he or she spends in gaining recognition from people into gaining commendation from God. That much energy and drive put into serving the King could only mean one thing: commendations from Him for serving Him well. How much better are His commendations than any kind word from a fellow human!

Corrupted from Simplicity

> But I am afraid that just as Eve was deceived by the serpent's cunning, your minds may somehow be led astray from your sincere and pure devotion to Christ.
>
> —2 CORINTHIANS 11:3

What does your to-do list look like? How about your daily calendar? I want to know whether they're clean, neat, and lightly organized, or crammed full of events, tasks, errands, and the like. Once you leave the office, how does your evening look: filled with plans, errands, carting children to and fro, or a quiet evening at home having dinner with the family and relaxing?

Plenty of incredibly busy people—with filled daily schedules and jam-packed evenings—have great relationships with God. They put Him on their schedules, making Him a priority first thing in the morning or at a specified time each day. But there are also many other busy, well-intentioned people who let daily tasks and events lead them away from a desire and intention to serve Christ fully.

In the midst of busyness, ungodlike teachings have a way of slipping into your mind—and taking over your heart. In this verse, Paul warns the church that false teachers are threatening their faith. He wants them to be aware of the false teachers and be prepared against their smooth talk. Those teachers knew how to get to the Corinthians when they least expected.

Satan also knows how to get to us when we least expect it. When we're most tired, most stressed, busiest, he slips in. He makes us doubt our abilities and question our place in life; most of all, our busy schedules pull us away from spending time in God's word—our best and only defense against Satan.

Go ahead, fill up your schedule. Keep to your busy life. But please, put God on your schedule and make sure you keep His appointments. A busy life could allow Satan to slip in sight unseen. You wouldn't want your daily achievements undermined by his evilness.

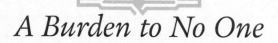

A Burden to No One

And when I was with you and needed something, I was not a burden to anyone, for the brothers who came from Macedonia supplied what I needed. I have kept myself from being a burden to you in any way, and will continue to do so.
—2 CORINTHIANS 11:9

Asking for favors is a way of life in many businesses. The adage "it's not what you know but who you know" applies in many situations. A young graduate looking for his first professional job may rely on his father's business contacts and reputation in the business world to land a prestigious job. A salesperson—no matter what she's selling—relies on contacts and sources to land the deal that makes her career. A seemingly kind and honorable coworker taps resources to get ahead.

Many times and in many ways, asking others for help is a good thing. The act keeps us humble and helps us learn to rely on someone other than ourselves. God tells us in several verses of the Bible that pride in oneself is destructive. It often keeps us from asking others for help. We want to do it ourselves, prove ourselves worthy, not admit that we need anything from anyone. So humbling ourselves and asking for help generally shows strength of character that God commends.

Being a burden to someone else is a different thing entirely. Think about your work situation. Can you picture someone who's a burden in your office? Is there someone who constantly asks for help, interrupts your work, seeks more information, more favors, more contacts—all for personal gain? Who knows: the burden in your office could be you, stealing time from your boss, resources from your coworkers, and supplies from the warehouse—a burden on the company overall.

No one likes to be thought of as a burden, which the dictionary says is something carried, oppressive, or worrisome. In this verse, Paul explained to his beloved church that he had deliberately not been a burden to them. Why? Pride wasn't the issue here. He wanted the Corinthians to see him as help, not as one of the false teachers who collected money from the people and then saddled them with ill teachings.

Do you want your coworkers to see you as help or as a burden? In which way do you think they currently see you? Use Paul's own example to guide you in your life. Bring love, teachings, and help, but don't weigh everyone down for your own personal gain.

Thorn in the Flesh

> To keep me from becoming conceited because of these
> surpassingly great revelations, there was given me a thorn
> in my flesh, a messenger of Satan, to torment me.
> —2 CORINTHIANS 12:7

A paper cut is more than a minor annoyance. Cut yourself in the morning, and you'll remember your foolishness all day long. Chances are, you'll remember it for quite some time and be more careful as you shuffle and file all the papers on your desk. That lingering cut on the tip of your finger serves as a reminder of the pain in the world and helps you make sure you avoid it as best as you can.

Scalding your tongue on a too-hot cup of coffee does the same thing. Torture your taste buds like that, and you won't eat or drink anything hot for quite some time—or at least you won't be tasting it.

The thorn in the flesh that Paul talks about in the verse here serves as a constant reminder to Paul not to become too conceited about his abilities in God. We don't know exactly what served as Paul's physical thorn in the flesh, but we can be pretty certain it was more than a pesky paper cut or scalded tongue. But Paul says he grew to be thankful for the thorn in his flesh, because it drew him closer to Christ. "That is why, for Christ's sake," he says, "I delight in weaknesses, in insults, in hardships, in persecutions, in difficulties. For when I am weak, then I am strong."

What is your thorn in the flesh? What hinders you from becoming too reliant on yourself—thus limiting your need for Christ? Your thorn could be a physical limitation, financial setback, any number of things. Are you thankful for your thorn? That's a hard thing to do, to thank God for something that hinders your ability. But God puts the thorn there to remind you of something very important: you need Him, and He wants you to need Him. If you were all-knowing and all-doing, would you really turn to Him as often as you do? I know I wouldn't.

Sufficient Grace

> But He said to me, "My grace is sufficient for you, for My power is made perfect in weakness."
> —2 CORINTHIANS 12:9

God says, "My grace is sufficient for you. . . ." He gives me and you and every one of His believers His personal guarantee that we will never need more grace than He can supply. What a powerful statement! Where else in life can you be guaranteed that you will never, ever run out of something you need? Your physical needs and circumstances change daily. You have no way of knowing that you'll have a job, that you'll always be able to provide for yourself. But no matter what happens, God promises a lifetime supply of His grace. That's all you need.

In 2 Corinthians 12:8, Paul says, "Three times I pleaded with the Lord to take it away from me," alluding to the thorn in his flesh.

Something out of Paul's control was interfering with His life. He begged his faithful God to remove the thorn in his flesh. God, with infinite power, said no. "My grace is sufficient for you, for My power is made perfect in weakness," God says. If God immediately healed us every time we asked, do you think we'd have such powerful relationships with Him? If God took away hurt, difficult circumstances, and painful emotions, do you think we'd talk to Him so often and see His mercy, love, and comfort in such a powerful way? No, of course not. We'd just go to Him every time we needed something—and then be on our way until the next time.

But that's not how God works. He leaves imperfections in our lives for a reason. He wants us to draw closer to Him, to need Him, to see how wonderfully He can work in our lives. He wants us, like Paul, to learn to love the thorn in our flesh and to understand that God's grace is all we need.

Reflect on this verse: "My grace is sufficient for you, for My power is made perfect in weakness." How do God's words affect your life, your personal situation? Know that no matter what, He will provide. That's His wonderful promise.

Spent for Others' Souls

Now I am ready to visit you for the third time, and I will not be a burden to you, because what I want is not your possessions but you. After all, children should not have to save up for their parents, but parents for their children.

—2 CORINTHIANS 12:14

In an age in which the average lifespan exceeds seventy years, more and more adults are finding themselves caring for their elderly parents. This relatively new occurrence has drudged up emotions, hardships, and sacrifices previously unknown by grown children who are used to their parents taking care of them until adulthood, and then they in turn take care of their children as their parents did before them. Simple as that.

But life isn't always simple. Elderly parents expect more of their grown children now. God, however, sees us as His children—and He doesn't want us to take care of Him or give Him anything of ours. Except, of course, for our hearts. As illustrated in the verse here, Paul says he is like a spiritual parent to the Corinthians. He, as a parent, wants to feed his children with spiritual knowledge and he wants nothing in return. You've probably heard the wise-crack "I want to live long enough to be a burden to my children." Paul doesn't want that, and neither does our God.

Instead, God wants us to be open to hearing His word. He wants us to learn from Him, love Him, serve Him. Money, material possessions, and things of this world don't mean a thing to Him. We are His children, and children generally shouldn't have to pay their parents' way. However, out of love, children often do give in return. That's how our relationship with Christ should be. Accept freely the love, teachings, and guidance He gives. In return, give Him your heart. What happens next is up to what your love for Him drives you to do.

Weak in Him

For to be sure, He was crucified in weakness, yet he lives by God's power. Likewise, we are weak in Him, yet by God's power we will live with Him to serve you.
—2 CORINTHIANS 13:4

T hey are weak, but He is strong," goes the familiar children's song of praise "Jesus Loves Me." Little did we know when we sang that song as children, complete with muscle-pumping arm actions, that we are the weak ones in the song. But it's always been abundantly clear that the strong one we're singing of is our faithful God.

Throughout history, unsuspecting people have pulled off heroic events. They range from a single person lifting a car off a pinned child to rescuing an elderly woman from the jaws of an alligator. I heard the latter one on the news this morning. An alligator grabbed onto a woman's arm as she swept brush out of the pond in her housing addition, pulling her toward the water. A female neighbor happening by witnessed the event and with brute strength pulled the elderly woman from the alligator's grasp. Asked how she found the strength, she said she didn't know—then she backtracked, saying yes, she did know where it came from. She implied on national television that God gave her the strength she never could have found on her own.

What issue has you pinned or caught in a trap? Is there something in your life you feel you can't handle on your own? Good news: you don't have to. God is here to do it with you. Great news: God is stronger than all of us, at all times. He's willing to use that power to help every one of us, if only we'll humble ourselves, acknowledge His power, and ask. "Ask and it will be given to you; seek and you will find; knock and the door will be opened to you. For everyone who asks receives; he who seeks finds; and to him who knocks, the door will be opened," Jesus tells us in Matthew 7:7–8.

Isn't it great to know that we don't have to live life as weaklings, relying on our own meager power to get us through? Life would be a pretty grim prospect without God's power on our side. God wants to share His strength; He wants to use it to your benefit and mine. Have you asked Him for help recently? Maybe it's time you did.

PART FOUR

Galatians

LIVING FREE

Key Elements

Purpose: to refute those who taught that Gentile believers must obey the Jewish law in order to be saved, and to release believers to faith and freedom in Christ

Author: Paul

To whom written: the churches in southern Galatia, a city founded on Paul's first missionary journey, and to Christ's followers everywhere

Date written: about 49 A.D.

Key Themes

- The law is a dead end. People can never be put right with God through relying on good works or keeping the law.
- Faith is the only way to God.
- We who have surrendered to the claims of Jesus are set free to serve the risen Lord.
- A follower of Jesus relates to God as a beloved son, not a fearful slave.

On a Mission for God

Paul, an apostle—sent not from men nor by man, but by Jesus Christ and God the Father, who raised Him from the dead. . . .
—GALATIANS 1:1

You know what it's like when your boss chooses you to complete a special assignment. You're excited that he chose you instead of one of your colleagues. You realize that your boss trusts you, believes in your skills and work ethic, and knows you're the go-to person to finish the job. That's a great feeling. If you're anything like me, knowing that your boss chose you makes you want to work ten times harder to do well on the project, putting your all into doing a topnotch job.

Or if you have kids—or remember when you were one yourself—you might picture yourself sitting in a classroom as the teacher asks for "special helpers" to take notes to the office. Walking those attendance sheets to the office was a chore—but it sure didn't feel like one when the teacher chose you to carry out the mission. No matter the age, we all love to be selected for a special assignment.

So imagine how the apostle Paul must have felt when his Heavenly Boss chose him to spread God's word. God chose him, Paul, a man who had previously persecuted Christians, to complete his mission. Paul was a man with a dark past full of skeletons and bad memories, yet God called him. What a thrill. Do you think he ever had butterflies in his stomach? Paul put his all into the task, going on three missionary journeys and changing the history of Christianity—all because God chose him, and because he loved his Father.

Do you feel the "just chosen" excitement when God asks you to do His work? Are you moving through life with a sense of assignment and intention? One by-product of being chosen is this recognition of personal purpose. Are you giving it your all and reveling in the fact that God chose you to do His work?

Don't let the novelty wear off. Don't let excitement for other things in life distract you from the mission of serving the one true King. Your mission is to follow God and do His work with abandon, all the days of your life.

On Stage Before God

Am I now trying to win the approval of men, or of God? Or am I trying to please men? If I were still trying to please men, I would not be a servant of Christ.
—GALATIANS 1:10

In writing, and in public speaking, knowing your audience is the key. In English and speech classes and in journalism schools across the country, teachers are hammering home the notion that writers must gear their stories, language, examples, and main points toward the people who will be reading their work. Why? Because readers do not pay attention to another's work if they don't feel the author or speaker is talking to them personally. Every writer is aware of being unable to write in a way that captivates and pleases everyone. The writer must carefully select the audience and then do the best possible work to retain them.

Our world today does its best to tell us who our audience in life should be. We have the impression that people play out their lives for their peers, for people of the opposite sex, and for those who exert power and influence at work. It's easy to get swept up in this frame of mind. Most of us certainly hear more in the media about how to please friends or loved ones than we hear about pleasing God.

Think about your day. Who did you "act" for today? Was it your boss, your coworker, your spouse? How many times today did you make God your key audience? How often did you consult Him before acting, or think of how your words or deeds would affect Him beforehand?

Paul didn't mince words in this verse when he told the Galatians they would be eternally condemned if they followed any teaching other than that of God. He said that he spoke so forcefully because he was trying to win God's approval, not the approval of the Galatians hearing his harsh—but true—words.

God is the only audience that matters. He determines whether it's curtains or time for an encore. He writes the final review of your life. So choose your words and actions wisely, and make sure God gives you thumbs up on your performance.

A Changed Man

> They only heard the report: "The man who formerly persecuted
> us is now preaching the faith he once tried to destroy." And they
> praised God because of me.
> —GALATIANS 1:23–24

Do the people around you know that you're a Christian? Is it evident in how you speak, act, and approach life—and at work, and even in front of those who don't know Christ?

It's one thing to profess faith at church on Sunday morning, but it's a much more complicated thing to let your faith shine while in the presence of non-Christians. A friend told me about an experience at her office. She had worked for a company for two years, professing to be a Christian but never striving to make her life look any different from those of the non-Christians in her office. One day she saw a fictional Christian novel in a coworker's mailbox. She struck up a conversation with the coworker about Christian novels, and eventually they shared their faith with each other. Her coworker's simple act of leaving the book in her mailbox for all to see witnessed to the office that she believed in Christ.

I'm happy to say that both of these women talk openly about God in their office now, and several other colleagues have joined them in openly professing their faith. They've even taken steps to engage nonbelievers in conversation about Christ. You'd better believe they now leave Christian literature in their mailboxes for all to see.

Although neither woman set out to destroy the faith, as Paul did (and I'm willing to bet you aren't persecuting Christians either), their initial action—or omission of action—did nothing to reveal a true faith in God. Just as the report mentioned in this verse told about Paul and his changed life, let the word spread about your changed life. Give people every reason to believe you're a Christian, no matter where you are or what situation you face. You never know who's watching.

Spiritual Pillars

James, Peter, and John, those reputed to be pillars, gave me
and Barnabas the right hand of fellowship when they recognized
the grace given to me. They agreed that we should go to the
Gentiles, and they to the Jews.
—GALATIANS 2:9

These apostles were on to something. They each had distinct strengths in leadership, and they knew it. James, Peter, John, and Paul understood their own temperaments and used that knowledge to decide who would do which part of the work.

For example, Paul becomes the apostle to the Gentiles and Peter is the apostle to the Jews. The book of Acts pictures Paul as the man with a heart for the outsider and Peter as the one with passion to reach the insider. In saying that James, Peter, and John have given Barnabas and himself the right hand of fellowship, Paul is saying they agree that their teachings are in line and accept each other as colleagues in sharing the gospel.

Together the men choose who will lead the Gentiles and the Jews, using their experience, background, and personal temperaments. What can we learn from this brief intersection between these first-century pillars of the faith?

First, consider the idea of being a pillar of the faith. It is easy to think of these men as giants when focusing on the end of their life and looking backwards. However, who would have ever voted Peter, the local fisherman, as a pillar-to-be? Pillars of the faith come out of the ordinary common stock of life. Any one of us can become a foundation of faith in our community by pledging our allegiance to following Jesus every day of our lives. A man or woman of faith who sets a goal to follow in the footprints of Christ is someone slowly becoming a foundation of faith.

Second, think about how there is room for many people all working in God's name. All of the apostles in this verse are working in their own way, but all for the same result. There is clearly unity among diversity. Not everybody has to express his or her faith in the same manner. We don't all have to be called to do the same work, or even in the same venue. This means there's a place for each of us to do His work. Now it's up to us to listen to Him and learn to serve Him where He intends us to be.

Private Power Supply

I have been crucified with Christ and I no longer live, but Christ
lives in me. The life I live in the body, I live by faith in the Son
of God, who loved me and gave Himself for me. I do not set
aside the grace of God, for if righteousness could be gained
through the law, Christ died for nothing!

—GALATIANS 2:20–21

Have you ever wondered what makes certain batteries last
longer than others? You know, the ones that claim they
"keep going, and going, and going." Every time my flashlight dies
just when I most need it most, I wonder about these obscure things.
What's really great are rechargeable batteries: plug them in when
their power is weak, give them a few hours, and they're good to go.

Watching commercials tout endless energy may make you
wish for some internal power of your own. Guess what? You can
have your own private power supply. All you have to do is give
your life over to Jesus Christ.

Stick with me here; I'm not saying that you'll never get tired
at the end of the day, or feel weary while shuttling off for another
eight or more hours at the office. What I am saying is that I'm not
running on my own power. I've got the power of Christ's resurrection to help me fight sin and live my life for Him.

Just think about the awesome power of God! When you give
your life over to Jesus Christ, you're essentially killing off your old
self, getting rid of the dead weight that slows you down. But tak-

ing Jesus into your heart renews your life and gives you power to live a better life, one that meshes your experiences with His and makes you want the same things for yourself as He wants for you.

What's more, fighting against God's power to change you because of what He did on the cross only wears you down. A sure way to feel powered up for the long haul? Rest in God's power to save you. Rest in the knowledge that God lives in you and carries you through—if only you allow Him to. Just think of yourself as one of those rechargeable batteries—plug into God regularly and He'll keep you shining bright.

The Law

So the law was put in charge to lead us to Christ that we might be justified by faith.
—GALATIANS 3:24

Many companies advocate job descriptions for new hires. On your first day at a new job, you might receive a photocopied page that outlines your main responsibilities. You think, *Great, I can handle this; this list isn't too long.* Well, if you did just what was on that list, it probably wouldn't take too much effort to complete the tasks in your forty hours each week. But what you've probably already learned—or soon will—is that just doing what's on the list, or what's given to you, isn't enough. The list is there to guide you to think for yourself, do a good job, and boost your employer.

In the verse here, Paul was saying to the Galatians that the law of the time wasn't just to be followed to the letter. The law was in place to lead people to Christ, to show them how to have faith in Christ. But it took more than blind obedience to get to the point. The Galatians had to learn to read between the lines, to learn the moral code behind the laws, and to learn about the Creator behind the moral code that gave them the laws.

In your spiritual walk, you might find yourself as the Galatians did in Paul's day, or as today's new hires presented with a job description do: plodding along, following the list, but missing the overall picture of God's faith. You know you're supposed to attend church on Sundays, so you do. You've learned that reading the Bible and praying each day are part of the Christian life, so you do them. Thankfully, you know the Ten Commandments and are careful to do what they say. Great, that's a wonderful start.

But are you getting the overall picture? Laws are designed to reveal the true will of God. They are designed to bring you closer to God, to develop a relationship with Him in which you trust Him completely and live by faith in Him. Look past the letter of the law to God's intent, and let it draw you into a vibrant love relationship. After all, life with God is really more about relationship than it is about rules.

Losing the Joy of Giving

What has happened to all your joy? I can testify that, if you could have done so, you would have torn out your eyes and given them to me.

—GALATIANS 4:15

Think back to last Christmas. We all know the true meaning of Christmas is to celebrate the birth of Jesus. In celebration, we give gifts to one another, symbolizing the gift our Heavenly Father gave us in the form of His son. But the way the world would have us see it, Christmas is all about giving the biggest, most expensive, and hardest-to-find gifts imaginable to everyone we know. Case in point: office Christmas presents and collections for the boss's gift. Christmas presents are so expected these days, it's as if you're obligated to give them, when in reality gifts are something you give freely because you want to. You give with joy because your heart tells you to do so.

In this verse, Paul questioned the Galatians' lack of joy in giving of themselves to God. He noticed that legalism had brought the Galatians down, making them feel obliged to serve their God and guilty when they didn't. The Galatians did what God requested because it was the law, not because they felt His spirit working in their hearts, calling them to live according to His will.

When we are in tune with our Creator, our will aligns with His. We want to follow His laws, we want to live as He commands, because we love Him and it is a joy to serve Him. But when we just do what we're told to do without fully believing in the cause—as when we're asked to "give liberally" to the boss's Christmas gift fund that we don't feel like giving to at all—it sucks the joy right out of the task.

Are you joyously giving your all to God? Or are you praying to Him, reading your Bible, and doing what He says out of a sense of obligation only? If you're not feeling happy about your contributions to God, just remember this: God gave His ultimate gift when He sent His son into the world, and again when He sacrificed His son on the cross. He did it because He loves us. Feeling that kind of love from our Father rekindles those loving, joyous feelings—and makes us want to give in return.

Stand Firm, Stand Free

It is for freedom that Christ has set us free. Stand firm, then, and do not let yourselves be burdened again by a yoke of slavery.
—GALATIANS 5:1

When you were a teenager, your parents likely set guidelines for living: be home by curfew, call when you're going to be late, tell them who you're with and where you'll be, and don't go anywhere alone. Surprisingly teenagers with clear guidelines—but not excessive, detailed rules to follow—feel the most freedom. Some people say that teens with guidelines feel more freedom than those whose parents exercise no constraint.

The thought that having to follow guidelines offers more freedom, not less, might seem contradictory. But when you think about it, it makes sense. Knowing your boundaries and then enjoying the freedom to act within them is more comforting than running wild, not knowing your place in life. The exception, however, comes when teenagers act outside the boundaries. Doing so often forces parents to enact stricter rules, hampering a teen's freedom in an effort to protect the teen from danger and mischief.

Apply that concept to what Paul says about Christ setting us free for freedom and not letting ourselves be burdened by a yoke of slavery. Imagine yourself as God's teenager. He has given you boundaries for how to live. He doesn't feel the need to give you excessive rules on every step you can and cannot take, so long as you stay within those boundaries. But the people of Paul's day felt the need to burden themselves with laws, rules, and special conditions. Putting an inordinate amount of restrictions on the Galatians took the people back to slavery, the very thing God wants to free us from.

It's easy to fall into this trap even today. Whether through prudence, misunderstanding, or disagreement with God's "guidelines for living," you are likely to encounter people who add rules to following Christ and nitpick every action. It's obviously good to keep tabs on living your life for God, but don't let others draw you back into slavery. Enjoy God's freedom and use it well.

Fruit of the Flesh

The acts of the sinful nature are obvious; sexual immorality, impurity and debauchery; idolatry and witchcraft; hatred, discord, jealousy, fits of rage, selfish ambition, dissentions, factions and envy, drunkenness, orgies, and the like. I warn you, as I did before, that those who live like this will not inherit the kingdom of God.

—GALATIANS 5:19—21

Reading that sexual immorality and hatred are part of a sinful nature come as no surprise. But what stands out in this passage are the words "selfish ambition." Do you characterize yourself as ambitious, especially when talking about your career? Generally speaking, in cultures like that of the United States, thinking of someone as ambitious is paying the person a compliment. But if you characterize yourself as such, would it be out of line to associate the word *selfish* with *ambitious*?

We usually think of being ambitious as a good thing. In the verse here, however, Paul lumps ambition with such sinful acts as debauchery, idolatry, hatred, and drunkenness. Not exactly how you'd like to be classified at work, I'm sure. But does the description fit?

There's nothing wrong with wanting to succeed at a career. But God clearly states that there's no room for selfish desires in His house. Selfish ambition means putting your eyes on yourself and your work, not turning your eyes to God and His work in your life. Friedrich Nietzsche once wrote, "Whenever I climb I am followed by a dog called 'Ego.'" The dictionary defines ego as "the self, especially as distinct from the world and other selves; self-love; egotism."

The Bible outlines that my ambition can be fueled by the desire to advance my own sense of self-interest, or it can be sourced in God. What distinguishes the kind of ambition is the source.

Take a minute to look at your career critically—and be brutally honest with yourself and with God. Do any of your actions, desires, or thoughts fall into the category of fruit of the flesh? Recommit to the wisdom from Psalms 37:4: "Delight yourself in the Lord, and He will give you the desires (ambitions) of your heart." Spend some time praying that God will help you align your desires with His, granting you His fruit of the Spirit as you march through life.

Fruit of the Spirit

But the fruit of the Spirit is love, joy, peace, patience, kindness, goodness, faithfulness, gentleness, and self-control. Against such things there is no law.
—GALATIANS 5:22–23

People inevitably talk about others, whether they gather around the water cooler, whisper in cubicles, or e-mail across the building. You have no control over that. What you do have control over is how you conduct yourself, which influences what people say about you. If you were a fly on the wall while your coworkers were chatting about you, how would they describe you? Would they use the words *patient, kind,* and *gentle?* If so, the fruits of the spirit may well be shining through you.

To produce the fruits of the spirit, you need one key ingredient: the Holy Spirit within you. In John 15:4–5, God says, "Remain in me, and I will remain in you. No branch can bear fruit by itself; it must remain in the vine. Neither can you bear fruit unless you remain in me." A grape pulled from the vine will not continue to grow. It needs the vine for nourishment and further development. Without the vine, the grape will wither and die.

God is our vine. No amount of good works, wishing, planning, or creating will produce the fruit of the spirit within you. The Holy Spirit puts the fruit of the spirit, traits that are found in the nature of Christ, in you when you make His will for you yours, putting aside your own desires. We were made in His image (Genesis 1:26), and it is through Him that we will exhibit the characteristics of Christ.

So how do you "walk in the Spirit"? A surefire way to draw closer to God and make His characteristics your own is to talk with Him daily and read His word. Have you ever noticed that you make better decisions when you're praying for God's guidance before you act and when you're reading His word regularly? By making it a habit to pray regularly and read the Bible, you'll have God and His will in the forefront of your mind. You'll think more about His will, and you'll be more apt to exhibit His traits.

Aristotle once wrote, "We are what we repeatedly do. Excellence, therefore, is not an act but a habit." Making your daily quiet times with God a meaningful habit produces the fruits of the spirit. In turn, coworkers associate your name with all that is good in Christ.

Keep in Step

Since we live by the Spirit, let us keep in step with the Spirit.
Let us not become conceited, provoking and envying each other.
—GALATIANS 5:25–26

Sometime around August or September of each year, executives meet in boardrooms, conference rooms, and offices across the country to figure out how to get their revenue in line with their projections. For the first six to eight months of the year, the bottom line looks as if it's on track. But as year-end spending drops, those in the know start to panic. They create charts and graphs, show them to their employees, and discuss ways to make revenue—the red line dragging along the bottom of the chart—align with projections, the black line gracing the top of the chart.

Does this example remind you of anything? Anything other than the meeting you sat through this morning? Let's spiritualize this analogy by making the projection line God's will for your life. The revenue line is your will, or where you actually fall on God's chart. How much variance is there between projection and revenue in your life?

At different times in your life your will and God's desires for your life come closer to each other and then fall away again. There's a direct correlation in how closely aligned your will is with His. The gap needs to be decreasing.

Paul was captivated by the thought that every minute of every day Jesus wanted to partner with him. As he further understood this, he used terms such as "walking in the Spirit" or "being in Christ." This life in God required a step-by-step alliance between Paul and his Savior. Many times, we forget the circumstances that surrounded Paul's life. He struggled with the same kinds of things we struggle with. He had issues of relationship, self-doubt, external hardship, and just about every other challenge that any of us have. Yet he understood the secret. It was staying close, with each step, to the life of Jesus.

Make every effort to live your life as closely aligned to God's as possible. You want your lines on the chart to draw nearer each other every day of your life—knowing the goal is that one day yours will overlap with God's.

The Original Do-Gooders

Therefore, as we have opportunity, let us do good to all people, especially to those who belong to the family of believers.
—GALATIANS 6:10

L et us do good to all people. What a powerful command. On a given day, can you think of at least one instance in which you failed to do good—or seriously wished you didn't have to do good? That's a hard command to live up to, even if you truly believe in Christ and strive to live for Him.

Take, for example, the office busybody. Every office has one, right? It's difficult to feel joy around someone who causes others grief—especially if you've been the centerpiece of one of her sordid tales. But God doesn't tell us to be nice just to those who are nice to us. He tells us to "do good to all people," and that includes the most difficult people we encounter.

Sure, nice theory. Now, how do we apply it to our lives? Remembering to treat others as if they were Christ ought to help. Recall Matthew 25:40: "And the King will answer them, 'I assure you: Whatever you did for one of the least of these brothers of Mine, you did for Me.'"

Why are we to do good to all? You never know who's watching. A friend told me this tale, and it might help illustrate the point. An intern joined my friend's company for the summer. Unbeknownst to my friend, the intern was struggling with her faith in God. At the end of the intern's session, she left a note for my friend that said how much she'd appreciated the way her mentor (my friend) had demonstrated a sincere faith in Christ and lived it out in her daily life. Upon further discussion, my friend learned that by including everyone in the office, not just those she enjoyed the most; by speaking only kind words; and by helping out at every opportunity, she had witnessed God's love in the best way possible to the intern. Without my friend ever verbally professing her faith, the intern just knew that God had to be behind an attitude like that. It renewed her desire to seek God wholeheartedly.

"Holy do-gooder" sounds like a phrase Batman and Robin might use. Actually, it was the apostle Paul who first thought up the idea and called for those of us who claim the name of Jesus to practice it.

Boomerang Living

Anyone who receives instruction in the word must share all good things with his instructor.
—GALATIANS 6:6

Once upon a time, anyone entering a business would be introduced to a mentor. The mentor would teach them about the business, guide their professional formation, and prepare them for life, not just the business at hand. The young professional would be forever grateful, sending notes, good wishes, and gifts to the mentor in appreciation of the elder's knowledge and devotion to teaching.

The practice of mentoring was in full force during the days of Paul. There were a number of schools that "platformed" various personalities and methodologies. Paul was taking this practice and applying a spiritual lesson to it. He wanted to reinforce the notion that we who have been shaped and influenced for the good have responsibility to return the favor. We are to share our bounty with our shapers.

Now, in our fast-paced, competitive lives, the way of the mentor, in the true sense of the word, has slipped a few notches. But for many, a pastor or spiritual leader serves the role of spiritual mentor. Are you supporting your church as you could? Are you giving back to those who have given to you?

In another letter, Paul talks specifically about the concept of giving. He wanted us to give out of a generous heart of appreciation. He wanted us to give sacrificially, proportionally, and without manipulation and compulsion—in other words, give back because we were given to in the first place.

Take a minute and e-mail, phone call, or somehow communicate a note of appreciation to those who shaped your life. If they are in need of financial help, make an investment in them. The size is secondary. The intent is primary. Return the investment.

PART FIVE

Ephesians

HIGHER GROUND

Key Elements

Purpose: to strengthen the believers in Ephesus in their faith by
  unfolding the purpose of the church, the body of Christ

Author: Paul

To whom written: the churches in Ephesus, and all believers

Date written: about 60 A.D.

Key Themes

- Jesus Christ is the centerpiece of God's agenda for mankind.
- We are part of Christ's body and consequently are called to live
  in harmony and union.
- Relationships in our family, work, church, and community are
  the venues for our authentic Christian belief to be translated
  into powerful Christian behavior.
- Jesus has agreed to walk through the ups and downs of life with
  us, each step of the path.

Other Person Prayers

I have not stopped giving thanks for you, remembering you
in my prayers.
—EPHESIANS 1:16

A friend recently told me a story about sharing his faith with a man who works for him. The new employee was in the office only half a day when the subject of religion first came up. Over lunch, the new hire asked my friend about his views of Christ—a perfect opening. During the next three weeks, my friend prayed earnestly for his employee, asking God to open the man's heart to hearing His word and for an appropriate opportunity to talk to him more about Jesus. My friend's church was having a special program that Sunday, so he invited his new employee, who said he would have to think about it. Several days later, the man approached my friend and asked, "Have you been praying for me to come to church?" My friend responded that yes, he had been praying for that and for an open heart for Christ. The new hire accepted the invitation to meet him at church on Sunday.

Praying for others works, even in the office. Paul tells the Ephesians in verses 1:16–19 that he has been praying for God to do great things in their lives. We too can follow Paul's lead. We don't have to restrict our prayers to just fellow believers, to people we know are praying for us as well. We need to pray that we will be effective witnesses to others, that God will give us opportunities to share His word with others. At the same time, we must ask God to open the hearts of those around us to hear His word.

Prayer works, there's no doubt about that. How else could you explain the story about my friend and his new employee? My friend had started praying for this man before he ever met him, praying that he would be blessed with a follower of Christ to work with. The very first day, the man saw something in my friend—God's spirit, no doubt—and the Lord led him to ask my friend about Him.

What wonderful things will you let God do in your life and in the life of your coworkers through *your* prayers?

Good Works

For we are God's workmanship, created in Christ Jesus to do good works, which God prepared in advance for us to do.
—EPHESIANS 2:10

In the business world, one often hears the instruction "Hire for attitude. With the right attitude, you can train any skills. But the right skills with a poor attitude won't get you anywhere." The theory behind this is that if you hire a person with a friendly, eager-to-learn, good-natured attitude, she will be more than willing and able to learn the skills needed to do the job. Her natural instinct will be to work hard, figure it out, and be of good cheer in doing so.

If, however, you hire someone who is technically gifted—very skilled and able to do the job you're offering—but has a stinky attitude, you won't care how great his skills are, because you won't be able to keep him around long with an attitude like that. He will think his skills are enough to succeed in the job, but no one will want to work with him.

Let's transfer this business maxim to our relationship with Christ. Good works alone, the equivalent of a technically skilled job applicant, won't get us into heaven because our lack of faith in God gets in the way, just like the bad attitude. In Ephesians 2:8–9, Paul says, "For it is by grace you have been saved, *through faith*—and this not from yourselves, it is the gift of God—*not by works, so that no one can boast.*" But if we have faith in God—truly believe in Him and put all of our faith in Him and Him alone—our good attitude leads us to perform good works. Good works are a by-product of our faith in God, not the other way around.

How is your attitude? Do you have the right attitude for the job of serving God—meaning, a strong faith in Him?

We All Need Peace

He came and preached peace to you who were far away and peace to those who were near.
—EPHESIANS 2:17

Everywhere you turn, someone's talking about peace. The context often varies, but the sentiment remains the same. Harried moms with crying kids and busy schedules want a few moments of peace and quiet. Secretaries wish for peace from the ringing phone, the boss's demands, and tight deadlines. The executive desires peace from personnel issues, money troubles, and public pressure. And, of course, we all wish for that elusive world peace.

How people find peace is one thing, but what peace means to them is another story. I'm sure your daily schedule dictates the kind and amount of peace you receive—or long for. It could be a cup of coffee while sitting on your patio, or a massage at a spa. Even five minutes alone with your office door shut might offer you a bit of relief. God has an even bigger meaning of peace for us: salvation in Him and a life of confidence with Him.

Paul explains in this verse that Jesus preached peace to everyone, because everyone needs it. When he says "you who were far away . . . those who were near," he doesn't mean physically close or far. He means spiritually close and far.

This concept still applies to us today. We all need peace, not just new believers and not just those who've lived a lifetime for God. God offers peace to all believers, and He knows that all believers need His peace. His message of salvation is available to everyone—with no prerequisites. All you have to do is ask. Put your life in His hands and let Him give you the greatest peace you'll ever experience.

How Wide? How Long? How High? How Deep?

> And I pray that you, being rooted and established in love, may have power, together with all the saints, to grasp how wide and long and high and deep is the love of Christ. . . .
>
> —EPHESIANS 3:17–18

Think back to your first day on the job as a professional. Remember how limited your scope of the company and of the business world was. You likely didn't understand much about your own specific job at that point, let alone how much your department, your branch of the company, or the entire corporation did. Forget about understanding the complexities of all the hierarchical levels. That would take years to understand, and it will change every time you think you have a grasp of it.

Sometimes there are things in our lives so big or so complex we just can't wrap our minds around them. How big is the ocean? How many stars are in the universe? How different are our lives from those of people in third-world countries? It's tough to really know the depth of these things. Another one that stumps many believers is how much God loves us. Paul says he wants us to understand "how wide and long and high and deep is the love of Christ."

God's love for us is so wide it covers everything we could experience in our lives; it covers the span of every one of our lives; it reaches the highs in our lives, and covers the low times as well.

There's nothing so big that God can't be bigger; His love can wrap around anything our lives drudge up.

This is pretty hard to understand, though, when we think about how our love for others is tested. We love our spouses, we love our families, we love our friends. But God's love for us is all of that and so much more. We don't have to understand how big the sky is and how many stars are in it, but we can still revel in its beauty. Too, we don't have to understand how God's love is so wide, long, high, and deep, but it is. The beauty is that we can revel in His love without truly grasping its complexity.

The Value of Unity

> Be completely humble and gentle; be patient, bearing with one another in love.
> —EPHESIANS 4:2

"Bear with me. . . ." That's a phrase we hear a lot at work. It's usually when someone's trying to figure out a tough problem, intercepting tons of phone calls in the midst of a meeting, or struggling to figure out the audiovisual equipment at a presentation. I know I've uttered those words countless times. This is what Paul says we should do: be patient, bearing with one another in love.

Even so, there is somehow a misconception among believers that becoming a follower of Christ automatically makes you a nice, likeable person—and that others will automatically be nice and likeable to you. Unfortunately, this is not the case. No matter where you are, whether at work or in a church meeting with believers, there's bound to be at least one person who rubs you the wrong way, someone who tries your patience, brings out your stubborn streak, and flames up anger inside you. God never said these feelings would go away just by believing in Him, and nobody here on earth is perfect. But God does instruct us to deal with difficult people by being humble, gentle, and patient.

The importance of exhibiting these characteristics is that we're all one as a body of Christ; we're a unit. Whether a military cadre, a marching band, a group of electrical components, or followers of Christ, a unit isn't very effective if there's division. Being patient and humble, bearing with our brothers and sisters in Christ—even those who do not follow His will just yet—helps keep our unit in God moving along.

Another reason to bear with those who irritate you is that we are extensions of God, reflecting His image to all those around us, including those who don't know Him. What kind of representatives of God are we if we allow annoying coworkers or a difficult boss to get the best of us?

Bear with your coworkers and others who cause you strife. Give them the benefit of the doubt, and get to know them. Showing patience and humility, and even befriending these people, is the best way to show them the true nature of Christ.

Change Your Stinky Clothes

You were taught, with regard to your former way of life, to put off your old self, which is being corrupted by its deceitful desires; to be made new in the attitude of your minds; and to put on the new self, created to be like God in true righteousness and holiness.
—EPHESIANS 4:22–24

Every fall, friends, church groups, and organizations across the country engage in an annual tradition: the bonfire. Loaded down with firewood, oodles of marshmallows, and pounds of chocolate, they set out to commune with nature, have fellowship with friends, and celebrate the rich fall weather. The fragrance of burning wood so sweet—until you get in your clean car and realize how smoky you smell. In my family, we shed the stinky clothes the second we get home; toss them into the wash; clean up; and put on fresh, clean clothes. We don't even want to put the smoky bonfire clothes into the laundry hamper for fear the smell will contaminate our other not-so-dirty clothes. Our bonfire behind us, we put off the dirty selves and look toward cleaner times.

God wants us to do the same with the lives we led before we found Him. In Him, we are new creations, living more righteous lives. Contact with our former ways only serves to contaminate the clean, crisp selves we've become. How? Think about your actions in the workplace before you became a follower of Christ. Every situation is different, but for example, did you harbor a negative attitude about certain coworkers in the past? Did you occasionally lie (stretch the truth) to make a deal or get out of trouble with your boss? Have you fudged your expense account in your favor—(stealing from the company)? Those are all ways of the past, the stinky clothes that need changing.

God is our shower and our washing machine. Living with Him allows us to shed the smelly past, clean ourselves up, and stay clean. He doesn't want us reverting to our old ways—thinking about past sins; associating regularly with people who brought us down; and allowing ourselves to revisit the past mentally, emotionally, or physically by putting ourselves in those old situations that stink up our current and future selves—just what God doesn't want from us.

Are you a new believer? Or have you believed for some time but just haven't put on your fresh clothes in God? Now's the time. Shed your stinky past; wash up in Christ; and look toward a brighter, cleaner future.

Settle It Before the Sun Goes Down

Do not let the sun go down while you are still angry. . . .
—EPHESIANS 4:26

Business relationships are touchy. Sure, you have more arguments with your spouse than you do with your coworkers, but there's a reason for that. You don't want to rock the boat at work; you don't want to jeopardize your position. By contrast, you know that at home you can bring up sensitive issues and talk about what's bothering you, because you're with someone you love who loves you back and is committed to making the marriage work. In business, though, there are no such guarantees. Your coworkers and boss don't have to like you, and if there's a difference of opinion, *hasta la vista* to you.

Even if you don't fight with those people at work, anger may still be an issue. In fact, it's probably more of an issue, because to stay in their good graces you keep it hidden, letting it fester inside you. Paul says in Ephesians 4:26, "In your anger do not sin. Do not let the sun go down while you are still angry. . . ." Harboring anger toward your colleagues could precipitate resentment, negativity, and hatred, causing you to fall into a pattern of sin.

So what should you do? Settle the issue before day's end. Ask God for guidance in ridding yourself of the anger you feel, as a prevention measure to keep you from sinning. For example, you might need to calmly confess to your coworker that what he said this afternoon really hurt your feelings and ask him if you can talk through the issue. Or if you're not ready for direct confrontation, maybe write him a letter, outlining your thoughts and feelings. Then pray on it, sleep on it for a night, and then decide what to do. Ask God to guide you, and acknowledge your anger.

Anger itself is not bad. We all experience it at times, and God gave us the emotion for a reason. But letting anger control your life *is* bad.

Quit Stealing

> He who has been stealing must steal no longer, but must work, doing something useful with his own hands, that he may have something to share with those in need.
> —EPHESIANS 4:28

If I asked you whether you steal from your office, your answer would most likely be an emphatic no. On first thought, that would be my answer also. Stealing is wrong; we know that. So we don't take what isn't ours, such as the computer on our desk at work, the filing cabinet we could really use at home, or the bottle of whiteout and box of colored pencils to help our children with an art project.

But there's more to stealing than that. Your employer pays you a set wage to work each day. Your boss expects you to work a certain amount of hours each day, to complete specified tasks before you leave, and handle myriad issues. You are supposed to do all of this to earn the wage you're paid. Here's where the stealing comes in. Coming in late, skipping out early, taking long breaks, pursuing personal projects during work time, and just daydreaming are all forms of stealing from your company. You're taking money from them that you did not earn.

Of course, most reasonable employers understand that people take a few breaks, talk with coworkers, and occasionally need to leave early. Within reason, that's OK. But making these things a habit is akin to stealing money from the CFO's petty cash drawer.

I challenge you to audit your time at work. Over the next few days, keep track of how many breaks you take during the day, how many times you spend twenty minutes here and there talking in someone else's office about issues not related to work. How many days did you arrive late or leave early, or stretch your lunch hour by a few minutes? Add up that time and subtract it from the amount of time you're supposed to be at work. How much money, according to your salary, are you stealing from your company during these lapses? It might be more than you think.

Keeping this issue in mind, make a greater effort to stay on task. You wouldn't walk out the front door of your office carrying a box of computer paper and a printer; what makes stealing your salary any different?

Not Even a Hint

But among you there must not be even a hint of sexual immorality, or of any kind of impurity, or of greed, because these are improper for God's holy people.
—EPHESIANS 5:3

You're in a meeting and a colleague starts to tell a joke. You listen to the first couple of lines and can see where the story's headed . . . straight into the gutter. You'd look impolite not to laugh, and you even find it somewhat humorous. But you hear a voice inside you saying . . . there must *not be even a hint.* . . . Do you risk being impolite to your coworkers, or do you risk your place in God's kingdom by disobeying His laws?

Every day Christ's followers are assaulted with vulgar language, crude stories, sexual images, and tales of greed and corruption. The things of the world manifest themselves in the workplace, where people spend hours upon hours with colleagues of varying beliefs, morals, and convictions—or lacking therein. Being around such things makes room for the evils to weasel their way into hearts of the unsuspecting. This is why God warns us not to allow even a hint in our lives, because a hint of immorality of any kind does not stop at a hint; it makes itself plain and clear, obvious to all who know us, in due time.

What's the harm in that? Plenty. For starters, it goes against all that God is. God is pure and generous, the opposite of impure and greedy. Once we allow immorality into our lives, we open the door for other intrusions that just draw us further from God. He doesn't give us this directive to shun immorality for our own sake. He also wants us to live pure lives as a good witness to others. The more they see of sin in our lives, the more susceptible they are to sin in their own lives. Happily, the converse is true as well.

Watch your language, actions, and thoughts too. Don't allow greed to rule your business life. Don't allow sexual impurity to rule your private life. Set your sights on the things of God—and ask Him to help you rule out the things of the world.

Carpe Diem

Be very careful, then, how you live—not as unwise but as wise.
—EPHESIANS 5:15

I remember taking classes along with a man in college who always studied hard, memorized every piece of information put before him, and listened eagerly and attentively to everything the teacher said in class, taking down notes almost word for word. A woman who sat near me also listened eagerly and attentively, but she took far fewer notes and memorized far fewer pieces of trivia. Guess who scored better on exams? Not the copious note taker. The other one. Why? Because she listened for the ideas, philosophies, and trends behind what she learned and figured out how to make that information come alive to her. The man, on the other hand, knew incredible amounts of trivia—but couldn't tell you for the life of him why it was important and how to use the information in his own life. The woman was wise; the man was smart.

Wisdom is the ability to discern inner qualities and relationships or good sense. It is to be commended and celebrated in today's world, especially in the workplace. So many people get to the top or near the top in an organization because of what they know; few stay at the top on what they know alone. They must have wisdom to make the right decisions. Cicero, a politician and philosopher born a hundred years before Christ, said, "The function of wisdom is to discriminate between good and evil." I agree.

God wants us to use wisdom to ferret out the bad in life—the things that corrupt us—and to turn to the good in life, like

Him and all that He stands for. Paul warns us in this verse: "Be very careful, then, how you live—not as unwise but as wise." Paul knew that evil thoughts, actions, and beliefs were pervasive in Ephesus—and everywhere, for that matter. He wanted believers to be prepared to handle the immorality, impurity, and evil things of the world. He wanted them not only to know the trivia behind these things but to understand how evil thoughts and actions would affect their lives personally—drawing them closer to Satan and farther from Christ.

Paul's message still stands today, and I can learn something from my two college classmates: it's not how much you know, but what you do with the information that makes you wise. The good news is that God can grant us the wisdom we need to discern between good and evil. It's up to us to ask.

Dressing for Battle

Put on the full armor of God so that you can take your stand against the devil's schemes.
—EPHESIANS 6:11

I've heard it said that work is a battlefield. Specifically, the boardroom, where tense negotiations take place, often serves as the battlefield on which corporate wars are won and lost. The corporate soldiers put on their armor—pride, hostility, greed, revenge, and other not-so-nice shields. When the battle is over, neither side wins if it hasn't done so on God's turf.

Unfortunately, workplace battles don't just happen in high-level business negotiations. We all face battles every day, sitting in our cubicles, chatting with coworkers, struggling to finish a project on time, while having to bear with an annoying colleague. The devil, ever the helper, shows up to all of these battles, ready to win us over to his side. Or at least try.

But wearing God's armor gives us a huge leg up on Satan. Ephesians 6:11 warns us to put on the full armor of God: "Stand firm then, with the belt of truth buckled around your waist, with the breastplate of righteousness in place, and with your feet fitted with the readiness that comes from the gospel of peace. In addition to all this, take up the shield of faith, with which you can extinguish all the flaming arrows of the evil one. Take the helmet of salvation and the sword of the Spirit, which is the word of God."

Only a God as loving as ours would outfit us from the beginning to ward off the evil advances of the devil. He's sending us into battle with the truth of His word to protect us. He has given us the breastplate of righteousness; when we know we're to follow God's word by shunning greed, immorality, hatred, and other favorites of the devil, we can't go wrong. Our feet prepared with readiness to stand firm against evil, and holding the shield of our faith in God, we're ready to ward off the devil's advances—even when they come in the form of a cursing client, a bullying boss, or a catty coworker.

God has given us His armor. But it's our job to put it on. He's counting on you and me to read His word; talk with Him daily; and surround ourselves in Him, His truth, and His love. We must take up His full armor if we want to win this battle.

PART SIX

Philippians

PERPETUAL REJOICING AND THANKFULNESS

Key elements

Purpose: to thank the Philippians for the gift they sent Paul and to encourage them in the truth that true joy comes from Christ alone

Author: Paul

To whom written: all the Christians at Philippi, and all of God's followers

Date written: about 61 A.D.

Key Themes

- The mountain peak portrayal of the humanity and humility of Jesus, the God-man, is unfolded.
- From a prison cell, Paul calls believers to always have joy and display contentment.
- Developing character and growing "in Christ" requires the Holy Spirit and personal obedience.

God Doesn't Quit

. . . being confident of this, that He who began a good work in you will carry it on to completion until the day of Christ Jesus.
—PHILIPPIANS 1:6

Some work assignments feel as though they started ages ago and seem to have no end. Sometimes, in the midst of a huge project, you might feel as if you're making no progress at all. You toil away day after day, but you've only begun to make a dent in what you need to accomplish. It's a discouraging feeling, yet you know you must go on. Your job depends on your finishing what you started—even when you feel that you can't.

In the same way, sometimes you might feel as if you're not moving forward in your spiritual walk with Christ. You started this project with Him ages ago, and your project won't end until you've met Him face-to-face, but you feel that you're not moving forward very far, very fast. The good news is that God won't quit on you, and He won't let you quit on Him. "He who began a good work in you will carry it on to completion until the day of Christ Jesus." Once you give your heart to Him, He claims you as yours and He won't quit working on you—changing your heart, cleansing your soul, refining your character—until the day you finally meet in heaven.

Whenever you're feeling down, like a runner way behind in the race, remember that God has promised to complete His work in you. And God always keeps His promises. So feeling as if you're not getting anywhere won't get you anywhere; you have to place your trust in Him and allow Him to do His work in you. He started it, and He won't give up until He completes it. Hang in there, toil away, and know that although your work life depends on finishing a difficult project, your whole life depends on allowing God to finish His project in you—no matter how difficult you may be.

Isn't it good to know that someone cares enough about you to make sure you get to the finish line?

Diagnosing Our Lives

. . . so that you may be able to discern what is best and may be pure and blameless until the day of Christ. . . .
—PHILIPPIANS 1:10

Nurses have the most contact with patients, and doctors carry the biggest burden. I noticed this at a recent trip to the doctor. In a normal twenty-minute doctor's visit, a patient interacts with a nurse for ten to fifteen minutes, generally. The nurse takes a history, finds out the reason for the visit, reads vital signs, and then notes findings in the chart for the doctor to read. Then the doctor breezes into the room for the last few minutes of the appointment, makes a diagnosis, and sends the patient on her way.

We might be tempted to ask why the doctors get paid the big bucks when the nurses are the ones doing the work during an exam. But there's a significant reason for this: doctors earn their living by discerning what your symptoms mean and by putting the weight of a diagnosis and treatment plan on their shoulders, not on the nurses' shoulders. Nurses do a lot of preliminary work, and the doctors make the final call—and often pay the consequences if they make the wrong call. They deserve the big bucks for taking on that responsibility.

Guess what? We're the doctors in our own lives. We are responsible for making a diagnosis in a given situation: whether to trust a colleague, how to handle a potentially volatile client, what to tell staff members at the next meeting about your failing company. We have added help in making our diagnoses and treatment plans: a direct line to God, our ultimate physician.

Paul calls us to discern what is best, and to be pure and blameless until the day of Christ. However, we don't have to shoulder the responsibility all on our own. God wants to help us make that judgment call. He's available twenty-four hours a day, for routine visits, emergency calls, and everything in between. Now, if only we had nurses to take care of the preliminaries in life. . . .

Hardship Has Its Rewards

> As a result, it has become clear throughout the whole palace guard and to everyone else that I am in chains for Christ. Because of my chains, most of the brothers in the Lord have been encouraged to speak the word of God more courageously and fearlessly.
>
> —PHILIPPIANS 1:13–14

Reach back in your memory and drudge up the worst experience you've ever faced in your professional life. It could be a job loss, not getting a promotion you were promised, flubbing up a major presentation, having to move across the country for a job, or anything of the sort. Now remember how you felt and acted during that time. Did you praise God for giving you an opportunity to learn from the events? Or did you whine and moan, acting unbecomingly and making a poor show of your faith? How we react in hard times reflects our faith.

The apostle Paul spent many years in prison for speaking out in favor of Jesus Christ. He could have moped around, losing faith in God, but he did just the opposite. He wrote letters, like the one found in Philippians; he pressed Christ's followers to continue speaking out for Him, even though the Roman law forbade it; and he encouraged believers to stay strong in their faith by staying strong as well even while in chains. Most of us would feel discouraged and even scared to talk about God if we were in the same situation. But Paul used his imprisonment to further God's kingdom, and others noticed.

Paul's actions of so long ago can serve as encouragement to us today. We're lucky that we live in a land in which we can speak freely about our God. But our jobs, family life, and even the situation in our church might cause us to feel discouraged and tempt us to turn away from God. We have to remember how Paul reacted to such a situation. We have to turn even closer to God, draw our strength from Him, and march on. How we respond to hardships in our life affects not only us but everyone around us. They're watching to see what we do when we lose our job; they're attentive to what we say when our boss gives us fits; they want to witness everything we do during tough times.

Don't discourage others and let them see the devil get you down; instead, draw on God's strength and allow them to see your faith in Him. Show them with your words and actions that God will get you through. Paul made it work in prison; and even though sometimes you may feel you're in prison at work, you're not; you can still hold that same resolve and make the best of hardships in life.

Monitoring Your Conduct

Whatever happens, conduct yourselves in a manner worthy of the gospel of Christ. Then, whether I come and see you or only hear about you in my absence, I will know that you stand firm in one spirit, contending as one man for the faith of the gospel. . . .
—PHILIPPIANS 1:27

In this age of technology, more and more people work out of their homes or in an office located far from their bosses. Headquarters might be California, while a small group of people work out of an office in Kansas. Headquarters might be Hong Kong with a small office in Kansas, for that matter. Because of the distance, it's increasingly easy for bosses to have no idea how their employees spend their days. They could be off on the golf course for all the boss knows . . . until word gets back, one way or another.

It's Murphy's Law that whenever you're doing something you shouldn't—like playing hooky from work to attend a baseball game—you'll get caught. Someone will see you and send word to your boss that you weren't behaving in the manner expected.

In the verse here, Paul addresses this when talking to the Philippians. He asks them to conduct themselves in a manner worthy of Christ—when Paul's there and even when he's not, because he will hear about them in his absence. He wants them to unify, working for the gospel of God, not spend their time arguing with each other, or acting unbecomingly.

Your boss might not see you all the time. Your spouse might not see you all the time. But that's no reason to behave any differently, because God does see you at all times. He calls on you and me to behave the way He would behave at all times, because He does see us, even when others don't. The notion of God watching our every step should bring caution to our mischief and confidence to our good conduct.

Is your conduct worthy of God? Even when no one's looking? Really?

Spiritual Cruise Control

> . . . for it is God who works in you to will and to act according to His good purpose.
> —PHILIPPIANS 2:13

The invention and implementation of cruise control into modern cars has greatly improved the traveling experience for people who spend a lot of time on the interstate. The driver, weary from trying to maintain a proper speed, sets the cruise control to the appropriate speed limit. The car, in all its wisdom and mechanics, takes over from there—so long as the driver maintains the direction the car takes. Cruise control takes much of the burden of highway driving off the driver—but only when the driver asks for it. It's such a blessing also because cruise control helps keep drivers within legal speed limits.

God is our cruise control. When we're weary and burdened, traveling a long stretch of road, He is there to maintain us. We have to set the cruise control, or ask Him for His strength and guidance, and He takes us from there. Just like cruise control, God keeps us out of trouble when we ask for His help.

Too tired to make it through another workday? Not sure whether you'll be able to hold your temper in the next staff meeting? Feeling the urge to give in to temptation? Just set your spiritual cruise control. Tell God your troubles, ask for His help, and allow Him to work in you according to His will and His good purpose, as Paul says in Philippians 2:13. God wants to help us. We don't burden Him when we ask for His help; that's what He wants to do. He wants us to give Him control of our lives. Our part of the equation: ask for His help and allow Him to do His work in us.

It's easy to give Him control in some areas; but other areas we feel uncomfortable giving up. Are there things in your life that you think are too big (or too small) for God to handle? Understand that this is what God wants to do: fuel you to a closer relationship with Him and guide you through the big and the small, the significant and the insignificant, the good and the not-so-good. You've got this wonderful feature in your life, cruise control with God. Now use it!

The Final P&L

> But whatever was to my profit I now consider loss for the sake
> of Christ. What is more, I consider everything a loss compared
> to the surpassing greatness of knowing Christ Jesus my Lord,
> for whose sake I have lost all things.
> —PHILIPPIANS 3:7–8

Profits and losses. Balance sheets. The bottom line. Present gain over previous year gain. Or loss. These topics populate every year-end meeting of every company, and many other meetings in between. Organizations say their main goal or mission is to help the customer, serve the customer, improve circumstances in the community, or better consumer relationships. Even though so many companies may truly want to help, I'd say the great majority of them still focus on money—their personal gain—when all is said and done.

The desire to make more money, to increase profits every year, often mires the good intention to serve consumers well. When it comes to choosing between a plan that makes life easier for customers and one that brings hard numbers to the bottom line, it's not surprising that so many companies choose a better P&L statement over their consumers.

Bad news for those organizations. God doesn't care one iota about our business gains if they are done at the expense of goodness and rightness. He doesn't care about our credentials as we do. He doesn't care how financially sound we are, or how far up the corporate ladder we've climbed, if it takes wrong steps to climb higher.

As Paul states in these verses, everything he has ever gained, whether credentials, success, or money, is nothing compared to what he has gained in His relationship with Christ. He also says he'd give it all away to know Christ more. This begs two questions. First, how important is your relationship with Christ in the whole scheme of things? Do you place your relationship with Him as high on the list of successes as you do becoming manager of your department or the executive in charge of the company? Second, what are you allowing to stand in the way of your relationship with Him? Are you allowing work, pride, status, a relationship, or some other worldly notion to prevent you from drawing as close to Him as you'd like?

When all is said and done, nothing matters but your life with and in Christ. Your money, your power, your status, your business itself will all go away. But what you have in Christ is the ultimate gain, and it's one that you'll cling to forever.

Working Toward Perfection

Not that I have already obtained all this, or have already been made perfect, but I press on to take hold of that for which Christ Jesus took hold of me.
—PHILIPPIANS 3:12

Every year, bosses resignedly settle in to prepare the most painful meeting they'll ever conduct: the annual review. With forms in hand, notes gathered near, they push themselves to complete the written part of the review and then call in their employees, one-by-one, to talk about performance issues, attitude, goals, and hardships. As far as I know, every manager gets the spiel beforehand: "No matter how good the employee is, there's always room for improvement. Don't give him or her too high marks. You want your employees to have something to strive for."

Does this sound familiar—whichever side of the desk you're on? All employees, whether new to the job or twenty-year veterans, still have a skill to learn, an attitude to correct, or a new goal to reach. Good employees want to push themselves further.

As an employee of God, are you still pushing yourself, working toward new goals, and perfecting skills and attitudes of the heart to make you better in His eyes? Even the apostle Paul, in the verse here, says he still presses on to better himself in Christ. God is your heavenly boss. You don't have formal annual reviews with God about your performance, attitude, and goals, but it wouldn't hurt to check in with Him—much more often than annually—and see where you stand. Ask Him what you need to work on, what you could do better, and what goals He has for you for the coming year.

Give God as much effort as you give your job (and even more). God cares more, pays better, and the benefits are second to none!

The Winner's Circle

I press on toward the goal to win the prize for which God has called me heavenward in Christ Jesus.
—PHILIPPIANS 3:14

I have a friend who loves to run marathons. She actually finds joy in hitting the pavement for twenty-six miles, sweating, aching, downright hurting—all to say she finished the race and made better time than in the previous race. Sure, lots of runners finish before her, but many others finish long after she does. The reward is in pressing on, finishing what she set out to do, and winning the prize, even if it is a T-shirt for participating or a hug of congratulations from her husband. No matter what, she presses on, completes the race, and receives her reward for a job well done.

Are there times she'd prefer to quit and ride in the car to the closest ice cream stand instead? Of course. But the point is, she doesn't. In this verse, Paul uses the analogy of a race or some sort of contest with meeting God in heaven as the prize to illustrate living an obedient life with Christ. I can't think of a better prize for any contest than meeting my God face-to-face.

Are there times in life when you'd like to quit the race toward God? Maybe it's when business is bad and the temptation to fudge the numbers a little hits. Or when you know your boss would never check out the items you put on your expense account—and hey, you need a little extra cash anyway. Maybe it's not so much an action, but an attitude of the heart. In rough times, do you allow negativity, anger, bitterness, or selfishness to rule instead of the attributes of Christ that He calls for in you?

Dropping out of the race may cross your mind. I admit, it occasionally crosses mine—but not for more than a split second. Because I can see my reward for a life well lived. God is standing at the finish line, beckoning me with a smile and the promise of heaven, to finish the race He laid out for me. He stands there beckoning you, as well.

Don't give up. Visualize the prize. Your pain during this race is nothing compared to the joy you'll experience on the other side of the finish line.

Disagreeing, But Getting Along

I plead with Euodia and I plead with Syntyche to agree with each other in the Lord.
—PHILIPPIANS 4:2

Have you ever wondered how two people who love the Lord and live for Him can argue with each other so heatedly? I've seen many of Christ's followers embattled with each other, living with unresolved anger, bitterness, and disappointment for years, while still serving Him in every other way. The arguing parties don't understand that their fighting isn't just a personal issue; it's one that affects the church, God, and even outside observers.

How? God teaches us to love one another, to live in peace with our brothers and sisters. Plenty of people know that; even those who don't live in His spirit understand the concept. When two people who love the Lord won't resolve an issue or let it drop, others notice the lack of love between them. They're setting a bad example for the faith, often without even knowing it.

God cares about our relationships. He doesn't want them to suffer, festering in anger and hatred; that's not what He's all about. Yet too often we let an argument, a difference of opinion, or a petty squabble consume us—often leading to sinning (Ephesians 4:26). This mandate not to let differences come between brothers and sisters in Christ also extends to unequally matched friendships. Do you have differences you need to patch up, either with a fellow believer in your family or church or with a colleague? Have you let past differences affect your relationship with others, or with God?

Paul pleaded with two women in the church to agree with each other in the Lord. I plead with you now, too, to agree with those who've caused you grief. Find a solution to your squabbles, praying together and asking God for guidance. Find some ground that is common that both of you can stand on together. Life's too short and too precious to spend it arguing—especially since you serve God more fully when you get along.

Anxiety-Free Living

Do not be anxious about anything, but in everything, by prayer and petition, with thanksgiving, present your requests to God.
—PHILIPPIANS 4:6

S tress has taken over our lives. Everywhere you turn, there's another news article, health magazine, TV show, or pamphlet talking up the effects stress has on our lives. Stress has been proven to cause hypertension, heart disease, stroke, diabetes, insomnia, and much more. Health foods tout relief from stress. Doctors advise that regular exercise and a full night's sleep reduce the level of stress. Spas jump on the bandwagon, marketing herbal treatments, massages, and all sorts of therapies to the overworked, underrested adults in our society.

What almost all of these sources fail to mention is that God is the greatest stress-reliever ever. No amount of massaging, exercise, or sleep will relax us the way God can when we put our worries into His hands. Sure, a massage is great, but it works only when combined with God's comforting hand. Better yet, we should allow Him to massage our hearts and overanxious minds with His healing hand.

A friend recently said that worry is the opposite of trust. Such a simple phrase, but it sums up this idea succinctly. When we put our anxieties on the Lord, it shows that we trust Him to take care of us. But if we hold on to them, we're telling God that we don't trust Him enough to handle our day-to-day stress. I guess in those situations we'd rather run on the fuel from stress than give it over to Him.

In Matthew 6:25–27, Jesus teaches us why it's not good for us to worry: "Therefore I tell you, do not worry about your life, what you will eat or drink; or about your body, what you will wear. Is not life more important than food, and the body more important than clothes? Look at the birds of the air; they do not sow or reap or store away in barns, and yet your heavenly Father feeds them. Are you not much more valuable than they? Who of you by worrying can add a single hour to his life?" In Matthew 6:33–34

Jesus says, "But seek first His kingdom and His righteousness, and all these things will be given to you as well. Therefore do not worry about tomorrow, for tomorrow will worry about itself. Each day has enough trouble of its own."

This is not to say that we aren't to show concern for the people and events that affect our lives. God does want us to care. But allowing anxiety to overrun us to the point of needing medical attention goes against God's will for our lives. Cast your cares upon the Lord, and then schedule that massage.

Think on These Things

Finally, brothers, whatever is true, whatever is noble, whatever is right, whatever is pure, whatever is lovely, whatever is admirable—if anything is excellent or praiseworthy—think about such things. Whatever you have learned or received or heard from me or seen in me, put into practice. And the God of peace will be with you.
—PHILIPPIANS 4:8–9

Daydreaming is part of most every businessperson's life. While waiting for the computer to boot up, thoughts fill your mind. While filing the day's business, you allow your mind to wander to things more interesting than the papers in front of you. The meeting runs long—and very boring—and your mind runs away on some dream. But what kinds of daydreaming do you indulge in? Would God approve of your thoughts?

The phrase "garbage in, garbage out" stems from the fact that whatever we dwell on is a product of what we put into our minds. Watching trash television, renting immoral and impure movies, listening to degrading music that glorifies everything God is not, and reading worldly novels and magazines won't do anything to draw us closer to God. In fact, those things work just the opposite. Whatever you spend your free time watching, reading, or listening to will come out in your day-to-day absentminded thoughts. So if your daydreaming at the daily staff meeting is something you'd be ashamed to share with others or to confess to God, then you're probably not putting the right things into your head.

Paul tells the Philippians to focus on things that are true, noble, right, pure, lovely, admirable, excellent, and praiseworthy. Judging from what I've seen on television recently, we shouldn't be watching much of anything these days, because very few, if any, of the words in Philippians 4:8 describe what is on network television. Yet so many of us, followers of Christ, allow ourselves to watch things we think we'd never do or say. Once we've watched enough times, somehow those words, ideas, and images creep into our thoughts—garbage in, garbage out.

If you're struggling with unclean thoughts, take it to God. Ask Him to help you keep your daydreams under control. True, noble, right, pure, lovely, admirable, excellent, and praiseworthy all describe God. So keeping our eyes on Him at all times, thinking about Him and how He would react to our thoughts ought to keep us on the right track.

The Secret Silver Bullet

I can do everything through Him who gives me strength.
—PHILIPPIANS 4:13

The quiet worker who toils away in his cubicle each day gains respect for his smart ideas. His boss praises him for a job well done—and then asks the worker to present his theories to the rest of the organization at the next meeting. The worker, terrified of the idea of public speaking, repeats the verse, "I can do everything through Him who gives me strength," to himself after agreeing to give the presentation.

The construction worker, uncomfortable with heights, must scale the scaffolding and hand off some tools. As he climbs higher and higher, he motivates himself with, "I can do everything through Him who gives me strength."

The secretary, long a confidant and keeper of secrets—and giver of advice—longs to share her newfound faith in Christ with a constantly troubled coworker. But she's timid, not sure how to approach the conversation or how to share the good news she's found. This verse, "I can do everything through Him who gives me strength"—one she has just learned—spurs her to take the next step. She invites her friend to lunch and shares the story of how God has changed her life and then invites her troubled friend to do the same. God comes through for her, just as He always does.

He always will. God is the secret silver bullet in the arsenal of a believer. He gives strength to those who are seeking Him and doing His work. Just when it seems we can't go on anymore, He comes through for us, showing His strength and power once again.

When the apostle Paul was jailed in Rome, he wrote Philippians 4:13. He had no idea how long he'd be in prison or whether he'd ever be released. But he knew his job was to spread the word of God. He wasn't about to let prison or any other obstacle get in the way of his job. How? He had God, his secret silver bullet, on his side. He knew that if his will was aligned with God's will for his life, God would take care of him. God would help him finish the job He had sent him off to do.

God will do the same for us. We need that kind of faith, that whatever we set out to do— so long as it's in God's will for us— we will be able to do, because of His strength and power.

Are you ready to let God do all He can for you and your life? Are you ready to spend your life working for Him? You've got the power, the weapons, everything it takes when you've got Him on your side.

PART SEVEN

Colossians

CHRIST IS SUPREME

Key Elements

Purpose: to combat errors in the church and to demonstrate that
believers have everything they need in Christ

Author: Paul

To whom written: the Colosse church and all of Christ's believers

Date written: about 60 A.D.

Key Themes

- Because Jesus is central and supreme, our lives are best constructed under His Lordship.
- Homespun religions might gain cultural traction but they all measure up insufficiently against the standards of the "true gospel."
- An activated faith positively affects one's personal life, family life, and commercial life.

A Hidden Power Source

To this end I labor, struggling with all His energy,
which so powerfully works in me.
—COLOSSIANS 1:29

One of the biggest struggles facing working adults, especially those with children to raise, is finding the energy, power, motivation, and endurance to get everything done. Day in, day out, they wrestle with their schedules—and their fatigued bodies. Sound familiar?

Every time my dog zips past me or begs me to throw the ball—for the hundredth time that day—I wonder where she gets her energy. I always wish I could bottle it up and store it for my own personal use when I need it most. I'm not talking about just physical energy; emotional energy to keep on keeping on would be nice, too.

Luckily for us, God is an endless supply of energy—and it's ours for the taking, if only we ask. Indeed, God has more energy than we could ever hope to expend, and it's stored up, ready for our use. So what's the energy for? To allow us to more easily spread the word of His love. He knows we can't do it all on our own power—something so many of us fail to realize, thinking we're Wonder Woman or Superman, able to do everything and be invincible. In Colossians 1:28–29, Paul writes, "We proclaim Him, admonishing and teaching everyone with all wisdom, so that we may present everyone perfect in Christ. To this end I labor, struggling with all His energy, which so powerfully works in me."

With God, it's not a matter of summoning up enough energy to get the job done. It's a matter of harnessing the boundless energy that's available for our use. He wants to give us every resource we need to do the job He has laid out for us. One of those resources is the motivation, power, energy, and gumption to say what we need to say to whom we need to say it—and at the right time (God's time).

What are you doing with God's energy? Are you trying to live without tapping into the divine source for energy?

A Firm Foundation

So then, just as you received Christ Jesus as Lord, continue to live in Him, rooted and built up in Him, strengthened in the faith as you were taught, and overflowing with thankfulness.
—COLOSSIANS 2:6–7

Tomato plants, at least in my limited experience, are fragile. They grow strong roots, but to live fully and produce delicious fruit they need help. It comes in the form of a stake, to which you tie the tomato plant, giving support and a strong foundation. With strong roots, nourishing soil, water, and that foundation stake, the plant can flourish—at least if it's in someone's yard other than mine!

We're like those tomato plants, though. We can't make it in life on our own. We need the rich soil of God's word to nourish our souls. We need the fresh, pure water of His strength and comfort to carry us in the tough times and through hardships. We need the stake, His supporting hand, to guide us in knowing which way we should go. His hand is there to lift us up, to show us how to grow, and to build us up in Him, as Paul wrote in Colossians 2:6–7: ". . . continue to live in Him, rooted and built up in Him, strengthened in the faith as you were taught, and overflowing with thankfulness."

The great thing is, with God's support, nourishment, and guiding force we find ourselves standing strong against all odds. The gusting wind, the blistering sun, and the pouring rain won't beat us down; instead, because of our healthy life in Him, those elements will only build us up. In the end, He'll produce the fruits of His labor in us—His creations.

Follow the Head

He has lost connection with the Head, from whom the whole body, supported and held together by its ligaments and sinews, grows as God causes it to grow.
—COLOSSIANS 2:19

Many a sitcom has garnered laughs with a skit that goes something like this: Two characters need to find costumes for a party. They wait until the last minute, and the only thing the costume shop has left is an elephant or cow or some other large animal that requires two people to maneuver it. Grudgingly, they agree to wear the costume, totally humiliated. After flipping a coin, they take their assigned places at either the head, or (sadly) the tail of the costume. Invariably, the tail end doesn't want to do what the head of the costume directs, and disaster ensues.

On a much higher level sit God and His children. He is the head of the operation called life; we are the tail end. This means we're the ones who must follow His lead—or disaster will ensue. In speaking of false teachers who proclaim the teachings of Christ but have no real faith in Him, Paul said, "He has lost connection with the Head, from whom the whole body, supported and held together by its ligaments and sinews, grows as God causes it to grow." Clearly, God must be in control—and we must allow Him to be in control of our lives—for us to grow and thrive in this life.

How do we do it? We give over every aspect of our lives to Him. We pray for Him to do His will in our lives, and pray that we be amenable to His doing so. We ask Him for guidance before we act—not after, when we'll invariably have to ask forgiveness for the mistake we made in not following Him. We read His word, the instruction manual on life. We allow ourselves to be humbled as the tail end in the operation. He has the strength, the power, and the plan; we're supposed to follow along. No matter what we've seen in those sitcoms, God will never steer us wrong.

Heavenly Minded and Earthly Good

Set your minds on things above, not on earthly things.
—COLOSSIANS 3:2

Flip open your daily planner for a second and see what's on your list for the day. How many appointments, meetings, mundane tasks, and fun activities do you have scheduled, and how full is your day? Now, knowing how a busy person thinks—and how hectic a busy person's day is, from personal experience—try to recount how many other meetings, tasks, and engagements are swimming around in your head, not even on the calendar yet.

The point of this exercise is to illustrate how full our days get with tasks and things. Yes, many of these things are good and necessary, like finishing an assignment, picking up the dry cleaning, and running to your kid's soccer game. But amid all these earthly things, our minds don't have a lot of room for heavenly things. To put it simply, that's not good.

In this verse, we're instructed to set our minds on things above (Godly things) and not on earthly things (unimportant things, in the grand scheme of life). This doesn't mean you can't think about what's on your plate for the week; rather, it means your ultimate goal must lie in Christ, and keeping your mind on His plan, not your boss's plan, will help you achieve your goal.

Athletes, performers, all sorts of people, really, say to reach for the stars. Well, God wants you to look past the stars—to Him.

When you set your mind on Christ—and keep it there—you'll make better decisions. How? By keeping Him in the forefront of your thoughts, you're more likely to run all of your ideas, actions, and words past Him, checking for the moral thumbs up. It's when you forget about God that you're likely to err in judgment, because you don't have Him looking over your work.

If someone says your head is in the sky, thank the person, because if you're doing it right this means you're focusing on the heavens, which is what you should be doing.

Spring Clean Your Life

> You used to walk in these ways, in the life you once lived. But now you must rid yourselves of all such things as these: anger, rage, malice, slander, and filthy language from your lips.
> —COLOSSIANS 3:7–8

I can't work when my desk is messy. It's a silly thing, but the mess gets in my way. My mind feels cluttered, my creativity is stunted, and, well, sometimes my mood just isn't right when I'm surrounded by too much mess. So what happens is I hold off on the important work that's ahead of me, in favor of cleaning every piece of paper off my desk, organizing my pens and other gizmos, and wiping all surfaces clean. A clean desk allows me to function on a much higher level.

Nevertheless, a clean mind, heart, and soul contribute to functioning on a much higher level than a clean desk does. So spring cleaning our souls is a worthwhile task. In Colossians 3:7–8, Paul writes, "You used to walk in these ways, in the life you once lived. But now you must rid yourselves of all such things as these: anger, rage, malice, slander, and filthy language from your lips." So how about it? Do any of these things clutter up your life? If so, what are you going to do about them?

Anger, rage, malice, slander, and filthy language, just from a workplace standpoint, could ruin your position in the organization and put your job at risk. Anger with your boss or spreading untrue or unkind stories about coworkers could do the same, as well as ruin any chance of friendship or a good working relationship, and filthy language is simply unacceptable in many circles. But there's an even more important relationship at risk if you don't clean these things out of your life: your relationship with God. There's no place for such ill manners in His kingdom; fortunately, He is a forgiving God, ready to forget that you've taken part in these things the minute you repent.

What are you waiting for? Let's spring clean our lives, and make a fresh start for God.

A Heavenly Wardrobe

Therefore, as God's chosen people, holy and dearly loved, clothe yourselves with compassion, kindness, humility, gentleness and patience.

—COLOSSIANS 3:12

The clothes make the man, so the saying goes. In today's workplace, sometimes this seems true. The right suit, the right tie, the right dress, and you feel more professional—and people see you as more serious about your work. There's even a shift back toward more formal professional dressing, away from the workplace casual style that has been so pervasive in recent years.

But I think we all know clothes aren't the cornerstone of success, unless you're wearing a heavenly wardrobe of compassion, kindness, humility, gentleness and peace. In Colossians 3:12–17, Paul lays out the steps to living a Godly life. The first step is in the verse given here, and it involves putting on the traits of God each day. Do you have these traits in your wardrobe? Do you wear them to work every day, or just to church on Sundays?

When you wear compassion and kindness to work, it's amazing how differently you see your coworkers. Instead of getting upset with them for messing up a project or spacing out at a meeting, you'll see them more through God's eyes. Maybe then you'll understand that there's more to their actions than meets the human eye—and you'll feel more compassion for their situation. Humility is a biggie in the workplace: one promotion, one raise, even one kind word from the boss about you in front of others, and your ego soars. That's when we start forgetting God is the one who brought us to the success, not ourselves.

Tomorrow morning, when you dress for work, feel free to put on that power suit or your favorite outfit. But please don't forget to wear your heavenly wardrobe as well. You, your coworkers, and especially God will be glad you did.

Giving Work Your All

Slaves, obey your earthly masters in everything; and do it,
not only when their eye is on you and to win their favor, but
with sincerity of heart and reverence for the Lord. Whatever
you do, work at it with your heart, as working for the Lord,
not for men. . . .
—COLOSSIANS 3:22–23

Businesses in the United States keep an eagle eye on their employees. According to the Communications Workers of America, they monitor nearly forty million U.S. workers using video cameras and tape recorders, and by viewing e-mail and Internet usage. Why? To keep an eye on job performance, compliance with laws, and cost control, sources say. Not all of those employees know they're being watched every minute of every workday. On the other hand, some companies do tell their employees up front that they're being watched. The implication: if you know you're monitored at all times, you're more likely to work diligently and less likely to behave inappropriately, including stealing and slacking off.

If we all followed Paul's advice in the verses here, we wouldn't need such prevalent and invasive surveillance: "do it, not only when their eye is on you and to win their favor, but with sincerity of heart and reverence for the Lord. Whatever you do, work at it with your heart, as working for the Lord, not for men. . . ."

How many things do you do throughout the day that you wouldn't want your employer to know about? Even good, honest people have their moments. That catnap you caught last Thursday after a late night out? Or the thirty-minute gabfest with your coworkers on Monday morning, recapping the weekend's events? We all waste time surfing the Internet while we should be working, but because we're at our desks, looking as if we're working, it seems benign.

But God doesn't want us to waste time at work. Yes, it's just a job, and your real job lies in serving Him. But still, He says to work at our jobs as if we're working for Him. I doubt God would be pleased if we all checked our stock prices or caught the score of the football game on our handheld devices while in His house Sunday mornings.

Give your job your all—even if the job's less than everything to you. It matters to God, because you're one of His workers and He wants you to set a good example. Give your boss something to watch on that surveillance tape: pictures of you working.

Do Right—Be Fair

Masters, provide your slaves with what is right and fair, because you know that you also have a Master in heaven.
—COLOSSIANS 4:1

In such a flat economy, it's tempting to cut corners to pad the bottom line. Reducing office expenses, monitoring wastefulness, and being frugal with the extras are all ways to improve the company's numbers. So is withholding rightful wages, bonuses, and benefits from staff members. But that's not the fair thing to do.

As a boss, manager, or decision maker, it's up to you to treat your staff members well and take care of their needs. It's good business sense to take care of the people, even in down times, because those people are the ones who will be there for you to help turn the business around. Removing Friday afternoon snacks, cutting back on vacation days, eliminating freebie sodas and pretzels in the break room, and refusing cost-of-living increases save you money—but lose you employees. This is a pretty strong reason to take care of workers during difficult times.

Need another reason? God says so in the Bible. No better reason for that, in my book. "Masters, provide your slaves with what is right and fair, because you know that you also have a Master in heaven." No, you're not a master or slave, but the concept still holds true. Take care of those who work for you, knowing that you're not the chief in command; God is. He instructs every person in charge of others to give them what's fair and right.

Here's another way to look at it: What if God, in a bad economy, chose to eliminate the extras He provides us—grace, mercy, love, comfort, salvation? We work for Him but don't receive anything in turn. How would we feel then? God is our boss, and He provides for us in good times and in bad. It's only fair that all people in leadership return the favor to their subordinates. Follow God's lead in all ways; it's good for business and good for your soul.

Five-Star Dialogue

Let your conversation be always full of grace, seasoned with salt, so that you may know how to answer everyone.
—COLOSSIANS 4:6

At your favorite restaurant, what is it about the food that you like? For me, it's the fact that everything comes perfectly seasoned; I don't even have to ask anyone to pass the salt and pepper. The flavor is sublime, and I'm not lacking anything. Of course, I only find this on the few occasions when I dine at a five-star restaurant. Our local hangouts? Well, not so perfectly seasoned.

In this verse, Paul instructs believers to let their conversation be full of grace, seasoned with salt. "Why salt?" you may ask. For the same reason baseball games, amusement parks, and other commercial events sell so many salty items. Salt makes you thirsty, wanting more to drink. So if you buy an inexpensive snack with salt, you'll most likely come back to buy the expensive drink that quenches your thirst. Paul wants all of us to explain our faith in God with grace—always kind and loving, not argumentative—and to season it with salt. This means giving them interesting information about what God does in your life and leaving them wanting more. You want to make nonbelievers thirsty for Christ.

One of the best ways to do this is to use personal stories. Just stating facts about God, using big theological words, may turn off the unchurched. Putting things into everyday language, and telling a compelling story about how your life has changed since accepting

Him, or how He helped you through a tough situation, or how much more at peace you feel on any given day should draw in your coworkers and friends. Everyone's interested in how to weather a crisis, personal or professional. Stress relief is one of the biggest health topics today, so why wouldn't they want to hear about how your stress level has dropped since you put your faith in God?

Ask God to help you be a better seasoning to others and to find the right words to say in these conversations. You want to give them plenty of information, yet keep them coming back time and again. Just like those pretzels and popcorn at the ballpark.

PART EIGHT

1 and 2 Thessalonians

JESUS IS COMING AGAIN

Key Elements

Purpose: to strengthen the Thessalonian Christians in their faith
and reassure them of Christ's return

Author: Paul

To whom written: the church at Thessalonica, and all believers

Date written: 51 A.D.

Key Themes

- I am to live my life out every single day as if this is my last day
  to serve Jesus.
- I must never forget that this life will not make complete sense
  and bring total fulfillment.
- I must derive hope, motivation, and urgency in contemplating
  the return of Jesus.
- I should see my daily labor as part of the divine rhythm of work
  and rest, while I expectantly wait for Jesus to return.

Formula for Heroes

> We recall, in the presence of our God and Father, your work
> of faith, labor of love, and endurance of hope in our Lord Jesus
> Christ. . . .
>
> —I THESSALONIANS 1:3

I t always feels good to be remembered for doing the right thing. To be an unsung hero is better than doing nothing of significance, but to have honest effort celebrated is preferable. Paul's commitment to remember the good works and heroic labor of those he was close to is truly stunning: "We continually remember before our God and Father your work produced by faith, your labor prompted by love, and your endurance inspired by hope in our Lord Jesus Christ."

We are surrounded by fellow believers living Godly lives. On the basis of Paul's example, one of our leadership opportunities is to thank God for the work of those people, and to let the folks themselves know that their effort is noted and appreciated.

Recognition of good work is a powerful motivation to keep doing it. The good work itself is a wonderful example for others to emulate. Doing good work and recognizing the effort before God and each other is a win all around.

Spotting a good deed requires a heart that pumps on appreciation, eyes that can distinguish the good from the mediocre, hands that are willing to reach out and give a pat on the back, and a self-image that is secure enough to let someone else get the trophy.

Who in your life are you thankful for? When was the last time you thanked God for that individual's labor? Have you thanked the person, privately or publicly?

Being Chosen

. . . knowing your election, brothers loved by God.
—I THESSALONIANS 1:4

To be chosen is at least as memorable as not being chosen. Both scenarios bring vivid memories. Because I was not an accomplished athlete—either in my dreams or in reality—when teams were chosen out on the playground I was often the last boy standing. Not fun, though I really didn't blame anyone. Being singled out as one of the appointed few, on the other hand, is not only memorable, it is worth remembering.

Here is a simple truth: God loves us and has chosen us. Regardless of what we might think of ourselves or how others might view us, regardless of the current circumstances that surround us, we have been made part of God's inner circle because He wants us there: "For we know, brothers loved by God," Paul contends, "that he has chosen you. . . ."

We often don't "feel the love" in a work context, and neither are we always chosen. Life out there just does not work that way. But God's economy is different. He does love us, and He has chosen us. Regardless of what else might happen, I can retreat to my desk and know that truth. Perhaps being aware of such great (undeserved) love and such single-minded (and undeserved) chosenness can give us a quiet confidence if the same things do not happen among the folks we spend our time with.

Becoming a Protégé

> . . . and you became imitators of us and of the Lord when, in
> spite of severe persecution, you welcomed the message with the
> joy from the Holy Spirit. As a result, you became an example
> to all the believers in Macedonia and Achaia.
> —1 THESSALONIANS 1:6–7

Who around you is worth imitating? A follow-up question: What in you is worth imitating? According to the logical progression in Paul's mind, finding a mentor leads to becoming one: "You became imitators of us and of the Lord. . . . And so you became a model to all the believers. . . ."

What needs to happen in my life, for me to be a model to others? To whom am I looking to find an example for me to emulate? There has been a surge in recent years of business biographies and autobiographies. These books show up on the best-seller list as well as in magazine profiles. From Lee Iacocca to Carly Fiorina to Sam Walton, we look for information and inspiration for our own pilgrimage.

In the same way, life stories of followers of Christ who have left their mark on their generation and culture provide a goldmine of rich examples. They have gone before us, and we can learn how they did it. Our goal is not to imitate every portion of their lives, or to venerate them. Only Jesus is the perfect example and worthy of our worship. But it is desirable to peer through a window into other lives that can help us in our walk. From David Livingstone to John Stott to Dietrich Bonhoeffer, their actions and words speak across the years.

Who around you is worth imitating? A follow-up question: What in you is worth imitating?

Knowing Our Customer

Instead, just as we have been approved by God to be entrusted with the gospel, so we speak, not to please men, but rather God, who examines our hearts.

—I THESSALONIANS 2:4

So much of business life comes down to knowing the customer, serving the customer, remembering the customer. So much of *all* of life comes down to the same thing. Our customer is not the boss or the project engineer. The customer is not our spouse or children. Our customer is God: "We are not trying to please men, but God, who tests our hearts."

What does it mean to please God instead of men? Are pleasing God and pleasing men always at opposite ends of the continuum, such that pleasing one means offending the other? No, of course not. Pleasing God means we have an inner gyroscope that centers us and helps us retain our bearing. With God as our focus we stay on track, even when others go in a different direction.

What happens when people lose their bearing and direction? What happens when the inner gyroscope ceases to work or is uncalibrated? Disasters such as Enron, Tyco, Andersen, and WorldCom. What happens when the inner sense of direction is correct? Miracles such as Chuck Colson following his conversion, William Wilberforce fighting successfully against slavery, Mother Teresa helping the poor in Calcutta, Jim Elliot reaching the Auca Indians in South America . . . and the list goes on.

Our customer is God. Service to Him is our privilege.

Leading Characteristics

You are witnesses, and so is God, of how devoutly, righteously, and blamelessly we conducted ourselves with you believers. As you know, like a father with his own children, we encouraged, comforted, and implored each one of you to walk worthy of God, who calls you into His own kingdom and glory.
—I THESSALONIANS 2:10–12

Bragging is a bad thing; a big ego is never attractive. Self-righteousness is a repulsive thing; arrogance pushes people away. So, is it ever appropriate to draw attention to your behavior or example? Paul certainly thought so: "You are my witnesses, and so is God," he says, "of how holy, righteous and blameless we were among you. . . ."

How is it possible for Paul to make statements like that? What prevents him from coming off as arrogant? First, what he said was true: he had indeed done the right thing and been a good example.

Second, his intent was to teach others in the faith; that was his motivation. One of the teaching strategies common in Paul's day was imitation, and he embraced this teaching strategy and oriented his life in such a way that other believers could copy it. Quintilian, the Roman educator in charge of constructing a standardized curriculum for the empire, chose imitation as the cornerstone for that effort. Students were to sit at the feet of their masters, and the masters were to be individuals worthy of imitation, both in the subject matter they taught as well in the way they lived their lives.

Third, Paul makes it clear that he is not perfect. As he says in Philippians, "Not that I have already obtained this, or have already been made perfect, but I press on to take hold of that for which Christ Jesus took hold of me" (Philippians 3:12). He is on a journey and is making good progress, but he has not yet arrived.

If what I say about my life is true; if my motivation is to teach others; and, if I let everyone know that I am not perfect, then my example can lead people closer to Jesus.

The Power of Good News

For now we live, if you stand firm in the Lord.
—I THESSALONIANS 3:8

Paul loved to hear the good news that people he cared about were doing well in the faith. That, he says, is when he really lives: "For now we really live, since you are standing firm in the Lord."

One of the attractive elements of Paul's walk with Christ is that it is so other-centered. So much of what Paul wrote dealt with how encouraging it was for him to notice the faith walk of others. Paul's focus was not turned in on himself; it was turned out on people of Christ who surrounded him.

It is true that we are self-centered as a people and culture, but I am not sure that we are any more so than people have always been. As a believer, though, I have the opportunity to focus primarily on others, and to measure my sense of satisfaction in life in part on the basis of how others are doing in their faith pilgrimage.

When the two of us began our business, the primary motivation was to help ensure that we finished well. We looked around us and saw folks who did well in one season of life self-destruct in another. We knew that creating a "kingdom and commercial covenant relationship" did not guarantee that at the end of life Jesus would say to both of us, "Well done good and faithful servants," but we felt that organizing our lives in a partnership of accountability created a context where our faith could flourish.

All of us believers need to absolutely rejoice when fellow believers stand firm in the faith of the Lord. Is your life organized to make that possible?

24/7 Alert Status

*. . . as we pray earnestly night and day to see you face to face
and to complete what is lacking in your faith?*
—I THESSALONIANS 3:10

I have to fight continuously to keep prayer a part of my life. It
often seems like a losing battle, almost an impossible fight. Just
as travel is one of the first line items cut out of a budget during
any economic downturn, prayer is one of the first casualties of a
busy schedule. Unfortunately, life is very busy. But then, there's
Paul and his cohorts: "Night and day we pray most earnestly. . . ."

We have a friend and business partner who is a refreshing
example in the area of prayer. A former CFO of a Fortune 100 company, and currently involved in two time-consuming entrepreneurial ventures, he constantly refers to prayer. Whenever we are
together, in a phone conference or in person, he drives prayer into
the agenda. Yesterday, when I dropped him off at the airport, we
prayed at curbside. The police officer who waited patiently at the
door of the car must have wondered what was going on.

Paul prayed constantly, and judging from the frenetic pace
of his life and travel I don't think it was because he had free time
available. He knew that without prayer the task was impossible,
and that absent prayer he would work hard and spin his wheels.
Our friend believes the same thing. How about you?

Continuous Improvement

For this is God's will, your sanctification: that you abstain
from sexual immorality. . . .
—I THESSALONIANS 4:3

When the concept of total quality management hit the business world, along with its emphasis on continuous improvement, the movement came with the usual cast of characters accompanying any new best business practice: disciples and skeptics. According to the true believers, continuous improvement was the panacea for all business woes. According to the skeptics (among them Dilbert), the only thing that would change were a few meaningless buzzwords, and the whole thing would move off the screen as a fad as soon as the next hyped idea showed up.

You don't hear much about total quality anymore, but continuous improvement seems to be a concept that remains part of the business psyche.

According to Paul, sanctification—the Biblical word for a follower of Christ's continuous improvement—is no fad: "It is God's will that you should be sanctified. . . . For God did not call us to be impure, but to live a holy life."

Our lives are to be characterized by a constant trend toward being Christlike; toward maturity; toward being loving, joyful, peaceful, patient, gentle, and self-controlled. Maybe some of that total quality terminology needs to be dusted off: continuous improvement, zero defects, and staying within upper and lower control limits. How is the sanctification process going in your life?

Elements of Ambition

> . . . to seek to lead a quiet life, to mind your own business, and to work with your own hands, as we commanded you, so that you may walk properly in the presence of outsiders and not be dependent on anyone.
>
> —1 THESSALONIANS 4:11–12

So much for the hype of life, and the constant need to be noticed: "Make it your ambition to lead a quiet life, to mind your own business and to work with your hands . . . so that your daily life may win the respect of outsiders and so you will not be dependent on anybody." Paul takes the desire to be high profile, always visible, constantly up front, and turns it on its head. To paraphrase his instruction: work hard, get the job done, and don't worry if you remain under the radar in the process.

Paul does not contend that a fast-paced, high-profile life is wrong. He does make it clear that it is not to be our goal. The goal is focused instead on the basics: accomplishing the task well, and in such a way that outsiders looking in will say "There's someone who really knows how to get the job done."

Sometimes fading back into the woodwork a little improves the quality. It also lowers the blood pressure. Not a bad deal on either count.

Now, there is ambition worth chasing. To discover a life that is full of genuine and deep quality is a rare treasure. Add to that a life that is running with rhythm and balance and you have discovered the sunken treasure chest. What better thing could we have toward which to channel our ambitious energy? In a world that wobbles and runs full throttle far too long, this kind of ambitiousness looks good.

Be Prepared

About the times and the seasons: brothers, you do not need anything to be written to you. For you yourselves know very well that the Day of the Lord will come just like a thief in the night.
—1 THESSALONIANS 5:1–2

We are always preparing for something: a sales presentation, the release of quarterly financials, meeting with a client, the Christmas rush, you name it. According to this verse, at least one more thing needs to be on our list: being always ready for the return of Christ: "Now brothers, about dates and times we do not need to write to you, for you know very well that the Day of the Lord will come like a thief in the night."

Jesus really is coming back any day now. Being ready for His return means orienting my life continuously toward His face, and it means yearning to hear Him say, "Well done, good and faithful servant."

How do I stay prepared? I keep grudges and bitterness out of my life. I forgive others quickly. I seek forgiveness when I wrong others. I remain honest. I listen to the Holy Spirit's quiet voice. I stay close to the truths of Scripture. I make my heart pure. I keep my behaviors Godly. I work hard.

Jesus will come when we least expect Him to. But we don't need to be unprepared. We have been given enough preparation time and guidance to perform the necessary house cleaning; we can welcome Him with doors wide open and a smile that says, "We're ready, and glad you're here."

Performance Reviews

And we exhort you, brothers: warn those who are lazy, comfort the discouraged, help the weak, be patient with everyone.
— I THESSALONIANS 5:14

There are incentives all around us that encourage productivity. The government measures productivity and reports to the rest of us regularly as to whether it's going up or down. Our annual performance reviews help gauge the quality and quantity of our work. According to Paul, we are to work hard and also "warn those who are idle, encourage the timid, help the weak, be patient with everyone."

Our life with Christ is a kind of balancing act, between admonishing when it is necessary (with the idle and the lazy), bringing encouragement where it is called for (with the timid, those who feel unable to speak boldly), helping the weak (those disenfranchised or physically unable to accomplish the task on their own), and bringing patience to everything all the time.

My life with Christ is an existence that requires the constant exercising of Spirit-infused judgment and discernment: Does this situation call for admonition or encouragement, or some of both? Should I be helping this person, or would that help enable lazy behavior? The list of questions is endless. The only thing I know for certain is that whatever I do must be done with patience.

Dear Jesus, as I head into this day give me patience and wisdom to know how to respond to the myriad people I will encounter. Thanks.

Thanks

We must always thank God for you, brothers, which is fitting, since your faith is flourishing, and the love of every one of you for one another is increasing.
—2 THESSALONIANS 1:3

We recently published a book titled *Behind the Bottom Line.* The premise is that, although the bottom line of organizational health is crucial, there are additional elements to life that also must be acknowledged and that inform the bottom line. Paul mentions two of those issues here: "We ought always to thank God for you, brothers, and rightly so, because your faith is growing more and more, and the love every one of you has for each other is increasing." In our own personal lives, both faith and love are to be seen as growth stocks.

Faith is vertical in nature; it addresses the extent to which I trust Jesus in the daily issues of life. Love, in this case, is horizontal in nature; it addresses how I relate to those around me, especially fellow followers of Christ.

Charles Swindoll once made the comment that the problem of life is that it is so daily. It is the daily give-and-take of professional life that both tests and strengthens my faith and my love. How do I grow the business? Will I get a promotion? What should our strategy be? How do we survive the downturn? These are all matters of prayer and faith.

Why did he do that to me? How do I relate to someone who rubs me the wrong way? How should I show appreciation for the work done by the project team? These are all matters of prayer and love.

Are faith and love growth stocks in your life? Would those around you agree with your estimation?

Display of Power

. . . since it is righteous for God to repay with affliction those who afflict you, and to reward with rest you who are afflicted, along with us. This will take place at the revelation of the Lord Jesus from heaven with His powerful angels.

—2 THESSALONIANS 1:6–7

When I have been wronged, and when I am burdened, I need justice and I need relief. I have to fight for both; otherwise I will receive neither. Obviously, no one cares about me as much as me. But is that really so? Listen to 2 Thessalonians 1:6–7: "God is just: He will pay back trouble to those who trouble you and give relief to you who are troubled, and to us as well. This will happen when the Lord Jesus is revealed from heaven in blazing fire with his powerful angels."

We feel the need to fend for ourselves in many parts of life. Either we take the initiative and figure things out or we suffer the attendant consequences. No one, for example, will do our taxes for us. Either we arrange to complete them or we wait for a visit from the IRS. Much the same is true regarding working our way through the business and professional issues that always seem to be on the horizon. Our job is to figure them out.

It would seem logical that we also need to take the same bold action if we have been wronged, cheated, stepped on, stolen from, lied about, or pushed aside. After all, who will act on my behalf if I don't? God will do it, as it turns out. I have the absolute luxury of not needing to add getting even, taking revenge, or making sure things are made right. We can cross those items off our task list because God has the ball on that. He will take care of things at a time of His choosing (which might be different from my timetable). But He never forgets. He has it on His task list.

Have you been wronged, or do you feel troubled? Sit back, relax, breathe deeply, and thank God that He is monitoring the situation.

Calling

> And in view of this, we always pray for you that our God will
> consider you worthy of His calling, and will, by His power,
> fulfill every desire for goodness and the work of faith.
> —2 THESSALONIANS 1:11

We are "called" individuals. Every one of us has been personally called by God to accomplish some task, which Jesus ensures has spiritual and eternal significance. Scripture speaks of calling in two ways: calling to salvation and calling to a work task, a life purpose. So Paul tells the Thessalonians that "we constantly pray for you, that our God may count you worthy of his calling, and that by his power he may fulfill every good purpose of yours and every act prompted by your faith."

What is your calling? What is the task God is asking you to accomplish? There is perhaps no more important question to ask, and no more important answer to pursue.

Have you come to the firm realization that you are not an accident or afterthought on God's part? You were a creation; He went to the blank canvas and painted your personality, your gifts, and even your calling. He has made you for a purpose and you will wrestle endlessly with this life until you settle His calling on your life.

Fortunately, we don't have to figure out the answer for ourselves. We don't have to engage in a personal intellectual summit. To be called means that God is speaking—calling—and we are listening and responding. God's job is to call, to talk. Our job is to hear. According to Henry Blackaby, the author of *Experiencing God,* if we are not hearing, it does not mean that God is not calling.

Are you able to get quiet with God and hear His voice?

Synergistic Relationship

. . . so that the name of our Lord Jesus will be glorified by you, and you by Him, according to the grace of our God and the Lord Jesus Christ.
—2 THESSALONIANS 1:12

There is an inevitable part of our work that draws attention to ourselves. It could be a nameplate attached to our office door, or it might be being called upon in a public meeting situation. We probably show up somewhere on the organizational chart, and there is a good chance that a phone extension bears our name.

Paul tells the Thessalonians that he prayed for them constantly, "so that the name of our Lord Jesus may be glorified in you, and you in him, according to the grace of our God and the Lord Jesus Christ."

Part of my inherent privilege is to make Christ known at my place of work. When people look at me, in everyday situations at the office, they should be able to look through me and see Jesus. For many of my colleagues, there is a good chance that the only Jesus they will ever see is the Jesus they see in me. My "good deeds" should be so evident to those around me that they whisper among themselves that something is different, something is out of the ordinary.

To glorify Jesus means to make Him known. We can make Him known by talking about Him, and that is sometimes appropriate. We can also make Him known by behaving like Him, and that is always appropriate.

How are you glorifying Jesus?

Marketing Strategy

Finally, pray for us, brothers, that the Lord's message may spread rapidly and be honored, just as it was with you. . . .
—2 THESSALONIANS 3:1

A good marketing strategy is music to our ears. Get the brand out there and known. Clarify the audience. Stay on message. Target correctly. Be efficient with media. Measure on the backside. So much comes down to good marketing, with its singular focus of promoting a product or a service.

Paul makes a request of the Thessalonians, which is essentially a marketing request: ". . . pray for us that the message of the Lord may spread rapidly and be honored. . . ." To spread a message rapidly and in such a way that it is honored is the quintessential definition of a good marketing campaign. Paul asks here that we give specific prayer attention to the successful spread of the message of Jesus Christ. He asks us to pay attention to how the message is moving to new audiences, and with what effect.

In the context of a busy professional life, I am not sure we think enough about that—about new and fresh ways to articulate the message, and about the impact the message is having on target audiences.

Let's pray that the message of Jesus spreads rapidly and is honored.

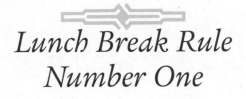

Lunch Break Rule Number One

In fact, when we were with you, this is what we commanded you: "If anyone isn't willing to work, he should not eat."
—2 THESSALONIANS 3:10

If you don't work, you can't eat. That is the final word, not out of Washington, D.C., in a debate between Democrats and Republicans but from Paul himself. Apparently there were members of the Thessalonian church who preferred to eat bread earned by others. The passage indicates that they did not think of themselves as lazy; in fact, they defined their existence as busy—too busy to work. It could very well be that they actually spiritualized that busyness as doing the work of ministry. To which Paul replies, "They are not busy; they are busybodies." Way harsh!

My clear responsibility as a follower of Jesus is to earn my own way in life, unless that is truly impossible. I don't mooch off others; I pay for my own food (and the other essentials of life). In the same vein, I should not support someone who ought to be earning his or her own financial way. My tithe and offering ought to go to those who are clearly in need (as defined by Scripture) and to those involved in legitimate, productive nonmoney-earning ministry.

According to Paul, we need to earn the food we eat. This means we are all hunters to some extent. We are to hunt for our own food.

Make sure you have not slipped into a lazy, deceptive spirit that thinks it is someone else's job to always take care of you. Be careful creating or feeding the spirit of codependency in others. Make sure you allow people in ministry to feel the weight of taking care of themselves.

Don't Quit

But you, brothers, do not grow weary in doing good.
—2 THESSALONIANS 3:13

Sometimes work is a drag. God told Adam, after the Fall in Genesis 3, that from that day forward labor would only be accomplished by the sweat of the brow. As anyone who has lived through multiple seasons of business life knows, there are no easy ways to make a living. Any job comes with its share of highs and lows, stresses and strains, successes and failures. In the process, we get tired and worn out.

As Paul closes his letter to the folks in Thessalonica, he makes a simple request: ". . . never tire of doing what is right." Get tired of other things, but don't get tired of that. Why? Because doing right is one of the hallmarks of a follower of Jesus.

Not every circumstance requires a right-or-wrong response. Much of what we face in professional life calls for judgment that is in the better-or-worse category: Should we go with this vendor or that supplier? Should we project this income or that revenue?

But then there are other judgments and decisions that require doing the right thing, such as keeping promises, honoring the law, and upholding moral standards.

Never tire of doing right.

PART NINE

1 and 2 Timothy and Titus

A MANUAL FOR CHRISTIAN LEADERS

Key Elements

Purpose: to encourage and instruct Timothy, a young leader in the church

Author: Paul

To whom written: Timothy, young church leaders, and all those who follow Christ

Date written: about 64–66 A.D.

Key Themes

- The love of money is the root of all evil.
- The qualifications for spiritual leadership are lofty, start early, and apply till our dying breath. Furthermore, they are more ethical than hierarchical.
- Good works are not the basis for salvation, but they are certainly the evidence of it.
- In prayer we have direct access to God, but if our prayers are to be effective they must be offered by a pure heart and a consistent life. The hands we lift in prayer must be holy hands.

Career Appointment

I thank Christ Jesus our Lord, who has given me strength,
that He considered me faithful, appointing me to His service.
—I TIMOTHY 1:12

Earning a promotion in your job is one of the greatest compliments of your skill, dedication, and attitude you can possibly receive. It says that your boss believes in you and your work and trusts you to handle even more responsibilities. I've never known anyone to call home and wail about getting a promotion; instead, it's something you call home and announce with pride and celebrate after work. You're pleased that someone noticed the good traits in you and rewarded you with a new title, job, and most likely a raise.

Now, multiply that feeling you get from earning a promotion in your job a million times to understand the depth of joy you should feel in being appointed to serve Christ. Serving Him isn't just another task to add to your plate, and it's not just another step up the career ladder. Serving Him is the highest promotion possible. It says that you've caught the eye of the most powerful, loving, and awesome boss—and have been found worthy of working on His team.

Usually, we thank other people for doing work for us. We don't often hear someone thanking us for allowing him or her to do our work. But that's how great an honor it is to work for God. The author of this verse says, "I thank Christ Jesus our Lord, who has given me strength, that He considered me faithful, appointing me to His service." Does this sound like someone who's doing

God's work grudgingly? Hardly. It sounds like someone who understands the sheer honor of being called out to serve the King, a magnified version of the joy felt when being promoted or called out to perform a prestigious task at work.

It's a joy to work for God. We're privileged to be in on what He does in this world. Let's not take it for granted, or do the work grudgingly. Let's call our family, share His good news, and celebrate our appointment on His team.

Second Chance

> But for that very reason I was shown mercy so that in me, the worst of sinners, Christ Jesus might display His unlimited patience as an example for those who would believe on Him and receive eternal life.
> —1 TIMOTHY 1:16

Where would we be without second chances? Not to mention, third, fourth, and fifth chances. We're lucky that, in most jobs, our boss understands that people make mistakes and doesn't fire employees after their first slip-up. Chances are, we've erred in our jobs more times than we'd like to admit, but we're still working there. And our boss still talks to us.

In many management circles, mistakes are something to value. Management leaders say that if you're not making mistakes, you're not taking enough chances. Then they stress the importance of learning from your mistakes—and those of other people.

God also believes in second chances. He has a good reason for doing so. In the verse here, Paul says that he, a sinner, received patience from Christ Jesus. Why does Jesus show us so much patience—and give us so many opportunities to do right by Him? Because He wants us to succeed and receive eternal life, and by showing His patience with us He draws even more people into His arms.

If God operated on a policy of one strike you're out, we'd all be in trouble—and not even here anymore, because it's a fact that we'll sin in our lives. It's what we do about that sin that matters. Have you thanked God for the opportunity to repent and change your ways? Have you used the fact of God's being so patient with us to bear witness to His greatness?

I once talked with an unbelieving colleague about God's mercy. This man said he could understand why God would forgive me, someone who has believed and tried to live by His word for years. But he couldn't understand the fact that God would forgive him, someone who'd lived in sin with his girlfriend for years, practiced many immoral habits, and shunned God's love most of his life. But I pointed out that Jesus says, in Matthew 2:17, "It is not the healthy who need a doctor, but the sick. I have not come to call the righteous, but sinners."

God wants to forgive us, because then we will understand how to forgive others. Then we will understand the error of our ways, and try to live in His will. Then we will better testify to His magnificent name.

First Things First

I urge, then, first of all, that requests, prayers, intercession and
thanksgiving be made for everyone—for kings and all those
in authority, that we may live peaceful and quiet lives in all
godliness and holiness.
—I TIMOTHY 2:1–2

Bad-mouthing a boss, manager, or leader is commonplace
today. Employees take pleasure in cracking jokes and bashing the boss, out of lack of respect, distrust, and dislike. But this
behavior only worsens what might already be a bad situation.

Imagine what work would be like if instead all the employees began praying for their leaders. If we all chose to lift up in
prayer the people we feel at odds with, many great things could
happen, not just for them but for us as well.

Paul wrote in this verse that first things come first: we are to
pray for "everyone—for kings and all those in authority, that we
may live peaceful and quiet lives in all godliness and holiness." Although Paul was speaking of political and governmental authorities, the argument could be made that his directive also applies to
our authorities in virtually all organizations—bosses, owners, managers, and team leaders.

Why pray for your boss? Because God allows us to help Him
change people and situations. The more we acknowledge others in
prayer, the more God will work in them and the circumstances surrounding them.

Praying for others carries an added bonus: it changes your heart, too. Every time you pray for another, you draw nearer to God. You show Him that you believe in Him and in His mighty power to act. Miraculously, He helps you through your prayers to see your boss through His eyes—and your heart will begin softening toward this person for whom you've previously felt anger, bitterness, or contempt. Praying for others is as much for them as it is for you. One action, double the benefit.

First things first: before you leave for work each morning, before you speak in anger, before you make a snide remark about the boss, pray.

What the Boss Is Looking For

. . . who wants all men to be saved and to come to a knowledge of the truth.
—I TIMOTHY 2:4

A big trend in management is to create job descriptions for every position within an organization. If a company is late jumping on the bandwagon, its leaders may go so far as to have employees help create job descriptions for the positions they are in currently. These documents include such information as daily, weekly, monthly, and annual job duties and overall job expectations. They serve two purposes: helping the boss evaluate job performance compared to the requirements, and giving the employee guidelines of expected behavior.

Whether you have a job description or not, you'll probably agree that knowing what's expected of you makes your job much easier. If your boss assigns a task that you don't quite understand, do you just wing it, or do you ask for clarification on what is expected? Clearly, the results are much better if you choose to ask for guidelines.

Our Heavenly boss was kind enough to provide us with a job description. Throughout the Bible He lays out what He wants from us, and in this verse He sums it up quite nicely: ". . . wants all men to be saved and to come to a knowledge of the truth." How's that for concise?

Some people argue that God only meant for some of us to find peace in Him. They think He chose ahead of time who He wanted in His kingdom—and whom He could do without. But this verse challenges that assumption; God clearly desires for every single one of us to be a part of His kingdom. Why wouldn't He? He created all of us; He takes pride in His creation and wants us to be with Him forever.

At work you follow your job description or your boss's orders because you want to succeed. You know that following those guidelines moves you along your career path. God, too, wants you to succeed. It's up to you, though, to follow the job description He's given you.

Leaving Instructions

Although I hope to come to you soon, I am writing you these
instructions so that, if I am delayed, you will know how people
ought to conduct themselves in God's household, which is the
church of the living God, the pillar and the foundation of truth.
—1 TIMOTHY 3:14–15

Leaving work for a long-deserved vacation often takes more
effort than originally thought. Somehow you feel you're the
only one who can do your job, and you feel that the operation will
crumble to pieces in your absence. So you leave written instructions. On everything. And everywhere. For everyone.

A bit much? Maybe. But those people left in the office while
you're soaking up the sun (or just staying at home, taking a nap
on the couch) appreciate your notes. Especially when they can't
figure out what to do next—and you've finally turned off your cell
phone and laptop.

You know how prepared you are when leaving the office,
wanting everything to go right. The apostle Paul must have felt
the same way while away from his people, because he left them—
and us—detailed, written instructions on a very important job: how
to live a Godly life. In his instructions, he covers everything from
sound doctrine, church leadership, and public worship to personal
discipline. Paul wanted Timothy, to whom he wrote this letter, as
well as church leaders and believers everywhere to know what God
expects of them. Fearful that they might miss something in his absence, he left tons of notes and instruction.

There are questions for you, though: Are you reading the instructions? Are you following them? You'd better do so as if your life depends on it, because it does.

Age Isn't a Handicap

Don't let anyone look down on you because you are young, but set an example for the believers in speech, in life, in love, in faith and in purity.
—I TIMOTHY 4:12

Wisdom comes with age." "Older and wiser." The list of quotations extolling the virtues of age goes on and on. It's often true that the longer one lives, the more one knows and the more experience one has gained. But age discrimination lawsuits and the plight of "older" people in search of jobs make it seem as if today the youthful are the most sought after.

However, in the organizational setting, the traditional notion that the young know nothing and the elders know everything prevails. As any recent graduate or young worker can tell you, it's hard to gain respect in the workplace for a baby-faced look, inexperience, and youthful ideas. Paul tells us, though, that age doesn't have to be a handicap. In writing this verse, Paul was telling Timothy, a young pastor, not to let others think less of him because of his age. Instead, he tells him to set a good example in all that he does—and that others, of all ages, will take note.

Do you feel that your age—whether you're young or not so young—interferes with how people see you? God doesn't care how young or old you are. He can use you in any state of your life, so long as you're willing to allow Him to work in you. When you're willing to let Him use you, He can speak through you anywhere and to anyone. Even if you differ in age from all the other people in your office, you can be an example to Christ, just as Timothy was an example at such a young age.

Age doesn't matter; what matters is how you speak, act, and believe. Don't give up because of worldly standards. Instead, use what you've got to God's advantage.

Relationship Guidelines

Do not rebuke an older man harshly, but exhort him as if he were your father. Treat younger men as brothers, older women as mothers, and younger women as sisters, with absolute purity.
—I TIMOTHY 5:1–2

Relationships at work are a sticky matter at times. You spend more time at the office than you do at home, which means you spend more time with other people than you do your own spouse or kids or friends. Yet you're expected to maintain an air of distance, while being friendly, supportive, helpful, and encouraging to coworkers. It's a minefield, especially as sexual harassment lawsuits abound.

What to do? Follow the rules Paul laid out in this verse: "Treat younger men as brothers, older women as mothers, and younger women as sisters, with absolute purity." If every person followed this simple rule, just as God intended, we would all save ourselves loads of heartache, trouble, and even money when it comes to defending ourselves in a lawsuit. Men and women alike often turn to advice columns, consumer magazines, relationship books, and the like to learn how to relate with one another. The truth is, God lays it all out for us clearly in the Bible. All we have to do is follow His word.

How does this apply to your life on the job? Say you work on a team with three other colleagues. As a project nears completion, you find yourselves staying late—and the conversation growing more intimate. The sinful you is tempted to engage in the sexual repartee; fortunately, the Godly you knows better. You realize that God wants you to see the women sitting across from you as your sisters or your mother—you'd never talk that way in front of them—and the men sitting across from you as younger brothers, with whom you must set a good example. When you picture those people as your mother, brother, or sister in Christ, it's a lot easier to refrain from the kind of talk or action you might feel led to partake in. This is exactly why God gives us the directive He does about relationships.

Remember the saying your parents probably used when you were a child: "It's for your own good"? Here, following these relationship guidelines is for your own good as well.

Take Care of Your Own

> If anyone does not provide for his relatives, and especially for his immediate family, he has denied the faith and is worse than an unbeliever.
> —1 TIMOTHY 5:8

What does it mean to you to be a follower of Christ, someone steeped in the faith? Does it mean attending church regularly? Reading your Bible daily? Praying at every opportunity? Looking to God in every situation? Providing for your family? "Wait—where did that last one come from?!" you might ask. The answer is, it came from the Bible.

Yes, providing for your family is a way of showing God your faith in Him. Paul points out in this verse that God considers family, especially immediate relatives, to be so important that a person is denying his or her faith—even worse than not believing at all!—if he or she fails to take care of relatives. And you thought you were working those long hours, bringing home the bacon, just to be kind. If only you'd known it was a directive from God.

How does this vantage point change your feelings about work, knowing that God *requires* you to provide for your family? I know it helps me when I'm not feeling up to the task of working through another long project to know that I'm doing this as part of my commitment to God, not just to earn another dollar. God is part of my family—the head of it, actually—and He provides for me. He says so in Matthew 6:25–34, as He describes how He takes care of the birds and the lilies of the field. In Matthew 6:26

He says, "Look at the birds of the air; they do not sow or reap or store away in barns, and yet your heavenly Father feeds them. Are you not much more valuable than they?"

Everything's more enjoyable when you're doing it for someone you love. In the case of providing for your family, you get to do it for several people you love: your earthly family members, and your heavenly Father. Consider it an honor.

Can't Hide What Is Good

> In the same way, good deeds are obvious, and even those that are
> not cannot be hidden.
> —I TIMOTHY 5:25

Two schools of thought prevail when it comes to gracious giving. The first takes great pleasure in giving publicly, whether to a university, church, or charity—or even to an office pool to buy a gift for the boss. People in this group expect acknowledgment or something in return for their gifts, like their names being printed in a brochure, announced at a ceremony, or inscribed on a plaque that hangs in the lobby. The recognition feels great, so they give more to get more.

The second school of thought on giving is that it's only good if done anonymously, receiving no recognition for the contribution. These people seek no glory for themselves, only for others.

Most of us would agree that God prefers us to follow the second thought on giving: do it privately. God knows our hearts, and that's all that matters. The same concept applies to every other good deed we do: we don't need recognition from our peers. God already knows, before we even perform the good deed, and he knows our motivations in doing so.

Helping a coworker finish an assignment to call attention to yourself? God knows. Helping a coworker prepare for a presentation, all because you care for her well-being? God knows that, too.

People may not be able to decipher your motivations. But God can—and you can't hide the good, or the bad, in your heart from Him.

How to Act with the Boss

> All who are under the yoke of slavery should consider their masters worthy of full respect, so that God's name and our teaching may not be slandered.
> —1 TIMOTHY 6:1

The boss has just yelled at you—for the third time today. He's still not happy with your report, even though you've made all his changes—three times, now. Your patience is growing thin; you're losing respect for the "creative genius" you so wanted to work for, before you found out about his moods and mismanaged business.

Sounds like a situation to drive anyone crazy, maybe to the point of making a scene, spreading the word about this terrible boss, and quitting. It's our choice whether to quit, but God doesn't leave much wiggle room about how we should act in such a situation. In 1 Timothy 5:25, God, through Paul, says that we must consider our masters (bosses) worthy of full respect. Why? Because treating anyone—our boss included—with anything less than respect undermines the working of the Holy Spirit in us. For example, what would you think if you saw your pastor, a man whom you respect and admire for his faith, screaming at an associate pastor for mixing up sermon dates? Then later you see him roll his eyes and make a face behind his secretary's back as she leaves the room. You'd be appalled. You'd think differently about your pastor. And you'd wonder about his faith.

Treating others with respect is what this faith in God is all about. We treat others as we'd treat God. Our bosses are no different, even though sometimes we'd like to treat them as though they were. We may not always understand their directives, and we definitely won't always agree with them. But it doesn't matter. We still have to respect them.

This doesn't mean we always have to follow every order the boss gives. Instead, it means we must approach the boss with honor and respect, handling the situation as God would and making a case for why we'd like to do something differently. We can disagree all we want; we just have to do it respectfully.

Great Gain

> But godliness with contentment is great gain. For we brought
> nothing into the world, and we can take nothing out of it.
> But if we have food and clothing, we will be content with that.
> —1 TIMOTHY 6:6–8

Have you ever seen the bumper sticker that reads, "He who dies with the most toys, wins"? Well, how about, "He who dies with the most toys still dies"? The second one hits it right on the nose—we can't take it with us when we go, so why work so hard to get it now? Yet that's what so many of us do day in and day out. We go to work to earn the money that buys the toys we think will make us happy. We spend more time at work earning the money for these things than we do at home enjoying the people in our lives, teaching our children how to live Godly lives, and worshipping the God Who carries us through life—and Who will provide us with an eternal home filled with more toys than we could ever earn in a lifetime.

Throughout the Bible, verses drive home the idea that things don't matter; it's the condition of our heart that really means something. In this verse Paul writes, "For we brought nothing into the world, and we can take nothing out of it." How true!

It's time for all of us to take a long, hard look at what really matters in our lives. For example, why do we work? To provide for our family, as God instructs in 1 Timothy 5:8? Providing for our families is a requirement from God, not just something we do because we want to. Or do we work to make enough money to buy all the toys we want, like a big-screen television, fancy new car, speed boat, or lots of high-tech electronics? Which of these reasons to work do we think God would most accept?

In the final verse here (1 Timothy 6:8), we're told to be content if we have food and clothing. We've got God, food to eat, and clothes on our back. But today's culture emphasizes the need for more, more, more. In God's eyes, though, what else could we possibly need that He can't provide? The answer is clear: nothing.

Bad Investment

> For the love of money is a root of all kinds of evil. Some people, eager for money, have wandered from the faith and pierced themselves with many griefs.
> —I TIMOTHY 6:10

This piece of Scripture has been repeated countless times throughout the years. Unfortunately, most people get it wrong, saying that *money itself* is the root of all evil. Money is a necessity in this life. We must have a certain amount of money to provide shelter, food, clothing, and everyday requirements for life. Beyond that, everything else is just extra.

It's the *love* of money that causes problems. Just look at all the companies that have failed in recent years. What's the root of their problems? Greed, an attempt to skim money off the top, not pay taxes, pull more for themselves wherever possible—and however possible. There's nothing wrong with earning a decent living.

But Proverbs 13:11 says, "Dishonest money dwindles away, but he who gathers money little by little makes it grow." At the heart of it all, Jesus says in Matthew 6:24, "No one can serve two masters. Either he will hate the one and love the other, or he will be devoted to the one and despise the other. You cannot serve both God and money."

Nowhere does the Bible say we should not invest our money, trying to earn a little more. Actually, in the parable captured in Matthew 25 Jesus tells about loaned money; He even talks about the value of investing wisely—whether it's time, talent, or in this case money. But the point is, we must come by the money honestly, earning it rather than scheming for it. Not to mention handling it well once we receive it, by tithing, giving to those in need, and using it for God's good. We must put our faith in God, knowing He will take care of us and give us everything we need. In doing so, we'll learn to rely more on God, and less on our own abilities and on dishonest schemes to gain more wealth.

Deep Relationship

Recalling your tears, I long to see you, so that I may be filled with joy.
—2 TIMOTHY 1:4

Every once in a while, a friend comes along who buoys your heart. You feel happier, more fulfilled, and more like your real self when in that person's presence. Friends like this, who know you intimately and still like you anyway, are a rare find.

Paul and Timothy obviously had this kind of relationship. In this verse, we learn that these friends cried upon parting—and Paul says he will be filled with joy upon reuniting with his friend. Thank God for friends like that!

The real issue to consider here, though, is this: What kind of friend are you? No, this isn't a quiz like what you'd find in popular women's magazines, because this one is based on God's word, not superficial fluff. A true friend, according to God's word, loves you as he loves himself (1 Samuel 18:1), is forgiving (Matthew 5:23–24), and is not vengeful (Romans 12:21). A real friend prays for you, does not gossip about you, shows genuine concern for your welfare, laughs with you, cries with you, holds you accountable, and offers support.

Think of your closest friend. Would he or she describe you as a model friend, on the basis of God's definition? Another simple test, stemming from Paul and Timothy's friendship: Do you feel sad when leaving your friend, and overjoyed on your friend's return? Better yet, does your friend feel that way about you?

Great Heritage

I have been reminded of your sincere faith, which first lived
in your grandmother Lois and in your mother Eunice and,
I am persuaded, now lives in you also.
—2 TIMOTHY 1:5

"Shas her mother's eyes and her father's smile." "Who does she take after?" "I see her grandfather's mischievous side in her."

Everyone likes to identify the source of traits in a child, whether physical or a personality trait or habit. They don't stop with mom and dad; people often see traits stemming from grandparents, aunts, uncles, and so on. There's a reason for that. Obviously we all pick up attitudes, habits, mannerisms, and beliefs from those we spend time with and those who are most able to exert influence over us—family members.

What beliefs have been handed down through your family? If it's a strong faith in God, great; don't let the heritage stop with you. Learning about God at an early age or from someone you trust helps solidify the faith in our heart and mind, so spread the word in your family. They'll likely listen to you more than to a stranger, especially when you're talking to your children.

If you didn't learn about God at home, that's OK. It's never too late to start a heritage—and how great it is to have it start with you! Talk to your relatives about God; tell them how He has worked in your life. Most of all, show it in your attitude and actions.

Who knows? Someday someone might be talking to your child or grandchild about the rich heritage you've passed on—spurring a new generation of believers.

Standing Proud

That is why I am suffering as I am. Yet I am not ashamed, because I know whom I have believed, and am convinced that He is able to guard what I have entrusted to Him for that day.
—2 TIMOTHY 1:12

Following Christ isn't always easy. He never said it would be, and that's part of the joy of serving Him: suffering in His name.

These days, suffering in Christ's name differs greatly from what it did in the early days of the church. In most Western cultures, we won't be jailed for speaking Christ's name, and we generally feel safe talking about and worshipping Him whenever and wherever we'd like. But those who follow Him—especially in countries hostile to the message of Jesus—do still feel the pressure of those who don't believe. They see the dirty looks, hear the rude comments, feel the heat of organizations pushing to get Christianity out of school systems and workplaces and governmental offices.

We can take comfort, however, in the fact that God knows we're suffering—and He rewards us for doing so. He wants us to stand up for Him, as Paul did, preaching the gospel even as he did from his jail cell, boldly and unashamed, in all circumstances. In Romans 5:3, he writes, "Not only so, but we also rejoice in our sufferings, because we know that suffering produces perseverance. . . ." Paul suffered, yet he still spoke boldly about Christ and His teachings. He still loved the Lord, no matter what happened. He was happy to suffer in His name.

How much pressure are you willing to put up with for God? You could easily not talk about Him at work, keeping your faith secret from nonbelievers—and thus eliminating much suffering in His name. But what would that say to God about your faith?

It's your call: you can stand proud and speak His name boldly, possibly suffering because of it, or you can keep quiet—and suffer those consequences later. Which will it be?

Behind the Strength

You then, my son, be strong in the grace that is in Christ Jesus.
—2 TIMOTHY 2:1

My daily workouts, a kind word from my spouse, talking with a friend, and a strong cup of coffee all give me strength to face the day. If I'm too tired to write another word, I pour a mug full of caffeine and revive myself. If I'm struggling with an issue, I call or e-mail my spouse, looking for words of encouragement or just an understanding ear. I love these sources of strength—but God is the true strength behind my each and every day.

Turning to God for everything, no matter how big and seemingly impossible or how small and seemingly inconsequential, is what we as believers should do to bolster ourselves. God cares about our every move, and He wants us to be well-equipped to fight the good fight. This means giving us the strength, physically, spiritually, intellectually, and emotionally, to go about doing His work.

Paul wrote the verse here in a letter to Timothy, reminding him to draw his strength from the *grace that is in Christ Jesus.* Grace, something undeserved, means something God gives to us because He wants to—not because we've earned it. He gave us grace when He forgave us of our sins and welcomed us into His arms. Here again, He's offering grace to live by—His strength, even if we don't deserve it.

There's no need to turn to things of the world to help in times of need (or even in times of plenty). Instead, know that God is there to help, whatever the issue. Be strong, Paul says. He's talking to us, as well as to Timothy.

In It for the Long Haul

Endure hardship with us like a good soldier of Christ Jesus.
—2 TIMOTHY 2:3

A soldier doesn't enlist for a cushy life. He understands that his days will consist of rigorous physical training where he's pushed to his limits and beyond. Mentally, he's pushed to do more and go faster than he ever thought possible. Most of all, he knows that he can't quit, because one day his life and his country's freedom will depend on his endurance, as we know all too well today. A soldier keeps on keeping on.

"Onward, Christian Soldiers," we sang as children. As adults we easily forget that we enlisted in God's branch of the military, and we have to push ourselves to endure everything that comes our way. But that's exactly what we're called to do: "endure hardship with us like a good soldier of Christ Jesus." Participating in God's militia isn't a one-day boot camp, or even a three-year enlistment in our lives. Putting our faith in Him and living for Him means living our *entire lives for Him*—and that doesn't come without consequences.

We may be ridiculed at work for our steadfast adherence to the Ten Commandments and all that they entail. We may lose a job for refusing to perform certain medical procedures, or for refusing to write about certain topics. The list of ways in which we suffer in God's name is endless—but, thankfully, our suffering will come to an end. As long as we polish ourselves up, keep in line, and follow the Boss's mandates, we'll join Him in heaven—and suffer no more.

Good Workmanship

Do your best to present yourself to God as one approved, a workman who does not need to be ashamed and who correctly handles the word of truth.
—2 TIMOTHY 2:15

After careful scrutiny of cost, ease of working together, and work quality, a company puts businesses on to the "approved vendor" list. This means that whenever an employee needs, say, a large photocopying and binding job done, she must use a vendor on the approved list in order for the billing and payment department to approve the expense and pay the bill.

In essence, making it on to the list means that a vendor has proven capable of completing the job in a friendly, professional manner and at the right price. This worker is someone who would have no reason to be ashamed of his or her work.

In the same way, we are to be checked out and (we hope) given the seal of approval by God. We are, in effect, "hired" by God to do His work. He wants us to serve Him well and to bring more people to know Him—it's that simple. But one day we will face the Boss, and He will inspect our work for flawed craftsmanship and defective materials. At that point, we will have to explain why we didn't use His resources more wisely, why we wasted time and slacked off.

It's humiliating enough to have this kind of conversation with our earthly boss. Just imagine the awkwardness, shame, disappointment, and fear that will go into our conversation with our Heavenly Boss when the due date for our life project comes!

God gave us His words in the Bible to prepare us for that day, a kind of manual for how to get on the approved vendor list. How closely are you following the manual? Will you make it onto the list?

Don't Argue; Teach Instead

And the Lord's servant must not quarrel; instead, he must be kind to everyone able to teach, not resentful.
—2 TIMOTHY 2:24

Everywhere you look these days, people are engaging in "friendly debates" that usually aren't so friendly. The topics cover the usual: politics, insurance, finances, and yes, religion. These debates don't take place just in homes and offices across the nation. TV talk shows and twenty-four-hour news programs have made debating the issues a daily occurrence. How do we followers of Jesus engage in those debates? Do they keep quiet? Do they shout louder than the others, in hopes of winning the argument?

Knowing what to say and when to keep silent is obviously a matter of spiritual discernment and judgment. God instructs His people not to quarrel, which the dictionary defines as "an angry dispute or altercation; a disagreement marked by a temporary or permanent break in friendly relations." So, to debate the issue is not out of the question. But quarreling is. To be kind and able to teach is always in order.

This message from Paul is important. For example, I know a man who has studied the Bible inside and out. He's very knowledgeable. But the thing is, he still doesn't put his faith in God, for whatever reason. He does, however, love engaging other believers in petty arguments about God's word, His intent, and his perceived flaws in "the system."

What's the correct response here? According to God, it is definitely not to get sucked into the argument. Instead, calmly sharing your faith and what you believe, and explaining what you know to be true, might get your point across quicker. Discussing God with others isn't a bad thing; getting sucked into an argument over Him, in which you might sin in your anger or frustration, is. Don't let it happen to you. Be prepared.

Get Ready

> But mark this: There will be terrible times in the last days.
> —2 TIMOTHY 3:1

There are certain events that I know ahead of time will happen: a big business trip, a conference, and so on down the list. Before each of these events, I think about how I will be relying on God more than usual, because I will be under more stress than usual. So I get ready. Just as I have to make my packing list, buy items I'll need to take with me, and make sure laundry's done so I can pack, I have to get ready spiritually to handle the stress.

I find myself praying more than usual during these times. I listen nonstop to inspirational music and read more books, including the Bible, that draw me closer to God—and it pays off. I'm more prepared to face the stress, the moods I might endure, the temptations I may come in contact with, and so much more when I know I'm grounded in Christ.

Of course, I know being close to Christ is important every day, not just in preparation for something big. But it doesn't hurt to know these things in advance and ask God for help in preparing the heart—and protecting the heart from these pressures. In the verse here, Paul instructs Timothy to get ready for the tough times ahead in the last days, the time between Jesus' resurrection and His second coming. Paul was telling everyone who lives during that time—including us—to make sure we're strong in the Lord and ready to face everything that comes our way.

Are you grounded in Christ and ready for the big day? If not, you'd better get ready; you don't know when He'll come.

Putting Truth into Practice

> They are the kind who worm their way into homes and gain control over weak-willed women, who are loaded down with sins and are swayed by all kinds of evil desires, always learning but never able to acknowledge the truth.
> —2 TIMOTHY 3:6–7

Knowing something and living something are two totally different things. As a kid, one conversation played out often in my home, I'm embarrassed to admit. It started with my not picking up my book bag off the kitchen counter or not cleaning my room when I'd been asked. Mom or Dad would tell me that I needed to get those things done, and my response would be, "I know," with a roll of the eyes and exasperated sigh. In return, they'd retort, "Well, if you know, then why haven't you done it yet?"

Good question. I'm better about putting my things away and cleaning my room now, but there are so many things that, like me back then, all of us know—but just neglect to act on. It's kind of like those people who are career students: learning anything and everything, but never getting around to putting the education into practice.

The same goes for studying the Bible, reading devotional or inspirational books, attending services and classes, but never putting faith entirely in God and following His word. Are there some things you're still holding on to that keep you from following Him completely? There may be some activities you still enjoy, though you know God has no place for them in His kingdom, or some attitudes that just don't jibe with what He asks of you. Those things are hard to give up, but it's necessary to release them if you want to have a real relationship with Christ. You can't just learn about Him and be welcomed into His kingdom. You have to purposely and deliberately make a decision to follow Him—and get rid of all that doesn't belong in His world.

Are you ready to do this? You've studied long enough. Now, put that knowledge into practice and reap the rewards He has in store for you!

Life's Instruction Manual

All Scripture is God-breathed and is useful for teaching, rebuking, correcting and training in righteousness, so that the man of God may be thoroughly equipped for every good work.
—2 TIMOTHY 3:16–17

Every new parent I've ever met jokes, "I sure wish babies came with instruction manuals!" The thought of a baby emerging into this world with a step-by-step manual for correct usage is funny, but new parents obviously find merit in saying it. The interesting thing is, although the Bible doesn't tell you how to change a diaper, feed a baby, or respond to a late-night crying session, it does tell you how to do just about everything else you need in life. It's our own instruction manual for life; best of all, it comes straight from God.

What's so different about this resource for life, compared with all the other instruction books you'll find in the bookstore? This one contains God's word; every word in the Bible stems straight from Him. He spoke through all the writers, telling them what to put down on paper, knowing that even today, hundreds of years later, we would still face the same issues and His word would still be valid.

Another great thing about this manual is that there's nothing sparse about it; God is complete in His instructions. As Paul writes in the verse here, God gave us His words "so that the man of God may be thoroughly equipped for every good work." God doesn't want us roaming through life unprepared. On the contrary, He has given us everything we need to survive and even thrive in life and in righteousness. Everything in the Bible is there for our benefit, to help us live more Godly lives, to teach us how to serve our God, and in turn how to love and serve others. He left no stone unturned, no subject untouched. He knew our concerns before we even came to be, and He answered them ahead of time.

All that's left is for us to follow the directions He has laid out for us—and to pass on this life's instruction book to everyone we know. As they say, real men and women follow the directions . . . of God, that is.

Oath of Office

> In the presence of God and of Christ Jesus, who will judge the living and the dead, and in view of His appearing and His kingdom, I give you this charge: Preach the Word; be prepared in season and out of season; correct, rebuke and encourage—with great patience and careful instruction.
> —2 TIMOTHY 4:1–2

Tradition calls for a person to take an oath of office when entering any kind of elected or appointed position, whether a governmental role, a church role, or that of parent teacher organization officer. It's a rite that solidifies in people's minds what it is this person will do while in office, and it holds the person to a promise of said behavior and actions.

When entering the role of Christ's follower, we essentially took an oath as well. Our promise? To be prepared to tell others about Christ and to correct and encourage others in their faith "with great patience and careful instruction." So, how are you holding up on your end of the deal?

One of the biggest tasks in the role of a child of Christ is spreading His word. As Paul wrote in the verses here, we aren't to spread His word just when we're in the mood to do so ("in season"). It's our duty to be prepared to tell friends, colleagues, relatives, neighbors, anyone we meet—about Christ whenever the opportunity arises. This means always being on the lookout for a moment of opportunity, and praying that God will open doors for us to talk about Him. We ask Him ahead of time to give us the words to say when the door opens and to lead us through conversations about Him. And we read our Bible regularly; the more knowledge we have, the better prepared we will be.

The other part of our oath of office entails correcting and encouraging others. Now, God doesn't picture us running around with red markers writing up every follower who makes a mistake. What He wants from us is a listening ear, a kind and sympathetic friend, but one who gently makes others aware of their sins in God—not to berate them, but to help them in their relationship with Christ. This is not an easy task, and it's why God gives directions on how to correct others. He says to use great patience and careful instruction—and His direction.

You've been in office a while now. Isn't it time you kept your promises?

Keep Your Head

> But you, keep your head in all situations, endure hardship,
> do the work of an evangelist, discharge all the duties of your
> ministry.
> —2 TIMOTHY 4:5

I n every organization, there's someone whom everyone admires for his or her ability to keep cool under pressure. No matter what goes wrong, this person doesn't appear shaken, calmly assesses the situation, prepares a measured response or logical solution, and carries on. We're none the wiser that, deep inside, this person is boiling with emotions and frustrations. But somehow he or she manages to keep it together for the rest of us.

When I look at people like that, I think of the verse here: "But you, keep your head in all situations. . . ." I feel that God is talking directly to me, reminding me that He wants me to keep it together, and for so many reasons. His reason behind wanting us to pull ourselves together likely has nothing to do with being admired in the workplace. Instead, God commands us to "keep your head in all situations" because it's when we lose control that we make errors in judgment, speak harshly, and get ourselves into trouble.

For example, if you find yourself in danger of ruining a project—and costing the boss a business deal—how do you react? The first-response reaction is to panic, possibly getting uptight, irritated, and snippy with others. When you're like that, you're much more liable to say things you shouldn't say and behave in ways you

shouldn't behave. This is exactly why God wants us to keep it together. Instead of overreacting, He calls us to slow down, think
about the situation calmly, and prepare a measured response or solution. In doing so, we're more likely to take other people's feelings,
moral issues, and God's direction for our lives into consideration,
thus making the right choices.

Coaches yell at athletes to "keep your head in the game" all
the time, reminding them to focus on the issue at hand and not
let outside distractions take them off course. The same can be said
for us: we must keep our head in the game, knowing what outcome we want in the end and not letting anything distract us from
getting there.

Avoid Alexander

Alexander the metalworker did me a great deal of harm.
The Lord will repay him for what he has done. You too should
be on your guard against him, because he strongly opposed
our message.
—2 TIMOTHY 4:14–15

Have you visited the religion section at your local bookstore
recently? If so, chances are you've seen on the shelves more
inspirational guides and books about spiritualism and new-age
mysticism than you've seen on the God we believe in. More and
more, people are accepting anything as religion, and expecting
everyone to accept that all religions are equal—and that all ver-
sions of "god" are equal.

What's really scary is that people who believe in other religions often call themselves Christians instead of blatantly opposing our message, as Paul wrote that Alexander the metalworker did. Therefore, it's harder to distinguish between what it is true and what is false in the way of God. Paul warns Timothy, and all believers, to beware of people who try to lead him astray or who oppose the message, because they might harm his faith.

Do you encounter any Alexanders in your daily routine? Perhaps a coworker who rails about the perils of Christianity, or another who touts the benefits of her "all-accepting" religion? Feel free to talk with these people, just as Jesus would have done. But be on guard against what they tell you; check out anything that sounds fishy in the Bible—where all truth is told. Never accept anything at face value, but check it out first. Prepare your heart for these meetings; pray that God will protect you, give you wisdom to know what is true, and lead you in growing in your faith—not being led astray by a nonbeliever.

Pursue a Blameless Life

Since an overseer is entrusted with God's work, he must be blameless—not overbearing, not quick-tempered, not given to drunkenness, not violent, not pursuing dishonest gain.
—TITUS 1:7

To hire the right person for a managerial position in any organization, large or small, it's most effective to first list the qualifications and characteristics you seek. Many of the qualifications and characteristics vary depending on what type of entity it is and its overall culture. But most organizations put such traits as "hardworking," "effective," "motivated," and "a strong leader" toward the top.

What many of them fail to include are the moral characteristics that—as we all know from the news in recent years—can make or break even the largest and strongest of organizations. In this verse, Paul calls for the leaders not to be overbearing, quick-tempered, given to drunkenness, violent, or dishonest. Do they really want folks of such high moral caliber? Yes and no. It's a tall order for many corporations to ask for these days. Pursuing dishonest gain? Quick-tempered? Overbearing? It's all around us in the business world.

Although walking in step with Christ's teachings may mean missing out on a few perks at the office (perhaps recognition, power, prestige, a bonus), we'll be all the richer having followed God and having put the wicked ways behind. But we should never think that good character goes unnoticed. It doesn't. God says, "I see it and am taking notes."

Our true reward for a blameless life is an eternity spent with our King.

See Life Through Pure Eyes

> To the pure, all things are pure, but to those who are corrupted
> and do not believe, nothing is pure. In fact, both their minds
> and consciences are corrupted.
> —TITUS 1:15

In a given situation, you'll find two camps of people: those who give the benefit of the doubt and look for the good in people and those who immediately find negativity, fault, and malicious intent. I'm sure you can think of people who fit in either category. Is there someone in your office who always takes what you say in the worst possible way, who always feels you're out to get him? Chances are, there's also a person in your office who always finds something positive to say, no matter how bad the predicament you're in.

The positive coworker likely isn't seeing life through rose-colored glasses; instead, she's probably seeing life through the pure eyes of God. As Paul says in this verse, "To the pure, all things are pure, but to those who are corrupted and do not believe, nothing is pure." If you're forever in step with God, praying daily, reading His word, following His will in all that you do, you're going to find it easier to see the good in those around you. Because you are more at peace with life by having God on your side, you'll be better equipped to let the harsh remarks from your boss roll off your back; you'll be more able to forgive a coworker who snaps at you, because you understand that he's just under a lot of pressure and is trying to finish a deadline; and you'll be more accepting of the pressures of your job, because you know your true reward lies in heaven.

On the other hand, if you're seeing life through a negative perspective, one built from years of hard-heartedness, sin, and corruption, you're going to see that negativity, hard-heartedness, sin, and corruption in everything others do. Paul is trying to warn us against this reality by showing us the effects of living a life in any way other than with God.

Sure, it's easy to commiserate with others and feel like part of the crowd when joining in negativity. But wouldn't you rather see life through pure eyes and enjoy God's perspective?

Sound Doctrine

You must teach what is in accord with sound doctrine. Teach the older men to be temperate, worthy of respect, self-controlled, and sound in faith, in love and in endurance.
—TITUS 2:1–2

Our society teaches that if it feels good, do it; if it looks good, watch it; and if it sounds good, believe it. Under this premise, many people live on the basis of half-formed ideas, misinformation, and whatever fly-by-night idea hits them. They are also the ones who live fragmented lives, never sure where they're going or how to respond to the curvy roads and dead-ends life throws in their path.

One way to escape living in such a topsy-turvy world is to follow the map we've been given in the Bible. In Titus 2:1, we're told to teach what is in accordance with sound doctrine. Sound doctrine is our foundation for life; it's our parameter for living; it's our map to a full and blessed life.

Sound doctrine is the exact opposite of doing what feels good, watching what looks good, and believing what sounds good. It's living grounded in the Word, it's spending time with Jesus in intimate prayer, it's willingly following what He has laid out for us. Sound doctrine is logical and well thought out.

Maybe you can relate. At work, how many times have you wondered who made up the rules or the processes you're supposed to follow? I know I've often wondered what logic lies behind some of the processes I've seen; actually, I often wonder if there even is any logic behind a lot of what goes on in the workplace today. With rules and methods like that, it make no sense to those following them; it's no wonder organizational loyalty, employee morale, and retention rate are on the decline. The answer? Sound doctrine, a logical, well-grounded map for living.

How does your road map look: a straight path to God, grounded in sound doctrine, or a topsy-turvy ride to who knows where?

Model Correct Behavior

In everything set them an example by doing what is good. In your teaching show integrity, seriousness and soundness of speech that cannot be condemned, so that those who oppose you may be ashamed because they have nothing bad to say about us.
—TITUS 2:7–8

Necessity may well be called the mother of invention—but calamity is the test of integrity," wrote Samuel Richardson, a British novelist from the eighteenth century. I have no idea what he was thinking when writing those words, but I can see how they relate to many situations in our lives here in the twenty-first century. It's said that a man or woman can be perfectly good while in a good situation, but we see a person's true nature only when he or she is caught in a bind.

How do you react when things don't go your way at work? When the copier breaks down for the third time today, your computer crashes, you're running late for a meeting, and your boss calls you on the carpet for turning in a less-than-perfect report, do you still "show integrity, seriousness and soundness of speech that cannot be condemned"? If so, I congratulate you on modeling correct behavior at all times. For the rest of us, however, there's a lesson to be learned from these verses.

Those outside the faith or those who are new in the faith don't observe us just when we're on our best behavior. Unfortunately, they see us in good and bad—and often they watch specifically for us to slip up. They want to see if this God we follow has really done such great work in our character that we can handle tough situations with grace and maintain our integrity. Like it or not, we become teachers the minute we choose to follow God.

What are you teaching those in your organization: integrity, or something less?

Obedience to Man = Obedience to Christ

Teach slaves to be subject to their masters in everything, to try to please them, not to talk back to them. . . .
—TITUS 2:9

Let's face it: sometimes your business relationship with your boss feels more servant-master than devoted employee–grateful employer. Stretching the analogy to say we're in a position of slavery might be taking it a bit far, but there are a few things to glean from this passage.

The author of Titus wants the people of his day—remember, it was a time when slavery was common and accepted—to understand that slaves and masters could and by all means should live a loving, responsible life together. He explains something we should remember in our business relationships: God wants us to treat our employers as we would treat Him.

In Ephesians 6:5–9, he says, "Slaves, obey your earthly masters with respect and fear, and with sincerity of heart, just as you would obey Christ. Obey them not only to win their favor when their eye is on you, but like slaves of Christ, doing the will of God from your heart. Serve wholeheartedly, as if you were serving the Lord, not men, because you know that the Lord will reward everyone for whatever good he does, whether he is slave or free. And masters, treat your slaves in the same way. Do not threaten them, since you know that He who is both their master and yours is in heaven, and there is no favoritism with Him."

How can you serve your boss as if he or she were the Lord? Show respect. Don't steal, whether in petty products or (as is more common) in wasting time. Be honest about your work habits, skills, and activities. In general, do whatever you would do if God were here in the flesh watching you work—even when your boss isn't. Not only will you earn favor in the eyes of your employer but you'll also earn rewards where it counts: in the eyes of God.

Speak Evil of No One

. . . to slander no one, to be peaceable and considerate,
and to show true humility toward all men.
—TITUS 3:2

Slandering others seems to be a way of life for some people. Not a day goes by when I don't hear a negative word about a colleague by a colleague. But this isn't something that happens just among nonbelievers. Followers of Christ are just as guilty of slander as the next person.

Slander isn't just what you say; it's also what you don't say or what you allow others to say. When a colleague regularly bashes another colleague, how do you react? Do you sit and listen, even nod your head and mumble agreement? Or do you explain that you'd rather not talk about others that way and move your conversation to something more appropriate? It took me a long time to learn that listening to such talk is just as bad as taking active part in the discussion. Really, would you want God to just sit by and listen while someone spoke ill of you? Of course not, and He never would. This means we shouldn't, either.

Plautus, a Roman playwright, had a harsh take on slander: "Slander-mongers and those who listen to slander, if I had my way, would all be strung up, the talkers by the tongue, the listeners by the ears." Lucky for us, Plautus isn't our judge, or we'd all probably be strung up in one way or another. But don't forget that God is our judge, and He doesn't like slander either.

Challenge yourself today by asking how you have slandered someone recently. Can you correct the harm you've done? Sure, it takes a lot of guts to admit to a coworker or friend that you've spread unkind things about him or her. But the alternative is living with the fact that you've disobeyed God. Next, think about how you'll prevent future ill thoughts from becoming ill words. Will you excuse yourself from inappropriate conversation? Will you ask your company to stop the slander? Will you keep your mouth closed next time you're struck with a slanderous thought? The final step: ask forgiveness from God for your loose lips or open ears.

With God's help and your willingness to cooperate, slander doesn't have to be a way of life for you.

Invest in Good Works

This is a trustworthy saying. And I want you to stress these
things, so that those who have trusted in God may be careful
to devote themselves to doing what is good. These things are
excellent and profitable for everyone.
—TITUS 3:8

Profit. There's that word again. You hear it everywhere in your
daily rounds: in the board meeting this morning, the monthly company e-mail update, the CEO report. Everyone's concerned
with profit—how much you've made, how much you've gained or
lost compared with last year, how much more profit you have than
your next three competitors. Sometimes it feels as if profit is all
anyone cares about.

Guess what? Even God cares about profit. In His case, though,
He cares about a different kind of profit from what you're used to.
In terms of your life with God, He considers your time with Him
an investment. You invest time, effort, love, devotion, goodness,
faithfulness. Just as in business and the stock market, you have to
contribute something to gain something. Generally, the more you
put into your business, the bigger rewards you'll experience.

The same holds true for your investment of yourself in
God's kingdom. The more you put into His business—the business of winning people to Him and of serving Him daily—the better your profits.

The good news: we can make all sorts of analogies comparing your investment in God's kingdom with investments you make

in the stock market. But when investing in God, you're not running the kind of risk you face with the stock market. In fact, His stock market holds absolutely no risk. It's a sure thing. As any investor knows, you can't pass up a sure thing.

Are you passing up God's profits?

Divisiveness: The Three-Strike Policy

Warn a divisive person once, and then warn him a second time.
After that, have nothing to do with him.
—TITUS 3:10

Many public schools and city governments have adopted a three-strike policy. Their hope is that two warnings are enough; the third offense is grounds for automatic discipline. Your organization may even employ such a policy in terms of verbal warning, written warning, and termination upon the third offense.

The three-strike policy may well have stemmed from this verse, in which Paul advises believers to warn people who cause strife in a church twice, and then cut them off. Sound harsh? Maybe. But, as Paul says in Titus 3:11, "You may be sure that such a man is warped and sinful; he is self-condemned." In other words, the divisive people had it coming.

Sin that divides a church works a domino effect. One person's sins cause division in the church. In that division, others begin sinning by way of slander, gossip, negativity, bringing others down; overall, their actions disrupt the true mission of the church, which is serving and loving our God with all of our hearts, all of our souls, and all of our minds (Matthew 22:37). The best way to deal with such division is to lovingly warn the offender, and even give the person a second chance. After that, though, the risk the church runs of allowing this person to remain is much too great. He obviously has chosen to sin and bring down the church; therefore, it's his fault the church has asked him to leave.

It's important to remember, however, that God wants you to rebuke others out of love, not out of hatred. In correcting others, you yourself shouldn't sin. In Hebrews 12:5–11, the author says, "My son, do not make light of the Lord's discipline, and do not lose heart when He rebukes you, because the Lord disciplines those He loves, and He punishes everyone He accepts as a son." Show the offending brother love and caring, while handling the situation. Remember, in treating the other person as God Himself would do, you just might show the offender the true nature of Christ and lead him back to the fold.

PART TEN

Philemon

A REPENTANT RUNAWAY COMES HOME

Key Elements

Purpose: to convince Philemon to forgive his runaway slave, Onesimus, and to accept him as a brother in the faith

Author: Paul

To whom written: Philemon, who was probably a wealthy member of the Colossian church, and to all believers

Date written: about 60 A.D.

Key Themes

- Every man and woman has value and significance because of the stamp of God in his or her life.
- Every man and woman is in need of forgiveness and acceptance.
- Christian love and acceptance should overcome any barrier or grudge in any relationship.
- Tactful persuasion, basic respect, and genuine kindness are powerful tools in dealing with and accomplishing results with people.

From Useless to Useful

Formerly he was useless to you, but now he has become useful both to you and to me.
—PHILEMON I:II

Onesimus served as Philemon's slave. He likely did a good job, performing physical labor and all the chores Philemon instructed him to do. But he wasn't useful, as his name means, until he found Christ. Onesimus ran away from Philemon. While on the lam, he met Paul, who led him to know Christ as his savior. In appealing to Philemon to take Onesimus back, Paul said, "now he has become useful both to you and to me." Onesimus's new status with the Lord spurred his usefulness; now he could work for both Philemon and the Lord.

If I asked you how useful you are, you'd probably say "very." Then you might list a dozen important things you do, your status at work, the projects you do, your role in the church, your family's reliance on you at home. Yes, we would all consider your contributions useful. But how useful are you to the Lord?

Part of being God's child is doing His work and doing it well. Throughout the Bible, we read stories of people giving up their lives to serve Him. They step out of their comfort zone and spread the news of His salvation. They serve others by feeding them, helping them with work, opening their homes to them, and just loving them. God considers our work for others working for Him.

On the basis of this definition of *useful,* how useful are you? To be more so, go out on a limb and talk to your coworkers about Him. Pray that He will give you the right opportunities and the right words to say; you just have to be willing. Or you could offer to help a coworker who's swamped, even if it means staying a bit late yourself. In doing so, you're not only helping your coworker and your organization but serving your Higher Boss too. The ways you can be useful are endless. Use your creativity and knowledge in the Lord to find more ways to help others—and increase your value to God's company at the same time.

Partners in Christ

So if you consider me a partner, welcome him as you would welcome me.
—PHILEMON 1:17

Achieving partner status in an organization means you've hit the big time. You've paid your dues, you've served your time. Now it's your chance to run with the bigwigs. But something you might not have anticipated is that partners are in it together, not separate. Becoming a partner, whether in a law firm, medical practice, or any other business, means you'll still be sharing the responsibilities and the joys. You're not on your own, for better or worse.

Partners generally work together to make decisions, set policies, deflect problems, and celebrate their successes. They welcome each other equally, knowing they're in it together for the long haul.

As partners in Christ, we should treat each other equally as well. In Philemon 1:17, Paul vouched for Onesimus, a runaway slave who had found the Lord. He appealed to Philemon to accept

Onesimus back and to treat him as a brother in Christ—not just as property and a worker. In his appeal, Paul teaches all of us an important lesson: as children of Christ, we are all equals. No one of us is more important than another, so we shouldn't treat each other as such.

Do you welcome all brothers and sisters in Christ equally? It's easy to get into your own clique or social group and forget about others in the church. But we're all equally important in God's eyes, and that's what matters. How you treat fellow believers shows God how you feel about Him. When you slight a newcomer in your church or turn your back on a long-time member, you've slighted God and turned your back on Him. But if you make a newcomer feel welcome and show affection for all of His children, He will feel your welcoming spirit.

Open your eyes to the diverse people in God's kingdom and see the good in them. Take time to get to know them and learn how to be friends, or at least friendly acquaintances. Remember, Jesus said: "I tell you the truth, whatever you did for one of the least of these brothers of Mine, you did for Me." So what are you doing for the Lord these days?

PART ELEVEN

Hebrews

MOVING FROM GOOD TO BETTER

Key Elements

Purpose: to present the sufficiency and superiority of Christ

Author: unknown

To whom written: Hebrew Christians young in their faith, and all
of Christ's believers

Date written: about 70 A.D.

Key Themes

- To understand and connect with the awesome God of the universe, I need only look to the person and work of Jesus.
- Jesus is superior to any angel, any patriarch, any hero of the faith, any man or woman, any religious custom or ritual, or any theory of life.
- God has always preferred simple, individual, authentic obedience over elaborate, perfunctory sacrifice.
- Though we are saved and secure in our relationship with God, through Christ we are encouraged to grow and mature in our spiritual skill sets.

The Word Rules

> The Son is the radiance of God's glory and the exact representation of His being, sustaining all things by His powerful word. After He had provided purification for sins, He sat down at the right hand of the Majesty in heaven.
> —HEBREWS 1:3

The years have given us a steady increase in the availability of words, and we use them in enormous volume. From scrolls laboriously penned using inefficient writing instruments on handmade paper, to books printed on a manual press, and now words available in infinite variety and language in digital form on the Internet, we've never faced having so many words accessible and in our face. If we determined quality of life by sheer number of words alone, we would all be the Bill Gates of our time.

So what do words accomplish? Some words that we encounter take our time; certain ones change our minds, a few of them grab our attention, and others ignite our imaginations. Words are the white noise of modern life. But not all words are created equal. There are words, and words, and words.

And then there is the Word, and the Words He spoke. Those words actually do something significant: they sustain us. "The Son is the radiance of God's glory and the exact representation of His being, *sustaining all things by His powerful word.*"

Of all the billions upon trillions of words to focus on, there are a few words that sustain all things: they give life, they keep things in perspective, they show direction, they allow us to see God, and they communicate truth. The King of kings is also the

Word of words. His words make it possible to determine which other words to pay attention to and concentrate on. He does not have the only words. But of all the words, His are always the last.

Watch for Drift

We must pay more careful attention, therefore, to what we have heard, so that we do not drift away.
—HEBREWS 2:1

A good piece of driftwood is fun to find. A great piece of driftwood is fun to display. But in neither case would I want to be the driftwood itself. Driftwood, if able to talk, would no doubt have a fascinating tale to tell about spending months or years in aimless travel going nowhere in particular, all the while being beaten up by water, sun, rocks, current, sand, and wind. But drifting probably isn't much fun for driftwood.

Organizational drift is deadly. When you ignore the mission or the core values for one reason or another, there is grave cause for concern. If a public company shows that tendency, it becomes the kind of situation we read about in the *Wall Street Journal*. Left unchecked, sustained drift (like Enron or Arthur Andersen) results in bankruptcy. Businesses literally drift out of existence, and their driftwood assets end up on eBay.

Personal drift is deadly, too. "We must pay more careful attention, therefore, to what we have heard, so that we do not drift away," says the author of Hebrews. Our existence is anchored by the words of Scripture, by the reality of the living presence of Jesus, and by the hope of an eternity with God. With those anchors in place, what can go wrong? According to the passage, we can forget. We can neglect to pay careful attention. Then we may start to drift. It might be moral drift, or intellectual drift, or emotional drift. The drift might look like anxiety, or anger, or immorality, or laziness. A drifting man or woman is a sad sight.

How secure is your anchor?

Band of Brothers

> For this reason He had to be made like His brothers in every way, in order that He might become a merciful and faithful high priest in service to God, and that He might make atonement for the sins of the people. Because He Himself suffered when He was tempted, He is able to help those who are being tempted.
> —HEBREWS 2:17–18

A true mentor is someone who has traveled a road before us and serves as a life example and offers advice. When an individual we respect explains his or her priorities, approach to life and business, nonnegotiables, and core values, a panorama of clarity opens to us as we wrestle with similar questions.

There's only one thing better than a mentor who has traveled the road before you: a mentor who has traveled the road before you and now also travels it with you. The best mentor would be like a great older brother: quick to help, able to sympathize, interested in every detail, understanding in our weaknesses, gentle, and willing to take our burden for us.

Jesus is the perfect friend and mentor. He was "made like His brothers in every way, in order that He might become a merciful and faithful high priest. . . ." He knows what we are going through, and He's always on call for us. When He says "Come to Me and allow Me to carry your burden," He is making us an offer that's difficult to refuse.

But we *do* refuse His offers, all the time. For some reason, we have a hard time actually believing that Jesus understands our situation, and that He really can take our burden. It obviously would be easier for us to hand off the burden on our back to someone we can see. It would be nice to be able to meet Him at Starbucks and have a long conversation over a triple latte. But our faith walk is an intimacy cultivated with the currently invisible God of the universe. We will see Him one day and spend eternity in His immediate presence. For the moment, though, we go to Him in faith and have exactly the same conversation with Him in prayer that we would prefer to have over coffee.

He knows. He understands. He listens. He takes the burden.

Focus and Fix

> Therefore, holy brothers, who share in the heavenly calling,
> fix your thoughts on Jesus, the apostle and high priest whom
> we confess.
> —HEBREWS 3:1

I remember vividly the first time I drove seventy miles per hour. It was soon after receiving my driver's permit. With my dad riding shotgun, I merged onto I-35 and accelerated. As the speedometer climbed I couldn't handle the speed; my eye was fixed on the road directly in front of the car—and the pavement was coming at me faster than my mind could process. I was nervous, stressed, and soon weary.

My dad watched and then made a simple suggestion: "Look down the road, not at the road." My eyes moved up ahead and everything fell into place immediately. All of a sudden, driving was fun. Nothing changed—except my perspective. But that change in perspective made all the difference between my liking driving and not.

What does it mean to "fix your thoughts on Jesus, the apostle and high priest whom we confess"? The answer is simple and yet difficult. Fixing our eyes on Jesus doesn't mean that we ignore what's going on around us and just read the Bible ("Forget the strategic plan; just give me Jeremiah"). Neither does it mean that we avoid colleagues who don't follow Christ, or gravitate only toward relationships with those who have daily quiet times.

Fixing our thoughts on Jesus means that we look through the situations we face all day at work and see Jesus behind those situations. Not only is He present as we walk through any given day, He also provides the perspective to deal with those situations correctly: with patience, wisdom, and correct response.

Dealing with what life tosses to us without seeing Jesus behind the issue of the hour is like tooling down the freeway looking at the pavement directly in front of the car. Stress is high, and a wreck is imminent. Instead, fix your thoughts on Jesus and see the rest of life through your peripheral vision.

Encouragement Vaccine

But encourage one another daily, as long as it is called Today,
so that none of you may be hardened by sin's deceitfulness.
—HEBREWS 3:13

It's a tough world out there, and apparently it's so tough it can harden us. "Out there" isn't some abstract place you'll never find. It could be as close as your office, the places you hang out, or the company you keep. Have you seen what hardening of sin does to a person? I'm talking about people who look at you without emotion, with a cold gleam in the eye. The people who are impervious to appeals for help or mercy, people who have no grace in them and are cynical, skeptical, and legalistic. These people live out there in the tough world; the scary thing is, that tough world is capable of molding us along those very lines.

Good news: there's an antidote, a vaccine that guards against this kind of hardened heart. The author of Hebrews calls the vaccine *encouragement*.

It is amazing what encouragement accomplishes. You've probably seen the effects of encouragement in your life. It's a pat on the back, a note of appreciation after a well-planned and well-executed meeting, a smile in the hallway. Encouragement is a promotion, and a genuine affirmation to somebody. Encouraging others reinforces good behavior, as you may have read in the *One Minute Manager,* a management book by Spencer Johnson and Kenneth H. Blanchard.

Encouragement does something much more valuable: it protects against becoming hardened. Daily encouragement is an antidote to the kind of hardening that sin can bring. Encourage others, and ward off the hardness in your life.

The Faith Variable

For we also have had the gospel preached to us, just as they did; but the message they heard was of no value to them, because those who heard did not combine it with faith.

—HEBREWS 4:2

Have you ever tried substituting ingredients when cooking? It just doesn't work. I know for a fact that baking soda and baking powder are not the same. Use the wrong one, and you end up with flat cookies—and a lot of wasted time and ingredients.

There are other times when just the right formula makes all the difference. For example, it's impossible to hold a corporate retreat without a whiteboard. Calling a meeting without at least one other person present doesn't make sense. It's nearly impossible to create a good document without spell-check.

The key ingredient for a Christ-centered life is faith. You just have to have faith, or the formula or recipe won't work. Faith isn't the cracked pepper of the beef stew; it is the beef. Faith is what distinguishes us from our colleagues who live without it. Without faith, our entire universe can account for what is available to the senses only, what philosophers call the material world.

But for a follower of Jesus, faith adds an entirely new element of an unseen world. In faith, we use such words as *hope* and *love* and other intangible concepts.

Our faith is not just faith by itself, and it certainly isn't faith in ourselves. Nor is it faith in the leader of the organization, as we all know! The faith that the author of Hebrews talks about is a deep and profound faith in Jesus Christ. Faith is what bridges the gap between ourselves and Christ.

Do you have the right ingredient for a Christ-centered life? Remember, substitutes just won't work.

The Rest Variable

There remains, then, a Sabbath-rest for the people of God;
for anyone who enters God's rest also rests from his own work,
just as God did from His. Let us, therefore, make every effort
to enter that rest, so that no one will fall by following their
example of disobedience.
—HEBREWS 4:9–11

The busy demands of job and career often shred the notion of rest. Work is almost omnipresent in its ability to follow us, what with laptops on the airplane, cell phones in our hands, and personal digital assistants on the wireless network. Every minute demands to be filled. Every open slot requires justification as to why we should not stuff it with phone calls, memos, and meetings. We can't afford to waste time.

Rest is the wasted time of an unfilled slot. The very purpose of rest is to muscle work out of a specific time frame to accomplish other objectives. Ponder Abraham Heschel's explanation from *I Asked for Wonder: A Spiritual Anthology*: "Six days a week we wrestle with the world, wringing profit from the earth; on the Sabbath we especially care for the seed of eternity planted in our soul. The world has our hands, but our soul belongs to Someone Else."

The Sabbath rest is a soul day, not a workday. It brings perspective and gives time for reflection. The idea that we work nonstop through the busy years of our career and then take our rest later, in retirement, is a man-made idea totally without God's endorsement. Rest keeps us on the right track, which is exactly what

Hebrews contends. We must make every effort to enter the rest, "so that no one will fall." Perhaps rest is less of a wasted time slot than we thought!

Words That Jump off the Page

> For the word of God is living and active. Sharper than any double-edged sword, it penetrates even to dividing soul and spirit, joints and marrow; it judges the thoughts and attitudes of the heart.
> —HEBREWS 4:12

A great book is a wonderful gift. Whether designed to convey information (such as *Good to Great: Why Some Companies Make the Leap . . . and Others Don't,* by Jim Collins) or to motivate you to take immediate action (*Who Moved My Cheese? An Amazing Way to Deal with Change in Your Work and in Your Life,* by Spencer Johnson and Kenneth H. Blanchard), words written on a page help convey a deeper meaning to life at work and away from work. Really good books can change your mind or behavior or motivate you to take action. That's one of the great aspects of fine literature.

Scripture, however, is in a league entirely of its own. Yes, Scripture can motivate you to action or change your mind. But it's something much more. Scripture is God-breathed by the Holy

Spirit. When read, it takes on life as the Holy Spirit in us uses His own words to bring about an effect.

Great literature forces me to interact with the author and his or her perceptions of a given situation. Scripture does the same thing—with the added element that the Holy Spirit who inspired the writing also lives in me and can use the words specifically to affect my life for the better. That's why Scripture is called "living and active."

Scripture is like a catalyst in a chemical reaction. When I read a verse, I activate the actual immediate presence of God in me. He uses the words of Scripture to talk to me and speak into my life. This is why Deuteronomy 32:47 can say, "They are not just idle words for you—they are your life."

It is sometimes difficult to take up a book that was written long ago and expect it to have much practical or immediate use for right now. The truth of the matter, however, is that Scripture is more relevant, helpful, useful, and life-changing than anything else we could possibly read. No matter how old the text is, the ideas held within are still living and applicable—especially when God is living in you.

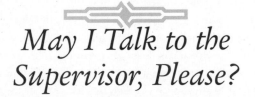

May I Talk to the Supervisor, Please?

Let us then approach the throne of grace with confidence, so that we may receive mercy and find grace to help us in our time of need.
—HEBREWS 4:16

I t is a fact of corporate life that the higher one goes in the organizational hierarchy the more inaccessible one becomes. Walking into the president's office doesn't hold the same look and feel as flopping down in the intern's cubicle. To commune with those at the top means running the obstacle course of gatekeeping assistants, busy schedules, tight agendas, and short time slots.

Then there is Jesus. Not the executive in the corner office, but the Son of God who sits at the right hand of God the Father. As the verse here shows, there is with Jesus complete accessibility along with eager willingness to give mercy, dispense grace, and help in our time of need. All we have to do is approach Him with confidence. He has the ultimate open-door policy. We don't need to make an appointment to speak with Him or curry favor with His secretary, but we do need to take the time to approach Him with confidence and talk.

Why can we approach Him with confidence? Scripture gives us a number of reasons. We can approach Him with confidence because He invites us to; because He has bought us with His own life; because He desires to take the burden off us. In other words, our relationship with Jesus allows us to take the most difficult, perplexing, unsolvable issues in our lives straight to the one person in the universe most willing and best-equipped to help us figure it all out. Going to confidence with Jesus takes talking to the supervisor to a whole new level.

Dealing Gently

> He is able to deal gently with those who are ignorant and are
> going astray, since He Himself is subject to weakness.
> —HEBREWS 5:2

When talking about a company's core values, you might use the terms *aggressive, cutting-edge, competitive,* and *entrepreneurial.* But "to deal gently" is not usually enshrined as a corporate core value. Try that one out on your boss and see what he or she says.

To deal gently is, however, part of the kingdom catalogue of appropriate behaviors. Jesus deals gently with us because He Himself once found Himself in the same position we face in our daily lives. Jesus understands, sympathizes, and walks in our shoes. He sits in our chair. He is well aware of the selfish coworker, the imperfect assistant, the difficult client, and the vendor who does not deliver.

He knows us, too—the critical spirit, the jealous look, the lazy streak. He knows our situation because He has lived in our situation. It's amazing to think that He knows exactly what we're facing in such a modern world, and that His principles are still valid hundreds of years after His earthly reign. But in a mysterious principle of spiritual transference, because He deals gently with us we too are to deal gently with others. "But the fruit of the spirit is," contends Paul, "love, joy, peace, patience, kindness, goodness, faithfulness, gentleness, and self-control" (Galatians 5:22–23).

Dealing gently with others is to be a hallmark of our existence and behavior. Even when people deserve an impatient response or a tight lip firmly set in disgust, we are to be gentle. When we think these people don't deserve such a gentle response, Jesus gently reminds us that neither do we.

The Remedial Class

We have much to say about this, but it is hard to explain because you are slow to learn.
—HEBREWS 5:11

I n the workplace, we all value the smart colleague. You know the one I'm talking about. He's the employee who's fast on the learning curve, the person who catches on quickly, the boss who's quick on her feet. Such folks are a joy to be around, and we work to be placed in those categories ourselves.

By the same token, we wouldn't consider it a very good day if a coworker told us over lunch that we're just a bit slow to catch on. But that's precisely the problem with some of us, according to Hebrews 5:11: "We have much to say about this, but it is hard to explain because you are slow to learn."

In the hustle and bustle of life, we just don't give enough attention to spiritual things. Our minds and time are engaged elsewhere—anywhere from the assignment you're working on now, to the pile of tasks cluttering up the corner of your desk, to the luncheon meeting, to the spouse and kids waiting on you at home. Whereas in a business context we're actively engaged in taking our learning to a new level, on the spiritual side we passively wait to be fed.

Does this sound familiar? God cares at least as much as your boss does about the level of your engagement with knowledge, truth, maturity, and competence. Are you giving your boss more effort than you're giving God?

Obviously, some of us need to pick up the pace. This means getting out in front of the curve and being more proactive instead of waiting for the spiritual input to come to us. It means setting aside regular time to commune with God and His word, and not always pushing that time aside.

Hopefully, when we meet Him face-to-face, the words from His mouth will be "Well done, good and faithful servant," not "You were slow to learn."

Time to Grow Up

Therefore let us leave the elementary teachings about Christ and go on to maturity, not laying again the foundation of repentance from acts that lead to death. . . .
—HEBREWS 6:1

When kids are small and act their age, they're cute. They talk funny, mispronounce words, misunderstand conversations, and reply in a completely different vein from the one you started out in. In short, they do things that make us laugh, and their childlike innocence is attractive and compelling.

But when kids grow up and remain immature, they move from childlike innocence to childishness. Does this statement bring to mind anyone you know? Childishness in an adult is anything but attractive. It's draining and sad, really. The author of Hebrews wants us to grow up in our faith. He says in Hebrews 6:1, "Therefore let us leave the elementary teachings about Christ and go on to maturity. . . ."

He wants our spiritual lives to evidence a spiritual maturity and a robust spiritual diet that aligns appropriately with our faith. Why, the author of Hebrews may ask, keep going back to second grade if we're able to graduate to third?

We can argue that the author of Hebrews—and God, for that matter—wants us to live a very professional, very Biblelike life. But unfortunately most of us lead a lopsided existence. We are either very business and sort of Bible, or sort of business and very Bible. For some reason, we rationalize the ability to be quite competent in one area of our lives but less than able in another. Scripture does not endorse a very-and-sort-of lifestyle. Scripture asks us to be very-very. This means we need to know our Bible and focus on the learnings that it teaches as much as we need to focus on business and best practices.

What is your next logical step in maturity?

Keeping Track of the Good Stuff

> God is not unjust; He will not forget your work and the love you
> have shown Him as you have helped His people and continue to
> help Him.
> —HEBREWS 6:10

Life is full of doing things that go unnoticed and unacknowledged. I'm sure you experience this every day at work. Does anyone notice that you filed all of the notes on the case you just finished working on? Not likely. Does anyone notice that you returned three phone calls this morning, answered four more, and replied to all of the e-mail piling up in your box? Probably not. You just do those things because they're a part of corporate culture, and because it's common courtesy. Fanfare is unnecessary.

But God doesn't forget your work. He notices everything you do, big and small, good and not so good. Hebrews 6:10 is really interesting if you read it closely. It says that God is not unjust; He will not forget your work and the love you have shown Him as you have helped His people and continue to help Him. He notices the love you show *Him* by helping *them*.

Whenever we do the right thing and lend a fellow believer a hand, God notices and does not forget. You might help a friend prepare a top-rate resume, make a phone call on a young intern's behalf, promote a worthy worker, or mentor and coach someone who wants to grow. These aren't all big things in the grand scheme of life. But whatever it is, in the context of this verse from Hebrews we bring blessing to others, and the blessing we bring is more significant than what a nonfollower of Christ brings.

Why? Because of the good deeds we do that accompany our salvation. When we give our heart to Christ, He in turn equips us to help others because of the gift of salvation He has given to us. He makes it so that we are able to help others more than those who have not experienced God's gift of salvation.

The bottom line: helping others helps Christ, and He notices. What kind of a follower and believer would we be if we turned our back on the one who gave us eternal life?

Looking for a Mentor

We do not want you to become lazy, but to imitate those who through faith and patience inherit what has been promised.
— HEBREWS 6:12

I t's no secret to anyone who's been in the workforce for a few years, especially in the same job or company, that staying challenged and fresh is difficult. In fact, it's downright torture sometimes to find something new that enthuses us in our jobs. The same thing happens to people who've followed Christ for a long time.

So how do you stay fresh, keep moving forward, keep learning new things, keep digging deeper? How do you prevent a lazy, been-there-done-that attitude from creeping into the daily routine of your life? Answer: find someone to imitate. Look for someone to emulate. According to Hebrews 6:12, "We do not want you to become lazy, but to imitate those who through faith and patience inherit what has been promised."

Our world gives us plenty of people to emulate. The modern media do a good job of serving up stories. It's up to us to filter which personalities and stories are worth digesting. As a follower of Christ, it's only natural to put Jesus as the one we want to emulate. Perfect.

But according to this and other passages, we are to identify followers of His who clearly show characteristics and qualities that we are attempting to build into our lives. When we find that individual, through a formal mentoring process or informal observation, our job is to incorporate into life the Godly things this person displays. In other words, we are looking for people about whom we really could say, "I want to be like this person when I grow up."

The kind of mentor we need changes as we move through seasons of life. For example, the question "What book has had the most profound impact on you?" probably would elicit differing answers from a four-year-old and a forty-four-year-old. "What kind of mentor do I need?" also demands revision over time.

Jesus is the only complete mentoring answer. Besides Him, we will have a patchwork quilt of folks helping us on our professional and spiritual journey. Who in your life is worth imitating?

The Power of an Indestructible Life

> . . . One who has become a priest not on the basis of a regulation as to his ancestry but on the basis of the power of an indestructible life.
> —HEBREWS 7:16

Since the events of September 11, 2001, we've all had a renewed awareness of how people and things can be destroyed without notice. In an instant, on a massive scale or with an individual bullet, what was is no more. Terrorism shows just how easily life is destroyed.

What or whom can you depend on in your life? Are you sure your job will be there tomorrow? If so, are you positive that the company's financial stability is in check and that you're still needed in the same way? Of course you can't guarantee that. Life has shown that the unimaginable certainly does happen.

How about your family: can you guarantee that nothing will happen to those you love? It's an uncomfortable, disagreeable thought, but one that is too often a reality in our society.

Things happen; life falls apart. Then there's Jesus, whose first work on earth was creation, not destruction. He himself is indestructible.

Jesus is indestructible; what a great word for our time! We know He does not change, but to think that he cannot be destroyed is a thought with genuinely current relevance. He is the alpha and omega, the beginning and the end. He is the one who suffered a humble death but now lives and rules the earth. He saves us and will never allow us to be separated from Him. He is the one we follow. He is indestructible.

Talk Through Me

Therefore He is able to save completely those who come to God through Him, because He always lives to intercede for them.
—HEBREWS 7:25

I have this friend, a business colleague, who always seems to bail me out of difficult situations. For example, in company meetings, when I'm floundering to get my point across—and obviously not making points with the rest of the crew—he knows how to intercede on my behalf. He uses this phrase, "I think what he's saying is . . ." and my colleagues see the light. I'm not sure how he always knows what I'm trying to get across, but he does, and I'm thankful.

So, how does God know what we're saying in prayer, especially when we don't really know what to pray and what to ask for? How do we pray with confidence in matters when we don't have confidence in what we're asking? We go through Jesus.

Jesus is our best friend, who always seems to bail us out when we're floundering and trying to find the right words to express what we're feeling to our holy God. Jesus intercedes for us, translating our prayers before they arrive at the throne of God. He adjusts our prayers to align with God's will, according to Hebrews 7:25. This is similar to the explanation of prayer Paul gives in

Romans 8:26–27: "In the same way, the Spirit helps us in our weakness. We do not know what we ought to pray for, but the Spirit himself intercedes for us with groans that words cannot express. And He who searches our hearts knows the mind of the Spirit, because the Spirit intercedes for the saints in accordance with God's will."

We therefore never ask God for anything that is inappropriate. The corrective measure is in place; the Holy Spirit and Jesus himself intercede and translate our requests, ensuring that what God hears is what is best for us. Our limited understanding turns into powerful, confident prayer requests.

I heard someone say once that the only bad prayer is no prayer. This explanation from Hebrews bears that out. We can plead the desires of our heart—as aligned to the greatest extent possible that we know to be true of Scripture—but even in areas where we don't know what to be pleading, we can articulate the best we can and the Holy Spirit will take care of the rest. Jesus lives to intercede on our behalf.

The Silver Bullet

Such a high priest meets our need—one who is holy, blameless, pure, set apart from sinners, exalted above the heavens.
—HEBREWS 7:26

In investing, we always want a silver bullet. In turn, we are always warned that silver bullets don't exist. Looking for a solution to investing in a downturn? No easy answer there. Trying to figure out how to go to market differently? It requires wrestling with global competition. Get out the *Wall Street Journal* and do some research.

Still looking for a silver bullet? Look no further than Jesus. "Such a high priest meets our need—one who is holy, blameless, pure, set apart from sinners, exalted above the heavens." As this verse spells out for us, Jesus is all we need. He is our complete answer, our only answer, and it's as simple as that.

The verse obviously has a whole lifetime worth of applications. My life needs to look like His life. I need to give my worries over to Him. I need to share my load with Him. I need to tell Him my uncertainties. I need to express my love and joy to Him.

The silver bullet is the single solution to any and all of our ailments. In the old days, it was an oil elixir sold by traveling medicine shows. The pitchman would preach from the back of the buggy: "You have no problem this oil cannot heal." The writer of Hebrews is no traveling medicine man, and Jesus is more than a six-ounce bottle of herbs and mixtures. But He does say that we can never find ourselves in a situation to which He is not willing and able to bring help.

Jesus is the silver bullet we spend so much of life looking for. It's as simple and as complicated as that: find Him, trust and accept Him, follow Him, and you'll search no more.

Brain and Heart Surgery

> This is the covenant I will make with the house of Israel after that time, declares the Lord. I will put My laws in their minds and write them on their hearts. I will be their God, and they will be My people.
> —HEBREWS 8:10

Core values have become a big deal to companies large and small. It's important to have a document somewhere in the entryway that declares the intentions of the folks sitting in their cubicles. You might see something like this: "We value teamwork, we act honorably, we strive to serve the customer, and to do so in a profitable and respectable manner." The word *core* in front of *value* is designed to indicate that this statement is something that reflects internal sentiments, not just an external gloss for the benefit of clients. In other words, core values are supposed to be intrinsic to the very fiber of an organization and to anyone who works there.

In the same vein, the Holy Spirit is our core value creator. He literally lives in us after we choose to follow Christ and, since He is the very being of God, puts the law on our minds and writes it on our hearts. So our interaction with the truths of God is from the inside out, not outside in. How do we activate those truths? Do they just show up automatically, with no action required on our part? Of course not. We activate the law in our mind and the law on our hearts primarily through the act of prayer and by studying Scripture.

Because the Holy Spirit Himself was the author of Scripture, when we read the words He wrote there is a mysterious spiritual interaction that occurs between His words and His being in us. By the same token, when we pray with the help of the Holy Spirit, the God who has been placed in us interacts with the God of heaven in a supernatural manner.

Wonderful things happen these days with heart surgery and brain surgery. As a follower of Christ, I have God placed in me, and the transformation of both my heart and mind takes place without any need for the surgeon to operate.

"I Do Not Recollect. . . ."

For I will forgive their wickedness and will remember their sins no more.
—HEBREWS 8:12

One of the standard answers in congressional inquiries is, "I do not recollect. . . ." Normally such amnesia coincides with what would be information damaging to the individual if it were remembered. The person, knowing he or she is in serious trouble, conveniently "forgets" any notion of wrongdoing—and forgets that the investigators and often the public know better than that.

Congressional and criminal investigations are engineered to find and fix blame; wrongdoers have designed the "I do not recollect . . ." response to deflect that blame. Thankfully, God does not operate like a special prosecutor with His children. He doesn't put us on the stand, lay out the evidence, and build a case against us. We do that to ourselves. In regard to our sin, God says, "I do not recollect. . . ." After we accept Jesus as our savior, when God looks at us He no longer sees our sin but instead sees the white robe of Christ's righteousness. The sacrifice of Jesus shields our sin from God's sight, and we are declared righteous. The biblical word is justification.

Unfortunately, we often remember what God chooses to re-member no more. We hang on to our sins, beating ourselves up over our indiscretions. But God has forgiven our wickedness and will remember our sins no more. As I've heard someone say, God finds the deepest portion of the ocean, throws our sins in, and hangs up a no-fishing sign. We, on the other hand, dwell on and recollect what God has long ago forgiven and forgotten, pulling our past out of the sea and suffering through our guilt once more.

The good news for us is that once we have asked for for-giveness, "I do not recollect . . ." is not a statement used to avoid blame. It is a reality of our freedom in Christ.

The Gift of a Clean Conscience

How much more, then, will the blood of Christ, who through
the eternal Spirit offered Himself unblemished to God, cleanse
our consciences from acts that lead to death, so that we may
serve the living God!
—HEBREWS 9:14

What is the worst thing you remember doing at work? Did
you lie to your boss about your hours? Manipulate an
expense report to land in your favor? Or make some other slip
that caused you great grief? Chances are that, like most of us, you
can easily remember the error of your ways. God, on the other
hand, can't.

One of the greatest gifts of a relationship with Jesus is a clear
conscience. Guilt weighs heavy; freedom from guilt lifts the spirit
and puts a smile on the face. Without the forgiveness of Christ, I
walk through life with guilt, like a low-grade fever that won't go
away. That bad situation is punctuated by something even worse:
acute bouts of even greater guilt that often surround events of great
wrongdoing or remembrance of such an event. A life without
Christ is by definition a life spent with guilt, and time spent attempting to forget about that guilt.

Jesus brings sweet freedom from all of this. He takes our
load of guilt on Himself so that we have to carry it no more. He
releases our mind and gives it the ability to not dwell on what

we've done wrong, but to focus instead on the solution that He provided in our salvation.

When we walk around with a load of guilt, it's like perpetually wearing a heavy backpack. We kind of get used to it, but nevertheless it weighs us down without our even realizing it. What does the freedom that Jesus gives us with a clear conscience allow us to do? According to Hebrews 9:14, "the blood of Christ, who through the eternal Spirit offered Himself unblemished to God, cleanse our consciences from acts that lead to death, so that we may serve the living God!"

Constituent Care

> For Christ did not enter a man-made sanctuary that was only a copy of the true one; He entered heaven itself, now to appear for us in God's presence.
> —HEBREWS 9:24

I met one of our congressmen at the airport recently. I introduced myself, and we talked briefly before he headed off to Washington and I boarded a flight to California. He talked about constituent care. He touched on how he fields requests and contacts from folks in the state, and on how he tries to help them the best way he can. You'd be surprised who calls him for help; the requests he fields range from help in dealing with social security to getting a green card to dealing with the IRS. They ask him for help when there's nowhere else to turn to, or when they just need someone on their side. Unfortunately, this one congressman can't be everywhere helping everyone with everything at all times.

The good news is, God can. It was wonderful, I'm sure, for people to have been in the presence of Jesus when He walked the earth. Biblical records show that His followers did not want Him to leave earth, and they were confused why He had to go.

Hebrews 9:24 details one of the advantages of trading locations from earth to heaven: "He entered heaven itself, now to appear for us in God's presence." Translation: Jesus is our twenty-four/seven constituent care advocate with God. He is there to plead our case and articulate to God our pressing needs. He can help us with everything our congresspeople can help with, and so much more. Unlike the helpful representative I met, God can be there at all times, helping with everything for everyone. All at once.

Where do you turn for help with your pressing issues? When you just don't know where else to turn and the situation seems hopeless, who do you call? Your congressional representatives might help with a need or two; your boss might put herself on the line and help you out; your family will pitch in as much as possible. But God is the all-time best constituent care advocate. You'll never encounter a busy signal, voice mail, or booked schedule. His line is open all the time, and He's there for you. Just call.

Hang In There . . . for a Long Time

You need to persevere so that when you have done the will of God, you will receive what He has promised.
—HEBREWS 10:36

We're all aware of the idea of perseverance. But we're in love with the need to hang in there. We hang in there while we wait for the phone call to come back from the client. We hang in there wondering whether the flight will go or be canceled. We hang in there with an intense focus on a project as it works its way toward the finish line. Perseverance, on the other hand, is an entirely different matter. Perseverance is for the long haul—years of waiting. Perseverance requires eons of patience; it is the ability to keep going even when the outcome is ambiguous.

A Long Obedience in the Same Direction: Discipleship in an Instant Society, which Eugene Peterson wrote a number of years ago, is a great book. More important, the title is accurate as it relates to perseverance. The Christian life is a long obedience in the same direction.

When the two of us began working together many years ago, we started with one simple statement on a napkin that defines everything we've done: "to finish well." We looked around us and saw folks who were not finishing well, especially at particular seasons in their life, and we decided that in partnering together we would have a better ability to work toward that outcome.

The partnership has developed into what we call a commercial and spiritual covenant relationship. Perseverance means that we arrange our lives in such a way that we finish well. We don't give up. We don't simply need to hang in there; we need to hang in there for as long as it takes, often for a very long time. We persevere.

Blind Faith

Now faith is being sure of what we hope for and certain of what we do not see.
—HEBREWS 11:1

Every day you make assumptions, predictions, forecasts, and stabs in the dark at work. You use what little information you have and make a not-as-informed-as-you'd-like decision. All that's left is for you to hope for the best. In a perfect world, we'd have every piece of information we need, and then some, before taking action of any sort. But alas, this isn't a perfect world. We rely on faith instead.

To understand faith, we have to close our eyes. Blind faith might not be an attractive concept, but Hebrews 11:1 could not be more precise: "Now faith is being sure of what we hope for and certain of what we do not see." Being a good steward of all available information means we see and perceive all we can. We ignore nothing. We engage our intellect fully. We think deeply. At the same time, we acknowledge that living by faith means there's stuff we can't see and information we don't have. We must realize that as a faith person we will fix our gaze on Jesus and let Him be responsible for all the questions we can't answer and all the data that's missing.

There's a book titled *If You Want God to Laugh, Show Him Your Business Plan*. What does the title indicate? That in the best of situations there is a dearth of good information; in the normal daily routine of life, enormous assumptions have to be made. The business life is full of what-ifs. We take the information we have, make assumptions, and take a leap. We're operating in the dark.

The good news about faith in Christ is exactly this: what seems like darkness to us is brilliantly obvious to Him. We might be blind, but we're not being led by the blind. I can handle that kind of blind faith.

Going, Without Knowing Where

> By faith Abraham, when called to go to a place he would later receive as his inheritance, obeyed and went, even though he did not know where he was going.
> —HEBREWS 11:8

Some of the most memorable trips we have taken as a family have been those where the destination was a mystery to the kids. My wife and I planned trips we thought the kids would enjoy and then gave the kids just enough information to keep them interested. The kids knew we were going on vacation and what kinds of clothes to pack. We told them what time to be up and ready to go. Beyond that, they knew virtually nothing. It was adventure of the highest magnitude—at least for them.

Our kids trusted us to take them somewhere they'd enjoy, and to keep them safe. They trusted that we were telling them the truth about what time we were leaving, what to pack, and that we were even going. They had faith in my wife and me.

Abraham had that same sort of faith in God when he went on his faith journey. "By faith Abraham, when called to go to a place he would later receive as his inheritance, obeyed and went, even though he did not know where he was going." He packed up, prepared, and followed where God called him to go—without so much as a map and a route highlighted. It's one thing to be willing to go. It's quite another to go without knowing where.

The utter reality is that no one knows where he or she is going. We think we do, but we really don't. We don't know what will happen one minute from now, much less twenty years down the road. Our perfectly planned careers, families, and accomplishments might change in an instant—if it's God's plan. A life of faith simply means acknowledging the obvious fact, and it means letting go of a future we're not able to direct anyway. It also means relaxing intentionally in the hands of Jesus and cheerfully allowing Him to show us the next few miles of the journey.

Built to Last

For he was looking forward to the city with foundations, whose architect and builder is God.

—HEBREWS 11:10

Have you ever read a management book that didn't talk about building a vision for your company? If so, I'd love to see it, because I never have. But these management gurus are on to something. Creating a plan for your career, your business, your life is crucial. You have to visualize where you want to be in order to get there—and, of course, pray that God will help you create your plan. Making your own without His help is pointless; He's in control, not you.

Having vision in a corporate context is absolutely crucial. It ranks right up there with mission and values. Abraham knew this business advice long before Stephen Covey wrote *The 7 Habits of Highly Effective People* or Brian Tracy tackled the topic. God had promised to make Abraham the father of a new generation, to have offspring more numerous than the stars in the heavens. God had also promised that the land Abraham stood on would be his forever. So Abraham looked at the hills, fields, trees, rocks, and rivers, and saw what? A city. He was a visionary—because he listened to God—and as visionaries are able to do, he saw what no one else did.

Articulating a vision means being able to paint some semblance of a picture of the future. In this context, Abraham was able to have a vision because he was tied closely to the voice of Jesus, who gave him a glimpse of what the future would hold.

Your vision as a believer is tied to the same source as Abraham's vision was. What do you see?

PART TWELVE

1 and 2 Peter

A LETTER TO SUFFERING BELIEVERS

Key Elements

Purpose: to encourage suffering Christians

Author: Peter

To whom written: Jewish Christians driven out of Jerusalem and scattered throughout Asia Minor, and all believers everywhere

Date written: about 62 to 64 A.D.

Key Themes

- Our salvation includes three elements: an expectant hope, an experiential faith, and an expressive love.
- Persecution and suffering should not steal our hope or deter us from standing firm.
- Submission is an essential ingredient to the Christian life, whether it be employees to their bosses, citizens to their governments, spouses to their mates, or saints to their Lord.
- God has given us all the necessary equipment to live the life He has called us to.

323

Preparing for Game Day

> Therefore, get your minds ready for action, being self-disciplined, and set your hope completely on the grace to be brought to you at the revelation of Jesus Christ.
> —1 PETER 1:13

Discipline is the key to an athlete's success. Athletes train hard, rising early each day and putting in many hours preparing for the big game. They eat foods that bolster their physical strength. They clock countless hours getting their bodies in top shape. They study tape after tape of game plays, mentally running through all the possibilities. They have to be sharp, alert, and ready for anything the game throws their way. Much like a businessperson entering a meeting: well-prepared, studied, sharp-witted, and ready to answer or solve any problem thrown on the table.

People toss around phrases that imply mental toughness is what counts; physical strength is just a little something extra. This is true when preparing for the game day with Christ. "Therefore, get your minds ready for action, being self-disciplined, and set your hope completely on the grace to be brought to you at the revelation of Jesus Christ." Meeting God is game day. Unlike athletes, we can't put the date of the game on our calendar and make sure we're prepared just for that day. We have to be prepared *every* day, because we don't know when Christ will return.

To be prepared, we have to exercise the things of our spirit even more than we exercise our bodies (or our boardroom banter). How? Keep God on the top of our mind. Visualize the goal; He is the goal. Everything we do must be in line with our goal. Therefore, we must exercise discipline of thought and discipline of action according to His demands. We must talk with Him daily, checking in to see how we're doing and letting Him know we're mentally still in the game. We won't let our opponents—the devil and the things of this world—psyche us out. God is our focus, and we've got our game faces on.

Are you ready?

Remain a Stranger

Since you call on a Father who judges each man's work impartially, live your lives as strangers here in reverent fear.
—1 PETER 1:17

In a tower on high, the big boss looks down. You often hear stories about what goes on in her office, but you wouldn't know, personally. You've never been there. She speaks to the employees through memos, e-mails, and a bevy of assistants and high-level colleagues. You fear her, as well as respect her. She runs a tight ship, and you're happy to be on it. But you know your place and keep your distance. You follow her orders when they come down through the pipeline. You don't want to disappoint the corporate expectations.

This isn't the kind of fear you'd see in someone who's afraid of physical harm or incurring the wrath of an angry dictator. Instead, it's what you'd expect of a person who admires and respects someone in a higher position.

God is our boss in a higher position. He talks to us in many ways, and we often hear stories about Him. But we've never seen Him face to face. Yet we still hold a healthy respect for Him, admiring Him and looking up to Him in all that we do. True, we're not strangers to God. He knows our names—unlike the boss on the top floor—and He knows every last thing about us. But this doesn't mean we can be casual about our relationship with Him. What He says, thinks, demands, or requests matters to us, and we're not to take Him lightly.

So when Peter calls us to live our lives as strangers in reverent fear, he doesn't want us to shake in our boots and keep our distance from God. He does, however, want us to know that there will always be distance between us and the Lord, until the day we meet Him face to face. Until then, we must look up to Him, respect Him, and follow His directives. Then one day, we'll get to see what *really* goes on in the tower on high.

Throw Away the Bad Stuff

> So rid yourselves of all wickedness, all deceit, hypocrisy, envy, and all slander.
> —I PETER 2:I

I have a couple of friends who detest grocery shopping. One look inside their perpetually empty refrigerator, and you can tell they don't much like shopping for food. They say, "It's a long, tedious task that we've not been able to find much joy in, especially when it comes time to pay the enormous bill."

Unfortunately, they're also not too good at eating all of their leftovers. Nor do they do particularly well with throwing out the leftovers. Instead, they tend to let stuff ferment in the fridge until they finally go to the grocery store again, come home with bundles of food, and dig out the old stuff to find room for the fresh, new food. It's not always a fun task, but they say it feels great, once it's all said and done, to have a fresh, clean refrigerator again filled with healthy, nourishing food—unlike the junk that's been sitting in there growing mold and stinking up the place.

Now that I've painted you a not-so-pretty picture, let's take it one step further. Going to God in prayer is much more pleasant than going to the grocery store (if you ask my friends). But sometimes we fail to go to Him often enough and bad stuff piles up in our hearts, fermenting, stinking, and growing, taking over all the good things we've still got in our hearts—like the wilting salad from two weeks ago taking over their fridge.

Wickedness, deceit, hypocrisy, envy, and slander all have a way of working themselves into our hearts, whether we like it or not. It's our job to clean out the spiritual fridge, ridding ourselves of the rotten things, and making room for the fresh stuff—things that are of God.

What's molding in your heart? Jealousy of a coworker? Bitterness toward your boss? Resentment over a missed promotion or perceived slight? Maybe it's that tendency to lie a bit on the job—telling tales to make yourself look better, land a deal, or get out of trouble. Whatever it is, it's time to throw it out. Get out the cleaning solution—prayer—and scrub your heart clean. Then fill it with nourishment—more prayer, God's word, fellowship with other believers—and enjoy the full feeling you get from God.

And please, don't let your moldy stuff accumulate, as these friends do with leftovers. Give God a clean home in which to live— and yourself the peace of knowing He's there.

Taste Test

Like newborn infants, desire the unadulterated spiritual milk, so that you may grow by it in your salvation, since you have tasted that the Lord is good.
—I PETER 2:2–3

I'm a coffee addict. I blame it on colleagues who suffer the same condition. For years, they've brought their steaming hot, deliciously fragrant cups of Starbucks into my office, tempting me to join the java club. You probably know what I'm talking about. No longer do people gather around the water cooler to chat. Now they gather around the coffee pot, discussing gourmet coffees, fresh-brewed versus instant, Starbucks versus QuikTrip.

Before this, my drink of choice was water. Several glasses a day of pure, healthy, nourishing water. I knew no better, so I craved nothing more. I was healthy. Then, desperate for caffeine and warmth, I gave in to the temptation. Now I'm hooked.

No one would confuse which drink is healthier, water or coffee. Water is pure, unaltered, healthy, nourishing, and everything I need in this world. The coffee, although it tastes good, is full of caffeine and other elements that don't add to my physical well-being. Coffee even tastes bitter; I add plenty of sugar and creamer to sweeten it and mask the bitter taste. You know, the devil does that to parts of the world that we think aren't so great at first. He dresses them up, sweetens them to our tastes, and then hooks us. Just think about it: impure entertainment; immoral actions, whether at home or at work; crude language and jokes with coworkers; manipulations and lies to get the job done. Suddenly we have developed an alien taste bud that needs to be satisfied.

I still love a good cup of coffee. My guess is that I always will. However, I need to upgrade my intake of pure, sparkling water.

What are you drinking?

What About the Bad Boss?

> Household slaves, submit yourselves to your masters with all respect, not only to the good and gentle but also to the cruel. For it brings favor if, because of conscience toward God, someone endures grief from suffering unjustly. For what credit is there if you endure when you sin and are beaten? But when you do good and suffer, if you endure, it brings favor with God.
> —I PETER 2:18–20

Your boss bawls you out constantly. She never gives you credit for a job well done. Or she takes credit for your work when it behooves her—and makes you her scapegoat when credit would cost her job. She can't make up her mind what she wants you to do with a project. The focus changes daily. She gossips all the time, making you uncomfortable, along with everyone else in the office.

Let's face it; not all bosses are good. In fact, many of them are terrible managers. But for some reason we stay put. We take the abuse they dish out, keep our nose to the grindstone, and pray for something better to come along. Above all, we still show respect and kindness, even when we feel the boss doesn't deserve it.

Peter tells us in these verses, in essence, to submit to our boss in respect, even when the boss is less than kind. He calls on us to suffer, endure it, and find favor with God. It might seem a little silly to stick with something we can't stand—and there's no reason we have to stay in a terrible job—but it makes sense to treat our boss, good or bad, with ample respect. Why? Because, even though we don't think bosses deserve it, God still loves them. Likewise, we don't deserve the grace, mercy, and love He heaps on us—but He still gives it anyway. So, being made in His image, we must follow along, showing love, mercy, and respect to those around us.

Besides, there are a host of things to learn about character from staying under the pressure load. The ability to persevere under hardship is a lesson we all must learn somewhere, sometime. The office is a great school for that course.

It's not easy, and God recognizes it. But He does still call for respect. That's what He gives us, and that's what He requires us to give others. It won't all be for naught; God will reward us in the end. We just have to hang in there till then!

Payback Time

> . . . not paying back evil for evil or insult for insult but with blessing, because to this you were called so that you may inherit a blessing.
> —I PETER 3:9

In our culture, being sharp-witted (or sharp-tongued) enough to hurl insults, barbs, and jabs at friends, coworkers, and even relatives is considered cool. Series of jokes—and even entire television shows—revolve around insulting other people. Millions of people pay to hear such insensitive remarks.

This form of "entertainment" has carried over into the office place. It's common, as you surely know, for coworkers to rib each other about clients, personal lives, job status, and many other things. It doesn't stop there; truly upset coworkers feel the need to let it all out. They berate, belittle, insult, and hurt their colleagues when they're upset, trying to make themselves feel better.

It's tempting to respond in kind when a coworker's acidic tongue strikes. It may even entertain others to hear your rebuttal. Choosing not to respond may make you look humorless, cowardly, or inept. But that's beside the point when you take into account God's feelings on the subject: ". . . not paying back evil for evil or insult for insult but with blessing. . . ."

Have you ever thought about praying for a coworker when he or she is less than gracious? The temptation to strike back in kind is overwhelming, and just then the last thing you're thinking about is blessing the offender. But that's just what God wants us to do. Someone hurts your feelings? Don't get mad, and don't get even. Just pray. Pray for patience to handle the situation; pray for guidance in whether to respond; pray for a kind, loving, and forgiving heart, not one of hatred and bitterness; pray that the other person feels God's love.

Think about a specific situation in which you answered back—but should have stayed silent. How would the situation have changed had you prayed to God for guidance instead of opening your mouth? Going jab-for-jab may make you feel better, but it won't do anything to please God—and He's your most important audience.

Do Your Homework

But in your hearts set apart Christ as Lord. Always be prepared to give an answer to everyone who asks you to give the reason for the hope that you have.
—I PETER 3:15

D o you remember what it felt like in high school to fear the teacher calling on you each day? The teacher had a way of knowing when you weren't prepared. Six classmates would raise their hands, falling out of their seats to answer. Yet you'd get the joy of struggling through the ordeal.

In college you learned—or maybe not—to be better prepared. Reading the text, reviewing your notes, and staying alert seemed to help. Even now, there's always a chance your boss will call on you to answer a question, present ideas, or even defend your place in the organization. Are you prepared?

Guess what: you also have to prepare to share your faith with anyone who might ask. "Always be prepared to give an answer to everyone who asks you to give the reason for the hope that you have," Peter says. You never know when someone will broach the subject with you, and if you're living as a witness to God's love and your faith in Him it's inevitable that someone will ask. Are you prepared to answer? What will you say to explain your faith and what God has done for you?

For instance, a friend shared a story with me. She prayed regularly for an opportunity to share the story of Christ's love with a coworker. She anticipated questions nonbelievers might ask and even brushed up on the answers. She was prepared for that one moment in time when someone would notice the light in her and give her the opportunity to share. One day, a coworker, battered and bruised from stress, rough deadlines, and difficulties in the job asked my friend what it was that made her so upbeat and positive in the midst of so much turmoil in the workplace. Now, there's an opening if I ever heard one!

Have you done your homework for such a situation? Be prepared. You never know when the Teacher will call on you.

All the Right Equipment

His divine power has given us everything we need for life and godliness through our knowledge of Him who called us by His own glory and goodness.
—2 PETER 1:3

During the tough economic times we've had in recent years, organizations are doing everything they can to cut costs. Chances are, you've been affected in one way or another. Some companies make cuts responsibly, only taking away the superfluous, leaving the necessary. But I've heard, more than once, that others are cutting to the bone. They're taking away the very things workers need to get the job done. A recent TV commercial even parodies this trend, showing all of the employees sharing one pen and one notepad, because they can't afford anything more.

The good news is that, as employees of God, we'll never find ourselves short of the equipment we need to complete the job. Peter says, "His divine power has given us everything we need for life and godliness. . . ."

God provides strength, knowledge, peace, mercy, love, and so much more. In Matthew 6:33, Jesus says, "But seek first His kingdom and His righteousness, and all these things will be given to you as well." As God feeds the birds and clothes the lilies, He also takes care of all of our needs, never leaving us without the necessities of life. If you find yourself lacking something, just ask! "For everyone who asks receives; he who seeks finds; and to him who knocks, the door will be opened" (Matthew 7:8).

Good managers make sure their employees have everything they need to succeed, and they are open to requests for additional items. God, the best manager possible, knows this. In fact, He invented the concept of keeping his workers fully stocked and ready to go.

Full Participation

Through these He has given us His very great and precious promises, so that through them you may participate in the divine nature and escape the corruption in the world caused by evil desires.
—2 PETER 1:4

Every day, people's names appear on mastheads, rosters, business documents, and anywhere else you can think of, even though they didn't do much to deserve the recognition. An intern spends a summer with a company, sitting in on meetings, making copies, and occasionally running a few numbers or glancing over a document or two. The intern and the boss both know full well that the boss is running the ship; the intern's just along for the ride. But sitting in on the activities allows her to have a hand in the project, at least.

Alternatively, a group is assigned a project. The majority head up the project, but a couple of newcomers sit in to get a feel for the process. They offer a few ideas, and their names make it onto the final result.

People like to feel a part of good things, even when they haven't done that much. Quite frankly, God allows us to have a hand in our lives to keep us involved. But there's no question that God is ultimately in charge of what happens. ". . . so that through them you may participate in the divine nature . . ." it says in this verse. God kindly grants us permission to participate; He wants our full attention and acknowledgment of what He's doing in our lives. This is the key point: God is the group leader, the foreman of the project, the workhorse who gets the job done. We're just along for the ride, and at our best we're allowing Him to do His job in us.

This is where we come in. We have to be amenable to the work He wants to do. We have to grant Him full permission to use us as He sees fit. In return, He adds our names to His organizational roster.

Adding to the Bottom Line

> For this very reason, make every effort to add to your faith goodness; and to goodness, knowledge; and to knowledge, self-control; and to self-control, perseverance; and to perseverance, godliness; and to godliness, brotherly kindness; and to brotherly kindness, love.
> —2 PETER 1:5–7

At the end of the year, companies make heroic efforts to push as much money as possible to the bottom line. They want their numbers to look good, showing those in the know (their corporate headquarters, or the stockholders) that they were able to meet and maybe even exceed the plan for the year. There's a push in the last quarter to cut costs everywhere possible, from withholding bonuses to not ordering extra batches of stationery and cutting down on business travel. Whatever it takes to add a penny here and a dollar there to the bottom line. In the end, the efforts make for a more profitable company.

We, too, have a need to push more to the bottom line. But instead of cutting items out of our budget, Peter instructs us to add several things to our operating costs, namely, faith, goodness, knowledge, self-control, perseverance, godliness, brotherly kindness, and love. Adding all of these things increases our self-worth and our worth to the King. Interestingly enough, adding these Godly traits to our personal balance sheet automatically takes away the draining, unproductive items that adversely affect our bottom line. With love, godliness, self-control, and the other traits mentioned, there's no room left for greed, hatred, jealousy, and things of an evil nature.

This is not to say getting your personal balance sheet under control is easy. Just as it hurts to cut the extras you enjoy out of the office budget (read: no more free colas and Friday afternoon snacks), ridding yourself of ungodly traits doesn't come easily. But you don't have to go it alone. God's here to help, if only you ask.

Don't Be Naïve

> But there were also false prophets among the people, just as there
> will be false teachers among you. They will secretly introduce
> destructive heresies, even denying the sovereign Lord who
> bought them—bringing swift destruction on themselves.
> —2 PETER 2:1

To be naïve means to be deficient in worldly wisdom or informed judgment. What's the cure? Information. The more
informed and better read we are, the harder it will be for people
to take advantage of us. That's the point Peter tries to make in the
verse: don't think you're immune to contact with false teachers and
the harm they'll bring to your life.

Peter wrote this letter hundreds of years ago, long before our
time. But the message still applies—maybe even more so today,
when it's often considered wrong to think one religion is best. Instead, we're supposed to be tolerant and accepting of all faiths, no
matter what they believe. The problem with that is we're much
more susceptible to hearing, accepting, and even believing something other than what Christ teaches. Peter says ". . . there will be
false teachers among you. They will secretly introduce destructive
heresies, even denying the sovereign Lord."

How can they secretly introduce destructive heresies? By engaging you in conversation that contradicts your beliefs. In the name
of tolerance, they'd find it unacceptable for you to disagree. Or, con-
sidering how prevalent television, movies, radio, and the Internet

are in our homes, there's no telling what false teachings we're picking up in these media. And we invite them into our homes!

Beware of what you allow into your home and into your mind. That simple sitcom you're watching doesn't teach God's salvation, though the characters proclaim to be followers of Christ; that movie portrays another way to get to God—something we know isn't true. Don't be naïve. Hold your ground, protect your heart, and know that God is the only way. Not sure if what you're hearing is true? Check it out in the Bible. That's what it's there for.

It Will Be OK

. . . if this is so, then the Lord knows how to rescue Godly men from trials and to hold the unrighteous for the day of judgment, while continuing their punishment.
—2 PETER 2:9

A lot of innocent or unsuspecting people have had their careers ruined as a result of greed and misdeeds in their organization. A few people err in judgment, costing hundreds to lose their jobs, retirement plans, life savings, and more. The unsuspecting bear the stigma of a collapsed company with corrupt leaders.

A hard pill to swallow, sure. But the good news is that carrying the reputation of a former employee of a corrupt company is a worldly title. The employees who kept their faith in God, were true to their word, and acted honorably—even amid scandal—will be saved by God. In 2 Peter 2:4–8, Peter outlines several instances in the Bible in which God saved righteous people who lived among the dishonorable people, among them Lot and Noah. He's speaking to us, here, by showing how important it is to hold on to our values, our faith, our devotion to Him, no matter what's going on around us. God knows the circumstances, and He will reward us for standing strong in the midst of corruption.

One final note: it's tempting to want to dole out punishment or revenge to those who neglect to follow God's ways, which might put you and your career on the line. But there's no need for you to sin out of your own anger or revenge. In the verse here, Peter says that God will save the Godly from trials and hold the unrighteous for the day of judgment, while continuing their punishment. The unrighteous will not go unpunished, but it's God's job to reprimand, not ours.

Stand strong in the knowledge that if you follow God, no matter the circumstances, He will bring you through just fine.

Keep It Between the Ditches

> They have left the straight way and wandered off to follow the way of Balaam son of Beor, who loved the wages of wickedness.
> —2 PETER 2:15

Back in Boy Scouts and Girl Scouts or on church camping trips, we all learned the importance of staying on the designated path the leader set out for us in the woods. Remember?

"For your own safety. . . ." The leaders warned of the dangers that lurked beyond the path, scaring us into obedience.

Our workplace might not be the campground of yesteryear (though it sometimes holds the same wild and dangerous feel). But there's still something to be said for sticking to the straight and narrow path, not venturing too far into the unknown of the woods. The path here is not made of trampled-down grass or sash-marked trees; instead it's marked by the words of God.

Today's workplace holds many opportunities to veer off God's path: corruption, lying, cheating, greed, jealousy, revenge. The list goes on and on, unfortunately. Peter talks in this verse about men following Balaam instead of sticking to the path God set out for them. Greed, the main motivator behind Balaam's misguided actions, is one of the biggest incentives for people who veer off the path today as well.

My advice? Keep yourself between the ditches. Follow God's path. Obviously, if He created the path, it will lead you to Him. All other paths lead somewhere you don't want to go.

Reminder Notice

Dear friends, this is now my second letter to you. I have written both of them as reminders to stimulate you to wholesome thinking.

—2 PETER 3:1

Forget to pay a utility or credit card bill, and you'd better believe you'll find a "friendly reminder notice" waiting in your mailbox in just a few days. Let a magazine subscription come within six months of expiring, and you'll also find a few reminders clogging up your mailbox. Doctors, dentists, even veterinarians send out reminders for visits. Some reminders we want; others, we could do without.

The kind of reminders Peter sent out were ones to live by. We still do. He sent reminders to his friends, fellow believers, to keep them on track with their faith in God. He wanted to encourage them to continue seeking God and to live in accordance with His will. In his letters he warned them against false teachers, encouraged them to diligently pursue a relationship with God, and tried to prepare them for Christ's return. No one ever wants their friends left behind; Peter was doing what he could to make sure it didn't happen to believers (then, and still today) with the letters he wrote.

What reminders do you have in place to keep you on track with God? Do you post Scripture verses around your office or in your daily planner? Do you have a prayer partner, daily devotionals, or an accountability partner or group to keep God foremost on your mind? It's no secret that people tend to think about the things they're surrounded by. If you surround yourself with the word of God, whether written, in your heart, or in the presence of fellow believers who spur you along, then you'll have an easier time remembering Him in all that you do.

If utility companies can send reminders, then surely you can set up a few for yourself to ensure your relationship with Christ. You wouldn't want your final bill to come back overdue!

Head in the Sand

> But they deliberately forget that long ago by God's word the heavens existed and the earth was formed out of water and by water.
> —2 PETER 3:5

Your daily planner is full. Sticky notes cover your desk, reminding you of tasks to complete. The phone rings off the hook, and every five minutes someone stops by your office or sends you an e-mail requesting a "moment of your time," which usually ends up being a lot more than a moment. Saying you're busy is an understatement.

Sometimes, amid such a hectic schedule, it's easy to conveniently forget tasks you find unimportant or not worthy of your time—at least not right now. For me, filing always takes a back seat. Sometimes correspondence waits a little longer than necessary. I just "forget" about it for a few days, until I can fit it back into my schedule. There's no harm in that; it just helps me reprioritize my limited time.

I'm sure you can relate. But do you know that some people conveniently forget that God created this world in which we live, and that He is our savior? Are you one of those people? In this verse, Peter says, "But they deliberately forget that long ago by God's word the heavens existed and the earth was formed out of water and by water." Sometimes it's easier to forget about God and His power, and that He will be our final judge when all is said and done. It makes us feel less guilty about our lives, because without God we're without judgment. We can file Him away for when we've got more time and when we're more together than now.

But without God, we're without grace, love, mercy, support, guidance, and so many other wonderful things that help us survive the daily grind. We can't stick our head in the sand and pretend that He doesn't exist—like the pile of work you tossed under your desk. God has always been there, and He always will be, fortunately for us. Let's not forget Him in our busy lives. We can't afford to.

Promises Made, Promises Kept

The Lord is not slow in keeping His promise, as some understand slowness. He is patient with you, not wanting anyone to perish, but everyone to come to repentance.

—2 PETER 3:9

Getting your timing in sync with other people's timing is sometimes difficult. When you say you'll get to an assignment "soon," your version and your colleague's version of soon might differ. You might be thinking "a few days," while he's thinking "this afternoon."

This varying timetable makes itself abundantly evident in marriage. She wants the cabinet door fixed, and says so. He assumes this means whenever he gets to it; she, of course, means right away. One of the best pieces of marriage advice I ever heard was that when asking for something to be done, give a reason and a clear timetable to help your spouse understand the urgency—and allay any miscommunication and potential problems.

However, this communication technique doesn't work when talking to God. We can't pray for a new job, a raise, or just whatever we want—and tell Him when and why we want it. He doesn't work that way. God has His own timetable for everything, and we must align ourselves to His plan, not the other way around.

In this verse, Peter reminds believers that God hasn't forgotten about the promises He made to come back for us. Instead, He is working in His own time, taking longer than many people want in order to give more nonbelievers a chance to find salvation in Him before it's too late. That's a good message for us to remember; God has a reason for everything, even if it's not clear to us. He promises that He will hear our prayers; however, He will handle the answering side of things when it fits into His plan.

In 1 Kings 8:20, the author says, "The Lord has kept the promise He made: I have succeeded David my father and now I sit on the throne of Israel, just as the Lord promised. . . ." Further proof that He will keep His word. Our part in this? Keep the faith, be patient, and understand that He's working for our good.

Primary Residence

But in keeping with His promise we are looking forward
to a new heaven and a new earth, the home of righteousness.
—2 PETER 3:13

Changing residence ranks high on the list of major life stressors, whether you're moving to fulfill a job commitment, to be closer to family (or farther from them), or just to relocate across town to improve your living conditions. The move likely involves spending lots of time online researching schools, neighborhoods, local governments, tax rates, pay scales, and much more. Not to mention finding just the right apartment or house to suit your needs.

A lot of effort goes into making the change of address go smoothly. Just imagine if at least that amount of effort went into securing our place in an eternal residence. God promises a place in heaven for those who follow Him faithfully—"the home of righteousness," as it's called in this verse.

Have you researched your future residence? Have you talked with the Landlord to see what kind of place you're upgrading to? Have you checked out the requirements of living there? How about the waiting list: is your name on it? You can ensure your place in heaven by doing all of these things. Your Bible is your prime neighborhood guide. It tells you what to expect, how to behave, and rules and regulations; it even outlines the joyous events that take place in your new neighborhood. Of course, it's always a good idea to talk with the Person in charge before moving. What kind of relationship do you have with your future Landlord? Do you see eye-to-eye on His policies? Do you trust Him to take care of you? Finally, you have to check out the waiting list. Giving your heart over to Him will ensure He has your name on the list—and your room ready and waiting when your time comes.

So what will your final mailing address say? Heaven, with Christ your savior? Or somewhere else? It's up to you to decide.

PART THIRTEEN

1, 2, and 3 John
LETTERS FROM A VERY OLD MAN

Key Elements

Purpose: to reassure Christians in their faith and to counter false teachings

Author: the apostle John

To whom written: the letter was untitled and written to no particular church; it was sent as a pastoral letter to several Gentile congregations and also written to all believers everywhere

Date written: between 85 and 90 A.D.

Key Themes

- While Paul uses the terms faith, hope, and love, John uses light, life, and love to describe the journey with Jesus.
- Walking in the truth is the posture for victoriously living the life of faith.
- We are to be transformers of the world, not adapters within the world.

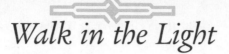

Walk in the Light

But if we walk in the light, as He is in the light, we have
fellowship with one another, and the blood of Jesus,
His Son, purifies us from all sin.
—I JOHN 1:7

To walk in the light of God means to have full knowledge of
God and a true relationship with Him. In the dark, you're
left to your own devices, and that's not a comforting thought.

When you're in the woods, a cave, or even your own house
without light, you're sure to stumble along the way. Walking in the
woods without light will cause you to stub your toe, run into a
tree, trip over a fallen log, or worse. But a lantern or flashlight can
guide your way, making the path clear and obvious. The light exposes dangers lurking in the dark and helps prepare you for what
lies ahead.

God is our lantern in the woods. He exposes the dangers of
this world when we walk in His light. In this verse, the apostle
John contrasts light and darkness. The light is God's word, truth,
and goodness. The darkness, however, is false teachings, words that
contradict God's words, things of evil nature. False teachers were
abundant in John's day, and by warning his people to walk in the
light he was challenging them to find out whether the teachers'
words were true by comparing them to what God says. This teaching holds true and is valuable for us today, especially in light of so
many new religions that claim to believe in God—but teach things
far from what God wants from us.

How do we walk in His light? By reading and believing His word only, by praying for truth and guidance, and by allowing Him to shine light on our path.

His Word Is His Bond

If we confess our sins, He is faithful and just and will forgive us our sins and purify us from all unrighteousness.
—I JOHN I:9

Once upon a time, people built businesses on the basis of their word and a handshake. Contracts weren't necessary. They upheld their end of the deal because of a sense of honor. They couldn't go back on their word.

My, how this world has changed. Now, even a written contract isn't a guarantee that work will be completed as promised. Contracts, lawsuits, and legal rulings serve to force one party to uphold its end of the bargain. "Get it in writing" is the rule to live by in today's business world. Just ask anyone who's failed to do so.

But we don't need a contract from Jesus to believe in His promises. He tells us He will be faithful and forgive us when we ask—and He stands by that word. Always has, always will.

Doubt it? Don't. Instead, see what the Bible says about God's faithfulness. In Deuteronomy 7:9, Moses says, "Know therefore that the Lord your God is God; He is the faithful God, keeping His covenant of love to a thousand generations of those who love

Him and keep His commands." In Psalm 117:2, we're told, "For great is His love toward us, and the faithfulness of the Lord endures forever." Need more proof that God keeps His promises? See Psalm 145:13: "The Lord is faithful to all His promises and loving toward all He has made."

God keeps His promises, even when your business partners and work associates don't. Yes, we all sin in this lifetime. God promises that when we seek Him with a repentant heart, He will forgive. There's no question about it.

Are you hanging on to lingering regret over sins, unsure He'll forgive you? He will, if only you ask. You have His word on that, and His word is good enough. Now, if only the rest of our world understood that. . . .

My Defense Attorney

My dear children, I write this to you so that you will not sin. But if anybody does sin, we have one who speaks to the Father in our defense—Jesus Christ, the Righteous One.
—1 JOHN 2:1

A man is charged in a court of law with stealing from the company at which he worked. He doesn't have much money to hire a prestigious defense attorney. Besides, he knows he's guilty. His heart once rested in God, but the strain of a hard life has led him off course, though he still believes in Jesus, our true defender. So he appeals to the courts: "Jesus Christ will be my defense today."

Sound far-fetched? Well, I can't vouch for His experience in the court of law, but Jesus does step in on our behalf when we find ourselves on the wrong side of God's "law." Now, God's plan isn't for us to sin, ask forgiveness, and then repeat. He doesn't want us to sin at all. But He knows we will, even if we truly believe in Him and want to live righteously. He is prepared to bail us out when the time comes. His Son, Jesus Christ, appeals to the Father, our loving Judge, on our behalf. The judge then expunges our sin from the record.

There isn't a better trial lawyer in the land. Our advocate understands our humanity and sin. He is more than acquainted with our frail makeup, and He doesn't look down on us. He rises to stand next to us and plead our case.

Here's proof that God, the Judge, works in our favor: because of Jesus' death on the cross, He has already paid for our sins. He has already paid the defense fee, and the Judge has already heard the case—and decided in our favor. There's an open-and-shut case if I ever heard one.

Love God, Not the World

Do not love the world or anything in the world. If anyone loves the world, the love of the Father is not in him.
—1 JOHN 2:15

We hear the phrase "loving the world" often. But do we really know what it means? People generally think of loving the world as loving material gain, physical desires, and ungodly activities. This is true, but there's more to it than that. Loving the world is as much what lies inward as it is outward displays of our heart's desires. Just as a company's actions are an outward display of its true values and motivations.

Your organization (most organizations, really) creates a vision or mission statement. Great. But to really get anywhere, everyone must truly believe the mission and lay out steps to follow it—and plan ways to stay on track, not to let outside influences interfere with a plan. An organization that truly follows its mission will show the world what's important at its heart by its actions.

A true follower of Christ, likewise, will show the world his or her true heart by the actions taken. What's in your heart? Greed? Lust? Pride? Envy? If so, your behavior likely shows those worldly actions. If love, joy, peace, and God's will are in your heart, your actions show that, too. Those are Godly characteristics, not worldly ones.

We're told in Philippians 4:13, "Finally, brothers, whatever is true, whatever is noble, whatever is right, whatever is pure, whatever is lovely, whatever is admirable—if anything is excellent or praiseworthy—think about such things. Whatever you have learned or received or heard from me or seen in me—put into practice. And the God of peace will be with you." If we follow this simple advice, there's no way we could follow the world, in actions or in thought.

Where does your heart lie?

God and Jesus—
The Ultimate Package Deal

No one who denies the Son has the Father;
whoever acknowledges the Son has the Father also.
—I JOHN 2:23

People love to buy things in packages. Marketing departments have known this for a long time. If they sell pens individually, consumers will think they're too expensive for just one nice pen. But if they package three pens with a notepad or a desk calendar—and charge a total of what each item would cost individually—consumers think it's a good deal. We see value in packaging like items, and we appreciate companies' putting all of our needs together in one easy-to-buy set.

Believing in God *and* Jesus is a package deal. It's impossible to believe in God but not in Jesus. They go together. Either you believe or you don't; it's as simple as that. But many people in this world believe only in one, without true faith in the other: "No one who denies the Son has the Father; whoever acknowledges the Son has the Father also."

Believing in God without Jesus just doesn't work. It's like technology. It never fails that I buy a piece of technology and once I get the item home I realize it won't work without some other cable, disk, or accessory. So what do I do? I have to run back out and spend even more money for the accessory to make the first purchase work. I don't just forget about the first purchase; that would be a waste of money and a silly idea.

People who want to believe in God need to realize that if you buy into one belief you must buy into the other, as well. Are you missing Jesus, the essential element in faith? If so, do as you'd do for technology. Get back to the source (talk to God) and get what you need. Don't let your belief in God go to waste without a belief in Jesus, too.

Born of Him

No one who is born of God will continue to sin, because God's seed remains in him; he cannot go on sinning, because he has been born of God.

—1 JOHN 3:9

Anyone who works for a company that makes and sells products to the public knows the rule: don't buy products from your competitors. Period. Doing so shows an utter lack of company loyalty, reduces your own company's profits, and may put your job in jeopardy. Likewise, you'd never sell trade secrets to your competitor, or cheer that company on, driving more business to it—and away from yours.

Yet every day followers of Christ buy from the competitor—Satan. We sell him trade secrets, we cheer him on by acting the way he wants us to act. It's a question of loyalty. Do we want God's company to succeed, or Satan's?

To make God's company prosper, we must stay loyal to Him. We must shun sin, live a righteous life, and watch His company flourish. We can't switch our loyalties to suit ourselves. God says that because we are born of Him—technically, we are His descendants—we will not continue to cheer for Satan's company. In 1 John 3:2, John says, ". . . now we are children of God, and what we will be has not yet been made known. But we know that when He appears, we shall be like Him, for we shall see Him as He is." God raised us, His children, properly. He has taught us right from wrong. His seed is in us.

We'd never shame our company by being seen buying a competitor's product. We need to hold that same fierce loyalty for our God. We can't shame Him by turning away from His teachings. Instead we must make Him delight in us, rather than sin and please the devil, the one Jesus was sent to protect us from.

Love One Another

This is the message you heard from the beginning: We should love one another.
—I JOHN 3:11

What does the word *love* stir up in your mind? Does it evoke feelings of affection for another person? In our culture, we use the word to say we really like ice cream, chocolate, our new computer. The list goes on.

In God's eyes, though, love applies to so much more than that. In 1 John 3:23 we're told, "And this is His command: to believe in the name of His Son, Jesus Christ, and to love one another as He commanded." God commanded us to love one another. Notice it isn't a suggestion or implication, but a command. The dictionary says to command is to "direct with authority; give orders to; to exercise dominating, authoritative influence over." I'd say God definitely has dominating, authoritative influence over us, and it's our job to obey Him.

He commands us—everyone—to love one another. This means loving the neighbor next door who snoops into your business, the irritating coworkers who never let you get any work done, and the rude sales clerk at your grocery store.

Let's face it: loving everyone is not easy. I can say with certainty that I'm not always the easiest person to love, either. My spouse can attest to that. But God commands us to do so, and He doesn't say it just once. In fact, He issues this directive many times in the Bible. He must be serious.

What does it mean to love one another? To help others, respect them, put their needs first. To consider them in your actions, to treat them as God Himself would treat them. It means not just action but an inner, Christlike love toward all people.

Don't worry, you won't have to remember everyone at Valentine's Day and anniversaries. One person is enough to take care of on those days. But you do have to remember them daily. God commands us to love one another, and that means always.

Check your heart. Do you love those around you? Even the ones who get on your nerves? God does. To be more like God, we must, too.

Share with Those in Need

If anyone has material possessions and sees his brother in need but has no pity on him, how can the love of God be in him?
—I JOHN 3:17

Giving at Christmas time is a wonderful way to spread the spirit of Christ to those in the community who have less than we do. But throughout the year, there are many people who need our help, and we turn a blind eye. Some of these people don't live in a homeless shelter or on the rough side of town. Actually, some of these people work right in our office. We work with them each day, pass them in the hallways, even dine with them at lunch. But somehow we turn a blind eye to their needs.

Maybe you think the person in need isn't deserving of your help. Maybe you think because he didn't help you last year when you needed it you won't help him either. Or maybe you simply think you can't afford to give. We all use any number of rationalizations, really, as to why we shouldn't have to help a brother in need. But the bottom line is that God instructs us to. In 1 John 3:17, John says that if we don't help others, we don't have the love of God in us. God commands us to love one another in 1 John 3:23, so if we don't have God's love in us and we don't help others, we're directly disobeying God's orders.

Helping another doesn't have to mean giving a huge monetary gift—though that is sometimes warranted and greatly appreciated by those in need, when you can do so. Instead, think about the little ways you can help. If you see a coworker struggling to buy groceries, make an extra casserole when you're cooking for yourself and bring it in to share over lunch. Or invite her family over for dinner occasionally. They'll appreciate the warm meal and you'll be able to witness God's love to them at the same time. Or if you see someone with car trouble and you're able to do repairs, offer your services. You never know whether or not that person could have afforded professional help and what your kindness might mean.

Think about others in need all the time, not just during the holidays. Helping your brother or sister in need does so much more than just getting a sibling through the physical difficulty; it shows your true spirit, and in turn shows him or her a glimpse of God.

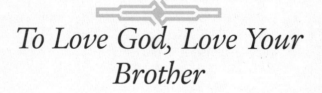

To Love God, Love Your Brother

And He has given us this command: Whoever loves God must also love his brother.

—I JOHN 4:21

A true test of your love for God doesn't come on Sunday morning, when the sermon is strong, the songs are powerful, and you're ready to praise Him. No, the true test comes when your coworker fails to get his part of the project done on time and you're forced to deal with the consequences. How you handle the situation; whether you yell at your coworker and feel harsh anger and resentment toward him; or whether you quietly pick up the pieces, assess the situation, and move on shows God how much you love Him.

Loving God doesn't count for much if we don't follow His instructions to love others. Just loving Him, while blasting coworkers, friends, and family for their errors and feeling something less than love for others, does not indicate true love and respect for our creator. Why should we love others? For a multitude of reasons, the first being that God tells us to. Many times. But the next is that God made us in His image. Every single one of us. Not just the people we like, not just ourselves, but everyone. How can we hate someone who was born in God's likeness? Whatever ill feelings we have toward others, God feels them from us too.

That's something for all of us to think about next time ugly feelings surface. We're not just hurting others; we're not just hurting ourselves. We're hurting God. It's safe to assume that's the last thing any of His followers want to do.

We Ask, He Hears

This is the confidence we have in approaching God: that if we ask anything according to His will, He hears us.
—1 JOHN 5:14

Approaching the boss and asking for a raise is one of the scariest things a person has to do in the office environment.

There's no guarantee that the boss will even grant you the chance to make your request, let alone hear you out when you speak. And getting the raise you request? That's a huge gamble in itself. So it's clear why normally confident people might be shaking in their boots at the thought of entering the boss's office for this reason.

We're lucky, though, that we can approach our heavenly Boss—the One who truly matters—for anything we want and we don't have to be afraid. God not only welcomes us into His office but listens to every word we have to say, every thought that's on our minds, every concern we're struggling to handle.

Here's the rub: "if we ask anything according to His will, He hears us," the verse says. Now, approaching God for a raise or a new car or just anything at all that we want doesn't cut it. God hears us when we ask according to *His* will, not ours. If our will is in line with His will, we'd never dream of asking for something He doesn't want to give us.

Aligning our will to God's is a process of praying for Him to show us His will. We must be open to following what He has in store for us and be able to pray that we will hear what He wants us to do and follow through on what He calls us to do, instead of praying that He will do our bidding. God doesn't work that way.

What have you asked God for recently that you feel He hasn't given you? List three things you've asked for, and then search your heart and determine whose will you were asking for—God's or yours. He will hear you; you've just got to know how to ask.

Grace, Mercy, and Peace

> Grace, mercy and peace from God the Father and from Jesus
> Christ, the Father's Son, will be with us in truth and love.
> —2 JOHN 3

Management books, self-help books, and improvement seminars extol the virtues of finding inner peace. They say it's the only way to get ahead in life. True, peace has its place in our lives. However, what these "experts" neglect to tell readers much of the time is exactly *how* to find inner peace. Or if they do explain how to find it, their way is much different from God's way.

How do you find peace during a hectic day at work? Do you reach inside yourself to find inner bliss? Do you play in your desktop Zen garden? Do you perform yoga exercises? Or do you meditate on the truths of God's word to bring comfort, healing, and renewal?

Reveling in God's truth and love is the only way to find true inner peace, as well as grace and mercy. John tells us as much in 2 John 3, in contrasting the effects of believing God's truth with what happens when you believe the false teachings of those who don't walk with God. Knowing that God loves us, that He wants to comfort us, and that He gives boundless grace and mercy to those who believe in His truths is all we need to find this inner peace. It's too bad so many people resort to expensive, time-consuming, or completely world-based methods to find something God has promised us all along.

Your challenge: next time you're feeling pressured, unloved, down in the dumps, or in some sort of upheaval, open the pages of your Bible. Read the stories about how God comforts, about the peace one finds when in step with Him; pray that He will bring that same peace to you. Then find a new use for your desktop Zen garden.

Not on Paper—Face to Face

> I have much to write to you, but I do not want to use paper and ink. Instead, I hope to visit you and talk with you face to face, so that our joy may be complete.
> —2 JOHN 12

E-mail has fast become one of the best time-saving devices in the workplace and in our personal lives. It takes a few seconds to shoot off a quick question to a colleague that would have taken five minutes to ask in person by the time you walked to the other end of the building, went through the formalities, got your answer, and returned to your desk. I've even been known to send an e-mail to a colleague sitting in the next office over from mine—when hollering around the corner or just peeking out my door would have sufficed.

This phenomenon of distanced communications continues when we get home. When was the last time you saw your neighbors in person and had a conversation with them? Can't remember? Neither can I. You drive home, park your car in your garage—using your garage door opener to let yourself in—and then stay inside for the rest of the evening, tied up with the computer, Internet, television, and other "personal communication" devices that keep us from communicating personally with others.

E-mail is great. Cell phones are wonderful. I couldn't do my job very well or very easily without those devices. But there's a time and a place for them, and a time and a place for more personal conversations. 2 John 12, though written many hundreds of years ago, could have been written today—if only the words "paper and ink" were substituted with "e-mail." As John explains, writing to one another serves a great purpose. But there are times when nothing can take the place of a personal, face-to-face talk with a friend, colleague, loved one.

We need that personal interaction to share joys and sorrows, to make a point more clearly, just to interact in a personal way with our brothers and sisters. Are you hiding behind your computer? Try once a day to get out from behind your desk and make a personal visit to a colleague when you normally would send an e-mail. Take time to get to know the other person—in person. Your relationship will bloom much more easily, you'll be better equipped to read moods and reactions, and you'll show that you care. Make your joy complete; leave the e-mail for the mundane writings.

Check Your Spiritual and Physical Health

Dear friend, I pray that you may enjoy good health and that all
may go well with you, even as your soul is getting along well.
—3 JOHN 2

I've heard people use the excuse that God will give each of us a
new body in Heaven, so they wonder why we need to worry
about our health here on earth. Usually this musing accompanies
a lack of exercise, poor eating habits, too little sleep, and immense
amounts of job stress. I've heard people argue that God doesn't care
about our physical bodies; rather, He just wants to make sure our
spirits are in good shape. I admit, on a particularly stressful and
tired kind of day, the last thing I want to do is go straight from the
office to the gym.

But God does care about our physical health. Why? Because
so often we're called to perform a service for Him that requires
physical health. If we don't take good care of ourselves, how can
we serve God fully? For example, part of serving God is helping
others in need and loving others. In my church, every time a family moves, the church is there to help. Not that anyone really enjoys it, but we do it because we love God, and He commands us
to love each other. Part of love is doing something you don't really
want to do for the sake of the other person. If the members of our
church were to let themselves go physically, how could we possi-

bly help our fellow believers move? We'd be letting them *and* God down just because we didn't care about our bodies.

On the flip side, in the office we often ask each other how we're feeling physically, concerned with one another's physical health. But how often do we concern ourselves with the mental, emotional, and spiritual well-being of those we work closely with? The apostle John says to his friend Gaius that he prays he enjoys good health physically and hopes his soul is getting along well. He shows his friend that he cares about him in more than one way, and that's how God feels about us.

Give yourself a spiritual and mental check-up: How are you feeling today in all regards? Are you in good shape, ready to do God's work? Or is it time to hit the gym—and your knees in prayer?

Imitation of Good and Evil

> Dear friend, do not imitate what is evil but what is good. Anyone who does what is good is from God. Anyone who does what is evil has not seen God.
> —3 JOHN 11

Who is your mentor at work? Is there someone in your organization to whom you look for guidance, assurance, teaching, and support? Throughout the Bible (notably Hebrews 6:12), God has told us about the importance of finding someone to serve as a role model in our lives. This leads us to believe He would approve of the mentoring process we find in so many businesses today.

But He wouldn't blindly endorse any mentorship. He'd probably ask a few questions first: Does your mentor exhibit Godly characteristics? Does your mentor follow Christ's teachings, including those that say to shun evil? Are you learning truth and love and goodness—or something else? It's easy to fall into the trap of emulating the actions of those around us at work, especially if they are people we admire. But God calls us to imitate only what is good. As we well know, not all that happens in business is good.

Now is a good time to audit your business relationships. Cast a critical eye on the ethics of your company and of those who serve as role models to you. Are there any areas in which they are not completely truthful, any shady business dealings that you know Christ would not approve of? Does anyone exhibit a hint of immorality in his or her business or personal life that you might be tempted to imitate?

". . . do not imitate what is evil but what is good. Anyone who does what is good is from God. Anyone who does what is evil has not seen God." Mentorship has its rewards, and even a person who exhibits some unethical tendencies might have something worthwhile to teach you. But be careful—once you trust the person to teach you the right way you'll be much less likely to question his or her other daily habits. That's one trap you don't want to fall into.

PART FOURTEEN

Jude

APOSTASY UNMASKED

Key Elements

Purpose: to remind the church of the need for constant vigilance—
to keep strong in the faith and to oppose heresy

Author: Jude, brother of Jesus and James

To whom written: Jewish Christians, and all believers everywhere

Date written: around 65 A.D.

Key Themes

- False teachers come in many flavors and spices, with the most dangerous being the kind of heresy that has enough truth to mask the poison.
- We must be careful to stay true to the very end and stand firm to the last lap on this earth.

Watch Out for the Dividers

These are the men who divide you, who follow mere natural instincts and do not have the Spirit.

—JUDE 1:19

Divided highways are a lifesaver for weary drivers. A physical barrier between a lane headed north and a lane headed south can protect innocent drivers from the weaving, crazy drivers coming their way. Islands that divide traffic are also put there for drivers' protection. But those who have said "curb check" a few too many times know that some dividers in life cause damage—to our fenders, wheels, and in the case of spiritual dividers, our lives.

For example, imagine a work team that gels well. The people work well together, communicate effectively, divvy up tasks to maximize efficiency, and genuinely enjoy each other's company. Then the boss hires a new hotshot to join the group. This person jumps in head first, pushing his ideas on the team, insisting they do things his way, and turning one person against the next. What happened here? A divider sprang up in the middle of this free-flowing group.

God calls for unity in His church; His believers must unify and work as one body to spread His word effectively. Many groups manage to gel, enjoying being together, divvying up the tasks of ministry, and working toward one goal: the kingdom of Christ. But it only takes one bad seed to form a divider right in the middle of God's team. Dividers such as these people are "clouds without rain, blown along by the wind; autumn trees, without fruit and uprooted—twice dead. They are wild waves of the sea, foaming up their shame; wandering stars, for whom blackest darkness has been reserved forever" (Jude 1:12–13). They split the body of Christ by being immoral, rejecting authority, and slandering God. Jude says dividers are "grumblers and faultfinders" who follow their own evil desires, boasting about themselves and flattering others for their own advantage.

Are you a divider, or a free-flowing highway? Do you grumble and find fault with others at work? It's an easy trap to fall into. But this negativity hurts more people than just yourself; if you do this, you're hurting God's kingdom by not portraying a loving and humble attitude. You're dividing God's team. How about rejecting authority? And slandering God? Do you partake in these divisive attitudes and actions?

Dividers have their place in our lives. The ones that save us, like those on split highways, are in good grace. But God has no place in this world for dividers that split what He stands for.

Being Nice Is Valuable

Be merciful to those who doubt. . . .
—JUDE 1:22

In a boardroom, consensus doesn't always come easily. I've sat at a table before in which eight distinct personalities debated one small issue tirelessly—for eight hours. Six people were on side A of the issue; two stuck to side B, but barely. They wanted to believe in side A; they tried to grasp the ideas behind side A. The debaters argued their sides well, but still the majority of the group believed that side A was the way to go. Unfortunately, they lost patience with those who disagreed—and they never did sway the dissenters to join their side.

What those on side A didn't know was that side B was painfully close to switching sides. But the hostile, negative attitudes of their opponents pushed them away.

Those people on the edge of the wrong side of Christ, and those who are on the fence about their faith, don't need lectures, hostile comments, and tireless arguments from the rest of us. What they need is love. Imagine what would have happened in that boardroom if the majority had patiently listened to side B's arguments, calmly addressed their concerns, and showed them respect and that they cared. It's always easier to win people to your side of things—whether an argument in a boardroom or a relationship with Christ—when you're calm, patient, loving, and concerned with other people's thoughts and feelings.

In this verse Jude says to be merciful to those who doubt. He's telling believers that there are false teachers and those who try to dissuade believers from their faith. But instead of showing hostility—fighting the way those without Christ would fight—we should use the kindness that comes from Christ to win them over.

It's a simple tactic, and one that's proven to work. Give it a try—in or out of the boardroom.